WATER OVER THE FALLS

ST. REGIS FALLS HISTORY

By
Paula LaVoy

World rights reserved. This book or any portion thereof may not be copied or reproduced in any form or manner whatever, except as provided by law, without the written permission of the publisher, except by a reviewer who may quote brief passages in a review.

The author assumes full responsibility for the accuracy of all facts and quotations as cited in this book. The opinions expressed in this book are the author's personal views and interpretations, and do not necessarily reflect those of the publisher.

This book is provided with the understanding that the publisher is not engaged in giving spiritual, legal, medical, or other professional advice. If authoritative advice is needed, the reader should seek the counsel of a competent professional.

Copyright © 2008, 2019 Paula LaVoy
Copyright © 2019 TEACH Services, Inc.
ISBN-13: 978-1-57258-468-6 (Paperback)
Library of Congress Control Number: 2008926807

DEDICATION

*To my three children,
Angela, Rebecca, and Daniel,
for their posterity.*

*In perpetual memory of my grandparents,
Douglas and Lillian Palmer.*

Many thanks to the people who helped me:

*First of all, to my husband and children for their love
and support.*

*Next, to other members of my family, friends, neighbors,
local residents and fellow genealogists, for encouragement
and suggestions.*

St. Francis Regis, Our Protector
The feast of St. Francis Regis has
been changed from June 16 to July 2.

CONTENTS

	Preface	*vi*
	Ode to A Town Gone By	*vii*
	Maps	*viii*
1.	The Beginnings	1
2.	Industry	10
3.	Business	21
4.	Religion	29
5.	Education and Sports	34
6.	Entertainment	61
7.	Law Enforcement	62
8.	Organizations	63
9.	Points of Interest	96
10.	Surrounding Hamlets	107
11.	Nature's Sweetness	113
12.	"Cry Wolf"	114
13.	Newspaper Clippings	117
14.	Family Genealogies	129
15.	Cemetery Records	202
	Bibliography	*363*
	Index	*365*

PREFACE

I became interested in St. Regis Falls area history several years ago when I started researching our family genealogy. I realized that many of our forefathers were very active in helping to give birth to the community. As I collected information and became more interested, I decided to compile the materials, have them published and share the area findings with others who might be interested.

Just as my parents, grandparents, and great grandparents; I grew up in this little mountain hamlet. Went to school at St. Regis Falls Central, married and moved away.

By the time my generation came to be, St. Regis Falls was no longer a booming, productive community. After the railroad was gone, so was the industry. And, of course, little by little, the town has slowly become dependent on other larger towns within a fifty mile radius for employment of the residents. The destruction by fire was also a great contribution to the demise of industry.

In researching and writing about this history, I have become more appreciative of the past, our ancestors and the community they built; only to become a time of the past.

I hope all readers will enjoy and appreciate the past I have worked over three years to compile.

Many personal thanks to all who helped in my research—local history and family genealogies.

"Bread thrown upon the water
indeed comes back to us."

ODE TO A TOWN GONE BY

by Paula LaVoy

Dying little town along the river bank,
Once you were so booming—
    but those days we can't bring back.
Once mill and industry,
    countless in the many
People came from distance to work
    and raise their family.
Bustling was the village with
    railroad tracks and all.
Traveling for miles and miles,
    through virgin timber tall.
Many came to seek their fortunes—
    and did with the towering pine,
The lumberjacks helped build the town;
    with stories, legend and song.
Now this little mountain town quietly it sits;
Still along the river bank,
With dying sobs; just memories remain.

St. Regis Falls, taken from the east looking west, after most of the large mills and industry had disappeared from town.

MAPS

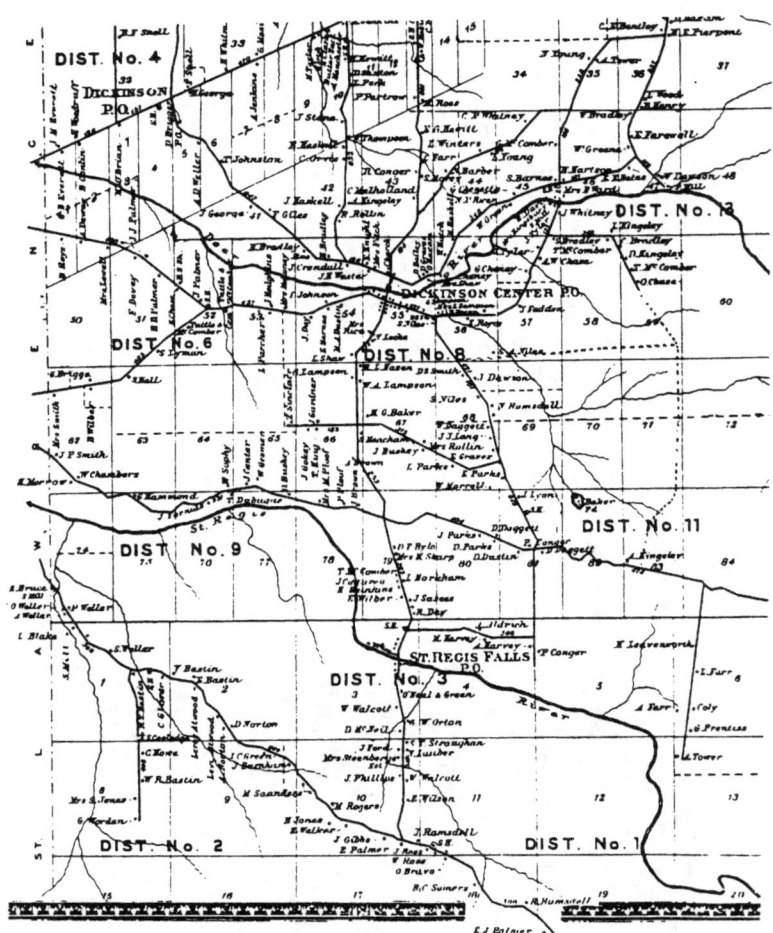

St. Regis Falls

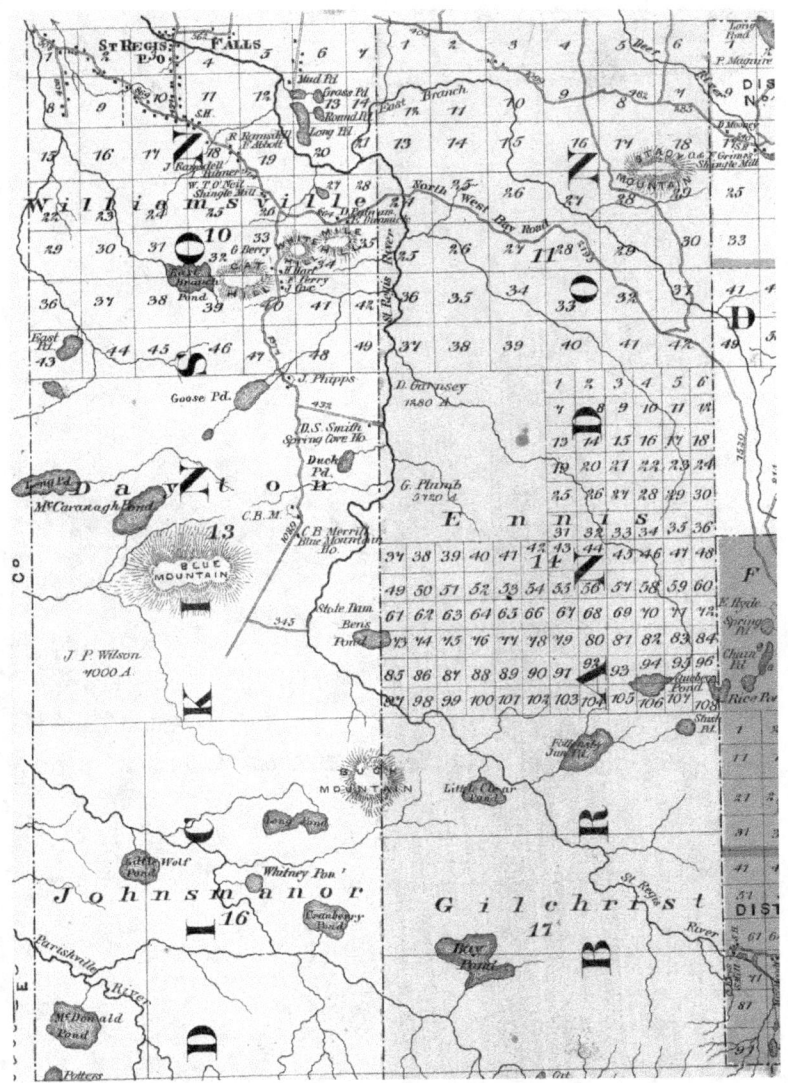

St. Regis Falls, from Beers' *1876 Atlas of Franklin County, New York*

View of St. Regis Falls, N.Y., ca. 1910

Chapter 1

WHY THE NAME, ST. REGIS FALLS?

Of course, we all know that being located on the St. Regis River and in the vicinity of the waterfall, the village quite naturally assumed the name St. Regis Falls. However, there was a time back in 1863 when this settlement was known as Linkinson. The first post office here was so named in honor of the Civil War president, Abraham Lincoln. After a few years, a change of name to St. Regis Falls was made.

The next logical question is, why St. Regis? Why not St. George or St. Gabriel? History records the facts as follows: in 1760 Father Anthony Gordon, a Jesuit Missionary, led a colony of converted Mohawk Indians to a small settlement fronting the St. Lawrence River and bounded by two rivers, now known as Raquette River on the west and St. Regis River on the east. This group arrived there on June 16th, which happened to be the "Festival of St. Regis". Thus was derived the name of the Indian tribe, the settlement and later on, the river.

Looking Down the River—St. Regis Falls, NY

St. Regis Falls, 1908

It is also known by few that before being known as Linkinson, the town went by Hammond Falls, about 1861, because of John and Charles Hammond, who were owners of the largest tract of land in the area, and builders of a sawmill here in 1860.

Another suggested name for the town was Greenville, about 1880, in compliment to Ira C. Green, a very active man in local politics. However, neither of these names lasted and the first official name was Linkinson.

However, this name didn't seem appropriate either, hence the town became known as St. Regis Falls, after its namesake, the river.

The village is located in the township of Waverly in the north-central section of Franklin County (once known as the "South Woods"), just inside the northern boundary of the Adirondack Park.

WHO WAS SAINT REGIS?

St. John Francis Regis was born in 1597 at Fontcouverte, France, of a family in the ranks of the small landed gentry. He was educated at the Jesuit College of Seziers, and at the age of twenty, became a Jesuit Novice. He was ordained in the year 1631 and celebrated his first Mass on Trinity Sunday. Missionary work was his lot for the remainder of his life. He worked mainly with the poor and oppressed, penetrating into the lost out-of-the-way localities of South-eastern France.

St. John Francis Regis

After several years of strenuous labor he effectively reestablished religious observance wherever a mission was conducted. In addition, many thousands of conversions have resulted through his preaching. A plea was made by Father Regis that he be sent on the Canadian Mission to the North American Indians. His request was denied, thus, he continued on with his work, taking the word of God to the wildest and most desolate part of the highland district, a region where no person went unarmed.

His last few years were spent in Velay, the capital city. The Jesuit Church proved too small for congregations, often numbering four or five thousand. Here he organized a complete social service, including prison visitors, nurses, and guardians of the poor, refuges for wayward women and girls, and a free granary for the poor. Several miraculous cures were the results of his prayers, including a return of sight to a boy and to a man who had been blind for years.

While conducting a mission prior to Christmas at LaLouvesc, he was stricken with pleurisy, from which he was unable to recover. Then on New Year's Eve, December 31, 1640, at the age of only forty-three, he died. His body remains to this day at LaLouvesc and his tomb is annually visited by fifty thousand or more pilgrims from all over France.

St. John Francis Regis beatified in 1716 was canonized in 1737. His "festival day" is June 16th.

THE HAMMOND BROTHERS

In the 1850s, the Hammond brothers, Charles and John from Crown Point, Essex County, began buying land near this vicinity and by 1860 a mill, built for them by Amos Harvey; with Hiram Cook, Julius Rising, and Kirby and Josephus Titus making up part of his work crew; was operating with Benjamin Babcock as mill superintendent. (This mill was sold and became the John Hurd Lumber Co.) This first purchase of land by the Hammond brothers to begin their mill may have been the first industry in what became St. Regis Falls.

The work crew that built the Hammond Mill were the first inhabitants in Waverly, except for perhaps two or three hunters and trappers. There were no roads, just trails and the Northwest Bay Road, which was a military turnpike that began prior to 1810—from Westport via Elizabethtown, Lake Placid, Saranac Lake, down through what is the Eleven Mile Woods Road into Santa Clara, St. Regis Falls and on through to Nicholville into Hopkinton.

After the railroad was completed in 1883, things started growing rapidly. The Old Hammond Mill was greatly enlarged and a store was opened, which had a trade of $75,000 a year. The establishment of logging camps sprang up throughout the vast timber lands. Steam power was added to the mill, and machinery was installed for the making of clapboards, lath and broomsticks. They also built a machine shop and a box factory. Real estate values quadrupled and the population was multiplied five or six times.

The highest recorded population, 2,270, was in 1890.

THE CONTRIBUTION OF JOHN HURD

The coming of John Hurd from Santa Clara, California to St. Regis Falls, about 1882, was an important mile-stone in the village. Due to the death of Charles Hammond, the mill passed to Thomas O'Neil, who formed a partnership with

Oren Richards. Richards failed soon after, and his interest was purchased by Samuel F. Vilas of Plattsburgh. O'Neil and Vilas operated the mill until its purchase in 1882 by Hurd, Hotchkiss and Mac Farland.

They rebuilt the mill and started a railroad from Moira south to St. Regis Falls. Mr. Hurd later extended the railroad to Tupper Lake. When the line was finished, he found that there was not enough traffic along the line to assure a dividend to the stockholders, and later the road was sold out by the bondholders.

Mr. Hurd built a mill in Santa Clara, which sold to the Santa Clara Lumber Co. Some time after the sale of the mill, a dispute arose over the title to the tracks to the lumber yard at Santa Clara. Ferris J. Meigs, manager of the lumber company, claimed the tracks were included in the sale of the mill property, and Mr. Hurd claimed that the tracks belonged to the railroad company. No settlement of the question seemed possible at the time, but later, Mr. Hurd built a large mill at Tupper Lake, on land the title of which he did not examine too closely. Mr. Meigs found out who owned the land—bought it, and made Mr. Hurd "cough-up" the tracks.

THE RAILROAD

When the thriving towns of the Northern Adirondacks of the early days are mentioned, we think of timber as the industry most responsible for this affluence. However, there was another very saleable commodity that would prove to be more inexhaustible, the scenery.  It could make this area the rival of such places as the Catskills and the Rockies. Some even compared it favorably to Switzerland. Added to the breath-taking scenery was unsurpassed opportunity for hunting and fishing.

The development of this region as a resort area was delayed largely because of the long and tedious stage rides necessary to reach the most desirable points. However, this was overcome by the opening of the Northern Adirondack Railroad which

St. Regis Lumber Co. #75

penetrated to the heart of the Adirondacks, making the most desirable areas easily accessible. Resorts sprang up as it was pushed through to accommodate the vacationer.

Mr. John Hurd built the railroad to provide access to some sixty square miles of timber land. It was first finished to St. Regis Falls, then to Santa Clara and Brandon in 1886 and finally to Tupper Lake in 1889—a total length of nearly seventy miles. Mr. Hurd, a venturesome men, had a monopoly, as no other railway touched near Tupper Lake. He ran into financial difficulties, however, went bankrupt and lost the property in 1895. The railroad was eventually acquired by the New York Central Railroad.

In 1883, construction of the Northern Adirondack Railroad was begun at Moira to run to St. Regis Falls and during the ensuing six years, it was extended piece by piece through Waverly, Santa Clara and Altamont to Tupper Lake. The first engineer to bring a locomotive up through to St. Regis Falls was John Smith. This shows the service provided by the railroad to the communities and resort spots from Moira to Paul Smiths and the consequent glory and glamour of an era that has passed.

The journey between the great cities of the sea-board and the silent forest could be undertaken in the most luxurious conditions of modern railway travel. The rail-bed and track were first class, being laid with steel rails and well ballasted.

It was equipped with all the modern conveniences for comfort and safety. The pleasure-seeker could now find beautiful lakes, forests, first-class hotels, pure, cold water (a rare item today) and clean, smog-free air to satisfy the most exacting.

In Dickinson, the railroad crossed the Deer River and ran four miles to St. Regis Falls. This was a community of considerable enterprise, having lumber mills, a box factory, and one of the largest tanning establishments in the state. The Waverly House seemed to be the most prominent of several hotels here. It was built by W. T. O'Neil in 1884, sold to Watson Page a couple years later and owned by L. C. Goodrich in 1889. It could accommodate fifty guests and the rates were $1.50 per day, and $5.00 to $8.00 per week. At St. Regis Falls, the St. Regis Falls & Everton Railroad had its western terminals and ran east six miles to Everton on the east branch of the St. Regis River, where the Everton Lumber Company had large mills.

The railroad had now ascended 960 feet. It crossed the St. Regis River and proceeded onward and upward to Shanley where the Alfred Lumber Company had mills. Near here also is the junction of the East and Middle branches of the St. Regis River, the former being the outlet of Meacham Lake and the latter of St. Regis Lakes.

Railroad Station, St. Regis Falls, NY

From Shanley's, the way continued three miles to Santa Clara, passing Cat Mountain, west of the road, and Conger Mountain, east. In this thrifty community with an altitude of 1600 feet, surrounded by mountains, the scenery was unsurpassed. It afforded the finest camping grounds for sportsmen and health-seekers. A new hotel in 1889 was the Santa Clara House with a capacity of 75. The price per day was $2.00 and the rate per week $5.00 to $14.00 for one of the better places. The population of the town of Santa Clara exceeded two thousand in 1890. "Uplands" and "Hill-crest" were later built by the Working Girls' Vacation Society as further indication of the salubrious, invigorating atmosphere that the area had to offer.

Many of today's children have hardly even seen a train, much less ridden on one. This, then, is the era of the railroad in the Northern Adirondacks from 1882 to 1889.

On July 1937, the railroad having given way to the automobile and the transport truck, the last of the rails and sound ties were taken up through to Tupper Lake. This was the demise of "John Hurd's Road".

The Dam Above the Falls

WHY THE NAME, ST. REGIS FALLS? • 9

New York Central Line timetable from July, 1912

Chapter 2
INDUSTRY

THE TANNERY

Chair Factory Ruins, St. Regis Falls, NY

In 1865, the Hammonds sold a parcel of land near the falls to Solomon R., Edward and Francis Spaulding of Boston, Mass., and James H. Young, where they proceeded to build a sole-leather tannery. This firm became Spaulding & Bumstead and did business until 1878, then failed.

Perley D. Moore & Co. then operated the tannery under lease for a year or two. Shaw Brothers of Boston then bought it about 1880, and converted it into an upper-leather works. After four years, the Shaw Brothers also failed and the tannery was sold again to Arey, Maddock & Locke, also of Boston. They changed the name to St. Regis Leather Co. History repeated itself; they also failed in 1901. However, in its day, the tannery was considered one of the largest tanneries in the world.

The building was then bought by William T. and H. E. O'Neil, who converted it into a chair factory, with a capacity of making

The Cascade Chair Co. was located downriver from the falls. This was once the tannery.

Looking up at the waterfalls

600 chairs per day. This was the Cascade Chair Co. Later it was transferred to the electric lighting plant. Both ran very successfully until 1909 when fire wiped them out.

A dam and pulp mill was then erected on this site by Alexander MacDonald and Dr. L. M. Wardner, named the Cascade Wood Products.

THE DYNAMO

In 1898, H. E. O'Neil installed a small dynamo in the planing mill of Watson Page Lumber Co., and organized the St. Regis Light & Power Co. Because of growing demand for electrical power it was moved to the chair factory. After a fire here, the power company was moved about two miles downriver to Ploof's Falls, in the township of Dickinson. A tub factory was operated in connection with the dynamo.

The original lighting contract in the village called for 100 lamps at the cost of $800 in 1909. The streetlights were on

There were other ways of transporting timber besides the river

from dusk until one A.M. and then from five A.M. until daylight. The flat rate for everyone was $1. In 1957, a new lighting contract was signed and new street lights were installed.

"THE JACK WORKS"

In 1927, John Johnston of Port Leyden came into the area and constructed a mill that would remove the bark from pulp wood, commonly called a drum barker. The supply came from upriver as far as Meacham Lake. Back in 1927, this supply seemed unlimited. Pulp wood was cut, carried to the river, dumped, and in time floated to the mill. River drivers in boats helped the product reach the mill. The mill, while over a hundred feet high, consisted mainly of a drum barker and many jacks and conveyer chains. A railroad siding was also used in the operation.

The pulp wood of spruce and balsam, in four-foot lengths, was caught in the river by a boom, then taken up a high jack or conveyer into the drum barker, then loaded on another conveyer, which carried it to waiting railroad boxcars. Each car held 16 cords, and six to eight cars were loaded in a shift. Two shifts of nine hours made up the regular working day.

Man in back row far left with cap is Ralph Gilbert Titus, circa 1907

Woodcutting Gang, St. Regis Falls

When the timber supply became exhausted, the mill was closed, leaving huge piles of bark fifty feet high, as if for a monument to the area's last major lumber industry.

THE MICA FACTORY

It was in 1911 when a company from Ottawa, Canada, moved into St. Regis Falls, for the purpose of manufacturing fireproof windows for use in coal and oil burning stoves, furnaces and for electrical equipment. Other uses of mica were; coating cheaper kinds of wallpaper, for giving toys and stage scenery the effect of having been frosted, as a lubricant in axle grease, manufacturing of explosives, making buttons and in flake form, for electrical insulation.

The mica itself was in the shape of large stones consisting of many layers of tightly compressed scale or sheets which, in order to be of use, had to be split paper thin. This raw material was brought here from Canada.

During the peak season there were as many as sixty employees engaged in this work, which was done not only in the factory, but in the homes of folks in town who split the mica on a piece-work basis. The splitting had to be done by hand using a very sharp knife.

The factory building was a two-story frame structure. After several years of operation here, the mica business slowed down due to the influx of substitute materials in the fireproofing industry and the factory closed, moving the equipment to Massena. Later, the local factory building burned. The old foundations are still visible on the corner of Purchase and Sabrey Streets and occasionally someone will dig out pieces of mica and perhaps wonder whence it came.

THE CREAMERY

The St. Regis Creamery was located on the upper end of Spring Street, this was called Buttermilk Hill. The milk plant sat on the right side of Spring Street across from the Hollister House. It was still in operation in the early 1930s. It was owned and operated by Henry E. O'Neil. Arthur O'Neil, at the age of 16 yrs., kept the books. Butter from this creamery was sent to New York City by railroad. Milk and cream was also sent by rail to Buffalo to the Fairmont Creamery.

THE CLOTHESPIN FACTORY

The clothespin factory was run by Francis Mayville around the time of the depression and into the 1940s. It was located in the building on River Street next to where Ross's Store is now. This was not a long-lived enterprise.

THE BROOKLYN COOPERAGE CO.

The Brooklyn Cooperage Co. started operations in the early 1900s. A subsidiary of the American Sugar Refining Co., in addition to processing the hardwood, they made staves and headings for sugar barrels. This company lumbered the hardwood from St. Regis Paper Co. lands. It also operated the railroad and locomotives number 1, 2, and 8 which were low-speed, high-powered and could draw huge loads.

When paper sacks became the way for sugar packers, the Brooklyn Cooperage Co. came to a standstill. This began the decline in industry of the community.

WHY THE NAME, ST. REGIS FALLS? • 15

The Brooklyn Cooperage Co. was located on both sides of the river near the bridge where the dam is. Photo taken in 1910.

Band saw

Circular saw

The Brooklyn Cooperage Co., on the corner of East Main and River Streets, on the east side.

16 • WATER OVER THE FALLS

Workers at the Brooklyn Cooperage Co.

The Brooklyn Cooperage Co., taken from the back of where the fire station is now, looking northeast to southwest.

A 1913 birds-eye view of St. Regis Falls, showing Woodman Stave, later the Brooklyn Cooperage Co. Barrel staves and headings were made for Domino Sugar Products, a subsidiary. The long building at center is the first railroad station, which also housed several businesses.

WHY THE NAME, ST. REGIS FALLS? • 17

Log Loader, St. Regis Falls

THE ROSSING MILL

Built in the early 1900s, the St. Regis Paper Co. established a rossing mill a half mile above the village (to the south), which shut down around 1915. It had a capacity of fifty thousand cords of pulp wood annually.

The Rossing Mill under construction located on the river near where the railroad bridge crossed the river.

Cows hauling logs to the mill

THE GIFFIN MILL

In the mid 1920s, Rollin Glenville Giffin opened the St. Regis Coal Co. He then added the sawmill operation shortly thereafter; this provided employment for some area people.

R. G. Giffin & Son, located in the middle of Mica Hill.

In the early 1940s, Rollin Jr. joined his father and the business became known as R. G. Giffin & Son. They expanded with the lumber business and also with building supplies—windows, doors, roofing, cement, nails, etc.

The Giffins bought logs from loggers and at one time, did their own logging on the cutting track. Mr. Giffin opened a "cutting home" and provided "bed and board" for ten or twelve loggers. Jim and Liz Camp, then Oscar and Martha McNeil operated this house. There was a team, which was used to skid the logs. Trucks and drivers transported logs to the sawmill in St. Regis Falls, where it was sawed into lumber. Reese Radloff and Carl Winters were sawyers. Slabwood sold for 50¢ a cord and boys who piled it earned 25¢ a cord.

When oil became popular as a fuel, the Giffins opened the first oil business in St. Regis Falls.

R. G. Giffin & Son continued, until Rollin Jr.'s retirement in 1975. At this point, the oil business was sold to McDonald Oil Co. of Moira. Two Massena men bought the sawmill machinery and moved it to Massena and tore down the sawmill buildings. Marshall Bros. of Dickinson Center bought the building supplies. Merle (Pat) Niles from Nicholville purchased the land, office, and remaining buildings.

1983—Jack LaBounty purchased the property from Niles and once again, building and plumbing supplies are available locally.

THE EVAPORATOR SHOP

The Vermont Evaporator Shop, established by a man from Vermont by the name of Robert Maroney, was located in the building between the present post office and the school. They made evaporator pans for use in boiling maple sap in the process of making maple syrup. This enterprise was in operation many years and closed sometime in the 1930s.

Shop foreman was Mr. Lyle Gleason. One of the workers at the evaporator shop was Edward McGarvey.

At one time, Mr. Maroney was town supervisor. He ran against John Fraser. During election night, residents of the village sang, "Johnny Fraser's hopes are dead. Bob Maroney's way ahead."

After the closing of the Vermont Evaporator Shop, Mr. Maroney purchased a farm on the Split Rock Road near Saranac Lake.

At the close of this enterprise, the building was then used as a garage run by Vernon "Dutch" Parks.

After the garage closed, the building was once again remodeled and used as a store run by the Winters Family. It is now the residence of Mrs. Regina Winters.

THE JOHNSON MILL

The Johnson Sawmill was built in the late 1940s by Orton Johnson. It was located on the south end of Spruce Street.

The logs processed here were cut into dimensions for the making of hockey sticks and were shipped to Canada and trucked to Watertown. Mr. Johnson also sold slab wood throughout the village area.

The Johnson Sawmill burned several years ago.

A SAWMILL

About 1868, Benoni G. Webb, from Bellmont, built a sawmill three-quarters of a mile below the village, (to the north). It was operated by Webb & Stevers until the firm failed, then it was acquired and run by Hubbard & Lowell. It burned in 1873. Charles H. Young rebuilt it in 1883, and in the course of two or three years sold it to J. W. Webb. R. P. Lindsay and then H. E. O'Neil followed in ownership. Hugh Raymo next had it and then in 1918 was owned by the Cascade Wood Products Company.

Bridge Crossing St. Regis Falls River near Sawmill

Sawmill and Bridge on St. Regis Falls

Pulp Mill, St. Regis Falls

CHAPTER 3
BUSINESS

HOTELS

The first hotel was built by Henry Bickford from Dickinson. Once named the Frontier House, it had many landlords, such as D. I. McNeil, Kenneth W. Kinnear, W. J. Alfred and Alexander Johnson. It was then owned by Evariste LeBoeuf, but was closed as a hotel because it was not permitted to have a bar.

The Waverly House

The Waverly House was built by William O'Neil in 1884. He then sold it a couple years later to Watson Page. The Waverly House then changed hands several more times to L. C. Goodrich, W. J. Alfred, and George Prespare. Then George Bishop ran it by lease. In 1898 the back addition was attached to the Waverly. The first basketball game was played in this part of the hotel.

The St. Regis House, formerly a store, was built by O'Neil and Parka, then owned by George Bishop, who remodeled it. However, it was closed because the town was "dry".

The Riverside

The Riverside, once known as "Ma Smith's", was owned by Mr. & Mrs. Otto Smith. When Otto Smith purchased this establishment it was a large, long building that went all the way to the corner (Tannery Street, now River Street). Mr.

Smith decided to decrease the size of the building. He hired Joe Ploof to take the center of the building out and put the two ends together. If you look closely at the picture, you can see in the middle of the building where it was attached. Note the gas pump at the right corner of the porch, and the stuffed bear in the corner at the right of the upper porch. The building in back of the Riverside was a blacksmith shop at the time this picture was taken.

The Hillcrest Inn, located on the opposite corner from the Methodist Church across from the school, was partially torn down and the large trees were cut. It has been the home of the Kenneth Johnson family for many years.

Waverly House, early 1900s

Main street, St. Regis Falls, looking north, ca. 1910

BUSINESS • 23

Looking north, the Brooklyn Cooperage Co. on the right; Ma Smith's (The Riverside Inn) far left side; the Commercial House, on left.

Main Street, St. Regis Falls

Taken in 1911, the 3-story building up the street at the left is the I.O.O.F. hall, before it was destroyed

Main Street, St. Regis Falls

Main Street, St. Regis Falls

Main Street and Hotel (Waverly House), St. Regis Falls

BUSINESS • 25

Meat Market, Main Street, St. Regis Falls

Main Street, looking north from the south side of the bridge.

Post Office and St. Regis Falls National Bank

The Newspaper

The Adirondack News printed its first issue March 14, 1887. The business was located on the south side of the river in the middle of the hill. The printing office was built first, then the living quarters were attached later at the right rear corner. The newspaper was published every Saturday, with terms of one dollar per year, in advance. Editor and publishers were Mark Rowell and Mr. Aldrich, with Grace Lennon, (Mr. Rowell's sister-in-law) also part owner and operator of the enterprise. *The Adirondack News* flourished until it closed its doors in 1933.

Our First Press

This old newspaper has been preserved on micro-film and can be enjoyed by everyone at the town office located in the firehouse building.

The old print building was torn down the summer of 1983—the residence section still remains and is occupied by the Darwin Kelley family.

The Bus Line

LaPoint's bus business was started in 1941 by Earl J. LaPoint. The buses ran to Massena and Malone from St. Regis Falls, and from Bangor to Massena. This line operated for thirteen years, until 1954.

The Bank

The St. Regis Falls National Bank was first chartered and opened its doors by Henry E. O'Neil in May 1905. It was first located in a small house on Spring Street next to the W. T. O'Neil house, more recently occupied by the Frank and Jane Young family. The president of the bank was W. T. O'Neil. Henry O'Neil, Alexander MacDonald, Frank Young, E. P. Tryon and R. N. Burns constituted the Board of Directors. When the bank moved to the present building, Henry O'Neil, otherwise known as Ed, was the president and remained so until 1916, at which time his brother, Arthur S. O'Neil became president. At the age of 21 years, Arthur was known as the youngest ever to be president of a bank. Then Mr. O'Neil moved to Ogdensburg and Burton Dupree became bank manager. The St. Regis Falls National Bank emerged with the Ogdensburg Trust Co. January 2, 1930. Percy Rowell was manager from 1942 through 1969 (27 years). Claire Kelley then held this position and at present, the manager of the Oneida National Bank and Trust Co. branch, located in St. Regis Falls, is Mrs. Joan Ploof Unwin. The Bank changed hands from the Ogdensburg Trust Co. to the Oneida National Bank and Trust Co. on Nov. 19, 1976.

Currency issued by the St. Regis Falls National Bank, signed by Alexander MacDonald and H. E. O'Neil, March 13, 1905.

Waverly House

EACH DAY IS A GIFT FROM GOD!

He has give us morning, brightness and sun,
Laughter to share and work to be done...

He has given us rainbows, flowers and song
And the hans of our dear ones to help us along.

He has given us prayer with its wonderful power
To lighten our hearts in a troublesome hour.

He has given us blessings to brighten our way
And always—the gift of another new day.

—Jean Kyler McManus

Chapter 4

RELIGION

Trinity M. E. Church

The First Methodist Episcopal Church of St. Regis Falls joined in 1882 with Dickinson Center as one parish. The church was erected in 1887–1888 at the cost of $3,100. The first trustees were; William E. King, Mrs. Esther MacFarland, Daniel W. Flack. Other trustees in the early 1900's were; J. A. Ketcham, and Leslie M. Saunders. The church and parsonage were first located on the south end of the present school site. When the school burned in 1926, the church was also destroyed

The old Methodist Church and parsonage, which was located on the school lot.

The old Methodist Church, after it burned with the school in 1926. The parsonage was moved by Joe Ploof to its present location.

by the fire; however, the parsonage was saved and moved to its present site by Joe Ploof, on the corner of Duane Street and Main Street behind the newly constructed church.

The April 16, 1887 issue of the *Adirondack News* reports that the old Methodist Episcopal Church main body of the church measured 38 x 40 feet, with a wing 26 x 40 feet. The basement was 38 x 40 feet and the tower was 60 feet high.

Methodist Episcopalian Church, St. Regis Falls

The St. Regis Falls Universalist Church organized as a parish church June, 1916, but not incorporated; it had no installed pastor, but had preaching on alternate Sundays by clergymen from Canton.

The First Free Baptist Church of St. Regis Falls organized March 23, 1893. The first corner-stone placed in 1894 and located on North Main Street just up from where the Methodist Church is now. The list of pastors were; James. A. Heath, 1893–1896; Nelson Ramsdell, 1896–1898; M. M. Shoemaker, 1898–1900; Nelson Ramsdell, 1901–1902; A. D. Walker, 1902–1904; F. E. Miller, 1904–1905; Myra C. Hoit, 1905; H. H. Stocum, 1909; S. D. Knapp, 1913; John

First Free Baptist Church of St. Regis Falls

Walker, 1914–1916; Peter S. Vining, 1917–1918. Trustees in 1918 were; Sylvester Meacham, Fred S. Ramsdell, Fred Lang, LeRoy Phillips, George Smith, and Oliver Brabon. The organization and continued existence was the results of the dedication of Rev. Nelson Ramsdell, who was still serving the church at the age of 84 years. The society entered into fellowship with the St. Lawrence Baptist Association in 1913. The church building was sold to the masonic lodge about 1931 and later torn down about 1935. This picture was taken about 1910.

St. Ann's Catholic Church—in mid Franklin County, Father G. J. Normandeau of Brushton sought out the catholic lumbermen of the "South Woods". While he felt that a more dreary and dismal spot than St. Regis Falls could not be found, he was greatly edified by mostly Canadian lumbermen who said the rosary together and sang part of the mass each time he visited them. By October, 1883, the village school-house could no longer accommodate the crowds for mass, and the following year, St. Ann's Church, first known as St. Regis Church, and renamed in

St. Ann's Catholic Church was located where the present church stands.

The Roman Catholic Parish Residence, St. Regis Falls, NY

1884, was incorporated on August 11, 1883; and erected on land deeded by Joseph Bushey on September 3, 1884.

St. Ann's Church incorporated with Rev. F. J. Ouellette as the first priest in the town, and continued his service here for more than thirty years until 1919, serving about 200 families. The first trustees were Joseph Bushey and Louis Quesnel. With a mission church in Santa Clara, St. Peter's, with Rev. J. Rodrique Lauzon serving 223 families. There were also services held in surrounding hamlets of Everton, Spring Cove and Brandon.

St. Ann's Church

The first Catholic Church in the town was dedicated by Bishop Wadhams on October 25, 1884. However, this church burned January 18, 1920. The second church (the present building) was built and dedicated July 1, 1923 by Bishop J. H. Conroy. However, on November 2, 1935 the inside was once again destroyed by fire. The church was restored in only one month. St. Ann's Church was then dedicated in memory of Paul and Josephine LeMieux.

Three separate lots for a cemetery were purchased in 1885 and 1889. Father Ouellette also purchased the lot for the rectory in 1891.

Resident pastors serving the St. Regis Falls community were; Rev. F. J. Ouellette 1884–1919, Rev. J. R. Lauzon 1919–1925, Rev. E. A. Tetrault 1925–1944, Rev. F. C. McMahon 1944–1950, Rev. J. L. Meehan 1950–1954, Rev. M. Jarecki 1954–1963, Rev. P. V. Beyette 1963–1973, Rev. L. O'Doherty 1973–1979, and Rev. P. Callaghan 1979 to the present.

Upper Main Street, from R. C. Church

Chapter 5

EDUCATION

The first school was taught in 1860 by Miss Amy Saunders; she was married and became Mrs. Philip Shuflet. Teachers were paid $1.00 per week plus their board. The original schoolroom was located in the rear of a log house, occupied in front by a family. The first schoolhouse was located at the same site as the present school and was probably a log cabin which was built about 1865. However, as the village grew they realized that better accommodations were needed. The large wood-framed structure was erected in 1886 at the cost of about $9,000. It accommodated more than 400 pupils and employed eleven teachers. The new school was named the St. Regis Falls Union School and was located in the same place as the present school.

In 1889 there were 426 students and the name was changed to the St. Regis Falls Middle School. It had gained an excellent reputation and by 1906, with such an increase in student body, warranted a new addition.

St. Regis Falls High School—One of the Best in Northern NY

St. Regis Falls Central School, built 1886

In January 1891, regents exams were given for the first time. The first graduating class, in 1894, consisted of Mr. W. Wardner, Overt Parks, Edith O'Neil (MacDonald), and H. E. O'Neil.

In 1907, Mrs. Mary Pritchard became the first commerical teacher. The class of 1907 was composed of Anabel (Hewitt) Green, Myrtle Griffin and Earl N. Weller.

Members of the St. Regis Falls School Board of Education in 1912 were; M. B. Ramsdell—President, M. A. Rowell, Dr. W. A. Wardner, Joseph C. Johnson, Alexander MacDonald, Mrs. Edith MacDonald, Mr. R. R. McLane, and Mrs. R. G. Giffin. Sr.

Members of the faculty in 1912 were; J. L. Blood—Principal, Miss Elisabeth P. LaPoint, Miss Mary C. Pritchard, Mr. G. A. Sealy—7th grade, Miss Myra Denning—6th grade, Miss Ora Somers—5th grade, Miss Parepa Lindsay—4th grade, Miss Grace Graffin—3rd grade, Miss E. Vaughn Conley—2nd grade, and Miss Eva Tryon—1st grade.

The school was vulnerable to fire, such as every other wooden structure, and it burned in 1926. A new brick school was built in 1927 and opened in 1928. During this reconstruction period, classes were held at various places in town. It was at this time that the school's name was changed again. It became St. Regis Falls Central and was centralized. Since the new brick school was built, there have been three new additions. The first addition in 1938 at the south end of the building, the second wing in 1956-1957 to the north end, and the third wing in 1968 at the north toward the back, with plans provided for the future to expand upwards. Santa Clara, Dickinson, and Nicholville were annexed in 1953 to St. Regis Falls Central School system.

The list of St. Regis Falls principals for the school were as follows:

Mark A. Rowell	(Sept. 1886—Jan. 1887) also taught
Miss Mary A. Cooney	(finished the term 1887)
Mr. Sands H. Austin	(1887-1888)
Mr. John A. Smith	(1888 term) Attorney
Mrs. R. R. McLane	(spring 1889)
Mr. W. G. Hitchcock	(Sept. 1888–June 1889)
Mr. Ralph Pringle	(1891–1905) resigned due to illness
Mr. John L. Blood	(1906–1918)
Mr. Newton Connally	
Mr. Carl Overton	
Mr. Harry N. McLane	(1927–1931) resigned
Mr. Stewart Powlesland	
Mr. Carl O. Daniels	(1933)
Mr. Lambert L. Spancake	(1933–)
Mr. James Meyers	
Mr. Harry W. Wager	(–1957)
Mr. John Sharpstene	(1957–)
Dr. Peter Bassette	Superintendent
Mr. Charles Marshall	Superintendent
Mr. Kenneth Mosher	Superintendent
Mr. Alan Tessier	w/ Mr. Michael Hunsinger as Superintendent

St. Ann's Catholic School—The information on the parochial school is sketchy. Only one parish report was recorded for 1888, which shows the school with 70 students, boys and girls. An annual Catholic Directory for the United States shows a parochial school at St. Regis Falls as follows:

1888, 1889 and 1900—Misses Philomena Amyot and Julia Pierce, teachers. Boys and girls numbered 75.
1901—Professor H. Contu plus assistant. Boys 26 and girls 27.

These directories show statistics for the previous year, so we might conclude that the school operated between 1887 and 1900. It was held, we believe, at the parish house, presently the parish rectory.

There was also a school in the mid 1870s located near the Wait Road across from the Brabon House.

Other one-room schoolhouses to educate the area children were located on the Trim Road—the Farr District, the Guide Board School, the Lake Ozonia School, and the Haynes Road School, which accommodated mainly children from Dickinson Center.

Breaking ground for the "new" school

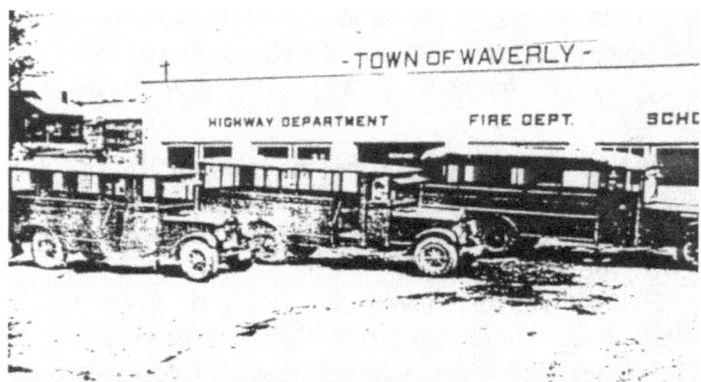

The first school buses, 1934. Alfred Deno is standing in the doorway of the bus on the right.

Where is this giant boulder?
Can you see anything unusual about it?

The present St. Regis Falls Central School, 1949.

EDUCATION • 39

THE BIRTH OF A LEGEND—THE WONDER FIVE: Remembering and Revisiting the Champions, by Allan Cummings

The autumn of 1932 found the village of St. Regis Falls, a logging town tucked neatly away in the foothills of the Adirondacks, sustaining the effects of the depression in much the same manner it found countless other settlements. People were concerned about their next meal, oblivious to the specks of flame which would ignite in Europe a few years hence and affect their lives in equal magnitude. Those who had radios were a minority, those with televisions were none. The news, when it traveled, was courted by newspapers, often stale by the time it met the reader's eyes. Those with an ear for country music would, in a few months, be saddened

"Wonder Five"
l to r: George Fisk, Gerald White, Willard White, Jim Rovito, Eugene Danforth, Keith Bennett, Earl Woods and Doug Binan. 1933.

by the death of the first real superstar of the industry, Jimmie Rodgers, America's Blue Yodeler. People who gauged their daily fortunes by those of sport's biggest name, rose and fell with Babe Ruth's homerun bat. More concerned themselves with the hope of better tomorrows with the emergence of Franklin Roosevelt into the presidential race.

Basketball? In St. Regis Falls, a town which even today would have to increase its population ten-fold to approximate its zip code (12980). Few citizens paid it more than token notice. Its gate appeal was suspect, at best; its effect on the community was even less. Schools the size of SRF could barely gather players enough to represent them in competition and contemplating any degree of success was, undoubtedly, in the minds of very few. Surely one would have to be a fanatic to engage him-self in thoughts of basketball prowess at a time when families were struggling just to feed hungry mouths.

Charlie LeMieux, coach at SRF High, was one of the few who had perhaps seen basketball headlines for the Falls before they were printed or merited. That his team would spread basketball-mania throughout the area and, indeed, throughout all of upstate New York, was less a secret to him than we might know, although its success quite likely exceeded his expectations. That he could reap the special feeling of satisfaction which is born through victory in competitive sports would provide rewards for the hard work that basketball practice was, and is. But it's not to be thought of that anyone could have predicted the lasting fame that would identify the Wonder Five to multiple generations through multiple decades. That basketball fever would be born, grow and rise to its highest peak in St. Regis Falls at a time when our country was at its lowest point is a coincidence of the strangest order.

The *Malone Evening Telegram* gave vent to the awakening of a new basketball spirit in SRF following an early season victory over Mount Assumption Institute in Plattsburgh. The Saints had opened their season by thrashing Waddington 31 to 14 and plastering Parishville, 56 to 17. They went to Tupper Lake in early December and put the Lumberjacks, a Class "A" St. Lawrence Valley League quintet, through a fierce contest, bowing by but a single point, 37-36. After staying the night in Tupper they traveled to Plattsburgh the next day and that evening, defeated MAI, also a team of "A" classification, 36-32, drawing the attention of Malone's resident sportswriter, the late Stanley Ferris. In the weeks to come he would crown them with their eloquent name, "The Wonder Five", and write about them with obvious delight. Often his columns would contain a generous helping of awe at their success, but he introduced them to his readers with a polite paragraph of respect.

> We take our hats off to little St. Regis Falls high school that is taking on the big clubs and battling them off their feet. The Saints...at Tupper Lake...lost out by a 1-point margin and followed this by handing MAI a 36-32 licking at Plattsburgh. St. Regis Falls has a classy bunch of basketeers and rank as favorites in the North Country league, a class "B" organization.

That win over MAI was the first in a string of unbroken victories that would total 16 before Ogdensburg ended it. With the passing of each triumph local interest increased and newspaper coverage became more widespread. Several class "A" teams fell victim to the onrush of the fabled little team, including Potsdam, Norwood, Canton, MAI (again) and later, in the best interests of local sports promotion, Malone.

St. Regis Falls became "that phenomenal team from the little mountain town" and Charlie LeMieux's little "wonder" team. One night they demolished Bombay, introducing the ball to the nets at an unprecedented rate in North Country League annals. At intermission they had a 40-to-8 lead. When the contest was reduced to statistics, the numbers would show 76 points on the SRF line score, 72 of which were by virtue of field goals. Never had an NCL team scored so heavily.

At that time in basketball history it was practically unexplainable that a team could score 76 points in one game. At this time in our story, it is no less a necessity for explanation that yesteryear's exception is today's rule.

Through the nearly forty years that have passed since the Wonder Five broke the popularity barrier in local sports, the game of basketball has changed its complexion markedly. The center jump after each basket was discontinued, giving possession of the ball to the defense. That would have somewhat of a neutralization in height differences but the post-war era saw the wholesale invasion of a scoring maneuver which would not only show complete disdain for height but would shove point totals up into the stratosphere. It was the running, leaping, jump-and-shoot affair we call the "jumper".

Its delivery, when properly executed in concert with the head fake or made swiftly when the shooter stops a forward movement without advertising, is all but guaranteed. Only marksmanship rests in the balance. While Charlie LeMieux's forces were creating their image in the early 1930s, the jumper as a factor in the game was nearly 15 years into the future.

And, while we're at it, remember that professional basketball as we know it today also would not appear until after World War II. Wilt Chamberlain, the game's greatest-ever producer of points, was yet unborn. Television, the game's and the world's biggest promotion stick was still but the brainchild of some hopeful inventor, if that at all. And, if you get the idea that the Wonder Five was a few years ahead of itself, consider that its reputation was built with the bare minimum of publicity facilities at its disposal. And, its success, fame and lasting image and the 76 points against Bombay were all accomplished without the jump shot.

It seems an impossible task to corner the very first man who shot a jump shot and milk him of his ingenious idea. For as surely as there had to be a "first" jump-shooter, he is just as surely not to be found. However, most professional basketball writers and historians give credit to Jumping Joe Fulks (now where'd he get that name) as the chief perpetrator of this near-unstoppable maneuver, although they stop short of giving him the patent. Fulks was the first big scorer who employed the jump shot in the early National Basketball Association days and gained undying fame for his artistry by scoring 63 points all by himself in just one game.

If it took basketball forever and a day to produce the one-hand flying shot, it took but the extra day to disburse it to a nation of players. Almost overnight every player from professional ranks to the smallest high school acquired this new, exciting and point-inducing tactic, which soon made 76 points a game a common team total. When, a few years later, the NBA adopted the 24-second rule, which gave possession of the ball to the opponent if a team did not shoot within 24 seconds after gaining title to the ball, the scores instantly zoomed over the 100-point mark and basketball was a game of run-and-shoot, run-and-shoot. And, because the jumper is easy to shoot but very difficult to block, shooting became what basketball was all about. Only in the 1963's when the Boston Celtics emphasized defense and won everything all the time, was the trend lessened. But the 100-point level was still an everyday attainment and promises to be permanent party to Basketball until they put lids on the hoops.

The Wonder Five, precocious, talented, dedicated and becoming nearly a household word in the Adirondacks, apparently had little regard for a turn of events in the game they excelled at, whether it was still over a decade away or whether it was never to be. They played good, crisp basketball, running patterns of give-and-go off the pivot, which was manned by the tallest of the starting five, 6'1" George Fisk. They were early exponents of the fast break and passed the ball unfailingly to teammates in open spots, operating as a team without regard to individual statistics. That the two forwards, Willard White on the left and Jim Rovito on the right, were the team's top scorers attested to the fact that plays worked off the post gave the forwards an open shot near the foul line on either side of the lane. Both were above average shooters as, indeed, was the whole team.

When the Big Team from the Little Town presented its lineup, four starters would be at least six feet tall. The fifth, 5'8" Doug Binan, who also was the captain, played right guard and was the best ball handler in school. As a unit they were a big team physically, usually having a height advantage over their opponents even when pitted against class "A" competition. Also, as a unit, they worked their game to a flow of smoothness that was unparalleled in the North Country League and was approached by very few in the highest class.

If their passing and cutting game (called "ball control") was effectively defended, they shot two-hand set shots from the outside with accuracy that rendered a tight inner defense useless. Their collective scoring ability through 27 games in the 1932–33 season would outweigh their opponents two to one (1032 to 507).

Deep into the 16-game winning streak, when January began hinting of February, the Falls was to meet Malone in what was billed as "the game of games". Natural rivals due to geographical proximity but in different classes of competition due to a gross spread in student enrollments, Franklin Academy, of the higher class, was pitted against SRF in response to public demand. Reporter Ferris, whose eyes kept a steady vigil on SRF's basketball fortunes, dropped the "little mountain team, etc." from his descriptive repertoire and let two words do all the work. His January 17th article warned of "the invasion of the 'Wonder Five' from St. Regis Falls."

> The Saints have played together the past few seasons, have been successful because they play as a unit. Willard White and James Rovito have been the main scoring threats but when they are bottled up Captain Binan in the back court takes up the burden and makes a good job of it.

Gerald White, the other guard, and Fisk at Center are also good shots from almost any angle.

An all-time record crowd will see the game good weather or bad and St. Regis Falls will come to Malone en masse for the game of games.

The above-mentioned James Rovito remembers that contest well. That one and several other "big" games, all publicized well in advance, most against teams of a higher league, each one guaranteed to draw a capacity crowd and each, almost without fail, ending to the delight of Wonder Five fans.

"That Malone game was really something", he told me a few weeks ago as we sat sipping coke in his Highhat Lounge on Main Street in Tupper Lake. "That was the biggest crowd I ever saw. Just about everybody from SRF was there. They even hired busses to take the people out. We beat FA 33–30," he said, brushing away four decades' time with a memory that the years could not baffle.

When I reminded him that a Malone sportswriter-fan was impressed by his ability to shoot with his back to the basket, he smiled at the memory of Ferris. He explained to me how he scored with the reverse lay-up but I must pass on to you the descriptive words of the best fan the Wonder Five had in Malone following their upset of FA:

> The Saints presented a fast attack with Rovito, a tall, powerfully built youth the mainspring...They proved past masters at off-balance shots, making these with a whirligig motion while tilted at a 45-degree angle, or further amazed the crowd with back-handed, overhead flips that passed through the cords without even grazing the rim.

When Jim Rovito talks about the "Wonder Five", one listens. Separating the romance of their image from the facts of their success is not necessary here, for no closer to the proverbial horse's mouth can an inquisitive ear bend. When the visitor wondered about the secrets to their success, his answers proved that despite the radical changes in basketball between then and now, several constants remain, each, when blended with talent and disciplined with knowledge, being conducive to victory.

> Practice. That and being in shape. We could run all day. I didn't smoke or drink and I don't think any of the others did either. We even practiced on the weekends and played every team we could just to keep in condition.
>
> We played as a team and Charlie (coach LeMieux) would not stand for any fancy stuff. If we tried getting cute or didn't make the right passes, he let us know it.
>
> He pushed us hard on defense. Ours was a man-to-man—I don't think we ever played a zone.
>
> We had to be careful there, though, because we only had seven or eight guys on the team and foul trouble could really hurt us.

Defense in basketball seldom excites fans like a sharp scoring play always does but its importance is a top priority on any winning team. The Wonder Five, for all their scoring capabilities were demons on "the big dee", as fans call defense today. They frequently held their opponents to one or two points a quarter and in the words of Stanley Ferris, "follow the ball like hawks and refuse to be faked out of position. The defense they put up is almost impregnable".

But offense will gain the headlines and Willard White, who scored 316 points, and Mr. Rovito, who contributed 252, saw their names splashed across sports pages in large type after most games. He will admit to a friendly rivalry between the two.

> But it never affected our team play. We were trained to look for the best shot and we worked hard to get it. George Fisk, (center) was just great at passing to us cutting through the pivot. He would never miss us if we got by our man.

Jim also remembered with nostalgic delight that writers in Tupper Lake, following the 1-point loss in the early going, referred to his set as "the longtoms".

Willard would say over long distance telephone lines from Cheektowaga, New York (near Buffalo) where he is a police sergeant, that his favorite shot was a one-hander from between ten and fifteen feet out.

"But a lot of my points came on the fast break," he said. "Fisk got the rebounds and hit us with a quick pass and Rovito, Binan and I would get down-court for a quick basket."

George Fisk, a superb leaper who practically owned the deed to the center jump, may have been overshadowed by the scoring feats of the forwards but his contributions to the offense, especially on the fast break, were attested to by them. The team's leading rebounder, he cleared the boards and rifled a pass to a forward at the point.

"Or sometimes, on a missed foul shot, I'd just bat the ball in that direction," he told me, "and either Rovito or White would be there automatically. Binan would already be headed down-court and we'd have a fast break going. That Rovito was the fastest big man I ever saw at getting down-court."

If that sounds like unbeatable teamwork, it was both that and the results of years of practice together that molded the team into a cohesive unit which always placed team ahead of indivdual.

And if Charlie LeMieux coached the team through its greatest hours, just as surely Carl Daniels, the Principal, laid the ground work for its success. It was he who took the boys in hand and, when the Wonder Five was still in the embryonic stage, pressed the stamp of teamwork into their basketball fibers.

In the words of Mr. Fisk, "he deserves all the credit in the world for our success."

Records will attest to the point productions of the front-line forwards but our out-of-town reporter was also duly impressed by Douglas Binan, the sparkplug little captain.

> The squad members are tall, clean cut and rangy without awkwardness. When Rovito, who specialized in flipping them in backwards, and White are contained, Binan, the captain and smallest man on the team, becomes the mainspring. The "mighty mite" is a thorn in their opponents' sides.

Mr. Curtis Benham, who lives on the Days Mills Road, was a faithful fan of the Big Five and recalls vividly the abilities of Doug Binan, ball handler.

> He was a great factor in their success. You can't say enough about him. He got the ball into the forecourt for them and was a whiz at dribbling.

I'll never forget a play he made in that big Malone game in early 1933, when we beat them 33–30. George Fisk tipped the ball to Doug who headed down the court, dribbled the ball right through his defender's leg and scored less than five seconds into the game! The crowd went wild.

As their winning streak matured so too did the precision with which they operated. The cumulative effects of the many hours of practice would sometimes emerge in unison and on better nights the Wondrous Warriors would be nearly on speaking terms with perfection. Whereas only routine effort was required in most of their games, the skills which were at their command also were properly tempered with victory's precious offspring—confidence.

When game pressures mounted and victory began flirting with defeat, the cool professionalism of the Fabulous Five guided storms before lightning struck. Panic, although not party to the team's play, was a definite by-product of it, easily recognized in the performance of their foes. The gifts of their reputation were many.

The popularity of the team became almost unbelievable as their victories and press clippings continued to increase.

"We practically owned the town," Mr. Rovito recalled. "We were given banquets, free suppers, free movie passes. It's hard to believe the way we were treated."

"Our strongest supporters were Percy Rowell, Earl LaPoint, and Mrs. Anabel Green."

"We were treated like royalty, and that's no kidding," adds George Fisk.

When this writer was attending SRF High the late Gene Danforth was resident coach and, in later years, athletic director. It was only after several lengthy discussions with Mr. Danforth, who was well-known and highly respected throughout entire upstate New York, that I went on public record with favorable comparisons between the Wonder Five and the Super Saints of 1969. At the expense of reiteration, I chose not to blend image with hearsay but searched for a credible analysis and knowledgeable comparison.

I, like all who knew Gene, maintained a high index of faith in his opinion. A man of well-chosen words but not given to offhand compliments, he bore witness to the play of both teams, first as a participant on the Wonder Five and last as a coach and consultant of the later-day Saints. From him, I knew, an intelligent comparison would be forthcoming which I could quote without fear of vicarious embarrassment.

Would they, I asked him one early January day of the super year, match up favorably against the Wonder Five if the changes in basketball over the years were given proper consideration?

With that thought in mind, he said, "I'd say they compare favorably. The changes have been many and have had such a speeding-up effect on the game that it would be difficult to say one way or the other who would win if they met. But I think that if we (the Wonder Five) played our game, where the emphasis was on ball control, we might beat them. However, if it was the other way around and the fast offensive game of today was the deciding factor, they might beat us."

When I asked Jim Rovito about Gene's role with the Wonder Five, he answered with words that would surprise not one single sports fan in town.

"He was a great shooter," said Mr. Rovito.

For those of us who knew that but little more, Jim continued,

> He was a terrific sixth man for us. He alternated as a substitute between the guard and forward positions and did a great job. He had an outstanding shot form the corner that he delivered with one hand. It wasn't really a jump shot but he shifted his body to a slanting angle and gave a little push with his feet when he shot it. He was deadly from that spot.

When the victory express completed its 16-game voyage on February 9, 1933, it was not without at least a hint of injustice, although if thoughts in that vein were present, words in kind were not forth-coming. But the loss came immediately following a 60-mile automobile ride through one of the winter's worst nights and cars of that day more closely resembled igloos than furnaces. The team, chilled to the bone, took the floor in an inadequately heated gym and were frozen out of the game before they were really ever in it.

Playing basketball with icy hands and frosted bodies is no harder than playing the guitar with boxing gloves on but the city of Ogdensburg, conquerors of the Wonder Five, would conveniently not make that comparison. Nor would a rematch of those two teams ever be staged.

For fans who delight in sports trivia and search for coincidences, the only St. Regis Falls varsity whose talents invited public debate about the Wonder Five and compared favorably with it, also met defeat at the hands of Ogdensburg Free Academy. The 1968-69 Super Saints, winners in 19 of their previous 20 games, in the last game they would ever play together, were 15-point victims of OFA in a one-game playoff for the Section Ten title.

And, to further feed the lovers of happenstance, the 1969 SRF team, like the Wonder Five in 1932–33, went undefeated through its entire regular league season. For dessert, both teams were represented by the name Danforth (Gene and Larry, his son).

The Victory March was halted on but one more occasion in the '33 season. After the loss to OFA, the Wonder Five's record was 18-and-2. They immediately regrouped and beat Bombay, Moira, Norwood and Chateaugay before Malone took their measure in a return match, 26-19, just before the playoffs.

Post-season games always generate more excitement in basketball and bring the campaign to its highest peak of entertainment and competition. Fans are continually reminded that class always tells in head-to-head playoffs and with the Wonder Five, class told in glowing terms.

They closed their fantastic year with a smashing exhibition in the tournament. On March 19 they scored a 55-29 win over Elizabethtown in which they piled up a 19-2 lead in the first quarter. Rovito and White, the two big scorers, were in prime form, getting 17 and 16 points respectively. Binan, the "mighty mite", added nine and Danforth six.

Then, the following evening, in true display of the image of their name, fame and glory, the Wonder Five became the first team in North Country League history to win a sectionals crown. They demolished Morristown, themselves victors in seventeen straight games, 44-16 in the Franklin Academy gym to capture the Class "B" championship of Section Seven. In so doing their record was upped to 24-3!

Listed below are the individual scoring totals for the year:

NAME	G	FG	FTA	FT	FT%	PTS.	PPG
W. White	27	144	52	28	.538	316	11.3
G. Fisk	27	25	24	13	.542	63	2.3
G. White	26	41	46	21	.457	103	3.9
J. Rovito	25	114	45	24	.533	252	10.1
G. Danforth	24	15	13	7	.538	37	1.5
D. Binan	23	61	74	45	.608	167	7.3
E. Woods	20	30	18	7	.389	67	3.4
K. Bennett	19	2	3	1	.333	5	0.3
* Besaw	7	10	9	2	.222	22	3.1

*Besaw played 7 games with the Wonder Five and then went to MAI at Plattsburgh.

Winning everything in sight in 1933 did for the Wonder Five what it does for nearly every team that gains title to a championship when the regular cast will return the following season. Scaling the heights and claiming the unclaimable for a town the size, or lack of it, of St. Regis Falls was not the biggest thing, important though it was. For in creating an image that was beyond local conception, wrapped in laces of gold and placed above mere mortals, the SRF quintet was placing demands upon themselves that were alien to other teams in their class. From then on they were EXPECTED to win every game they played.

All great teams, even super ones, lose one now and then. No one ever invented a team that never lost. "You can't win 'em all" it may be, it rings soundly with words of truth. SRF's Fantastic Five, if not actually exempt from the law of averages, was quite slow in obeying it.

They dropped a couple games early the next season when several regulars were ineligible but would return in the second half to reinvent their magic of 1933. They would capture another championship for the colors of SRF and would carry on for years as a town team with an even higher victory percentage. But the glory of their times would always radiate from a swift rise to fame that put St. Regis Falls, a mere semi-colon on the map, into up-state New York's sports spotlight.

And so, when time and eternity, in their inevitable merger, collaborated against the Wonder Five, its players were disbursed into the world with a common bond that would identify them forever in the eyes and minds of area citizens. Their credentials for fame were ample testimony to their deeds.

Jim Rovito, four decades, three wars and six presidents after the actual fact, still is asked if he's THE Jim Rovito of Wonder Five fame by people whose parents watched the legend during its construction. His son, a two-time All-Northern basketeer and now a teacher in Malone, courts remembrances to his father regularly from his associations in a town where the Wonder Five played only as visitors, and infrequent ones at that.

Basketball may have had several face liftings since the mid 1930's but the Wonder Five is now—and will be for generations to come—the yardstick by which success on St. Regis Falls basketball courts is measured.

The "Wonder Five" Basketball Team was not the school team, but the town team.

EDUCATION • 53

SRF basketball team, 1913; youth at far right is Melvin John Gibbs

SRF basketball team, 1915

St. Regis Falls School, ca. 1919

St. Regis Falls School, Fourth grade, 1921.
Mrs. Inez Hill, Charlie LaRose, Vivian Priore, Bertha White, _____ LaVare, Mable LaRose, Elmer Garuske, Leroy Woods, Kenneth Parks, Earl Scully, Stanley Sawyer, Raymond Ames, Eric Palmer, Harry James, Albert O'Neil, Cornelius _____, Edward Ploof, Lindon Hicks, Daisy Barkley, Ethel Kelley, Bernice DeLaire, Viola St. Dennis, Anna Dufrane, Mae Whitromb, Margarette Lagray, Leona Ploof, Marion _____, Annabel Niles, Idella Palmer, Ella Owens, Carmen Brabon, Ethel Rivers, Loretta Farmer, Rita Sculley, Lena Delaire, Lenore LaRose

EDUCATION • 55

St. Regis Falls, 5th Grade, 1922
Miss Kate Humphery, Henry Austin, Albert O'Neil, George Goodrow, Murray Mayo, Thomas Goodrow, Leroy Woods, Eric Palmer, Eford Cummings, Kenneth Parks, Cornelius Thoay, Raymond Ames, Edward Ploof, Viola St. Dennis, Vivian Priore, Daisy Barkley, Jeanne Prailly, Elmer Garuske, Bernard Arquite, Leona Ploof, Mae Whitcomb, Annabele Woods, Florence Dougal, Mildred Ashton, Anna Dufrane, Leonare Larose, Loretta Farmer, Lena DeLaire, Idella Palmer, Margarette Hewitte, Bernice DeLaire, Marion St. John, Carmen Bramen

Mendelson, Harvey, Frank Parks, Izzo, Sharpetone, Wager, Bandy, Baker, Dufor, Chebensky, Giffen, Cumming, LaMieux, Russell, Benham, Young

St. Regis Falls School, ca. 1919
The second girl on left is Pearl Potter, and sixth from left is Daisy Barkley-Fadden

St. Regis Falls, 4th Grade, 1922
The rightmost boy is Leroy Fadden; top row second girl is Pearl Fadden, who died of appendisitis at 18

EDUCATION • 57

St. Regis Falls, 5th Grade, 1934
Left to right, top row: Douglas Lapoint, Harold DeLosh, Carleton White, Marie Clark, Gorgianna Bagnato, Glencie Palmer, Harold Ford, Ethel Supernault, Basil Horton, Elaine Alridge, Audrey Betterly, Rose Deno, Laura LeMieux (teacher), Margaret Clookey, Audrey Decar. Front row (seated): Glenford Niles, Ester Martin, Almond Wait, Charles DeCar, Floyd DeBuque, Keith Smith, Bucky Gokey, Arthur LaVair, Pete Morick

St. Regis Falls Central School Band
Left to right, top row: Roslie LaChance, schoolteacher, Nelson Fadden, Clarence Cook, Earl Parker. Bottom row: Betty Haskel, Sylvia Winters, Constance Cook, Betty Marsh, Jack Lemar, John Tripany, ?, Barbara Powell, _____ Tripany, Elsie Bishop, Arlene Conley.

Ruth Barkley-Jackson;
SRF School in
background

EDUCATION • 59

Saint Regis Falls, Freshman Class, 1946–7
Left to right, top row: Frank Parks, Robert Ploof, Robert Cox, Wallace Story, Perry _____, Harry Haynes, Ralph Parker. Bottom row: Robert Boyce, Betty Goodrow, Claire Hunkins, Della Mushtare, Terica Payne, Freeda Genoway, Donald Richards

60 • WATER OVER THE FALLS

St. Regis Falls Junior Varsity, 1946–7
Standing, left to right: Coach Sam Izzo, Orville Perry, Nelson Fadden, Emerson Betterly, Earl Parker, Tom Barrett, Principal Harry Wager. Kneeling: Keith Marsh, Howard Palmer, Clyde Kelley, John Marsh

Chapter 6
ENTERTAINMENT

The first moving pictures were at Tryon's (the building that was next to the bank, which burned in the spring of 1983). There was a stage on the second floor, an area about 30 feet by 50 feet. Many meetings and live shows were held there. The time period was around 1903.

The Star Theater, 1909, was located in the Bishop's Hotel Building where the parking lot of the present custard stand is on Main Street. The Star then relocated to River Street, then called Tannery Street, across from where Ross' Store is now.

The Pastine Theater, 1913, owned by F. W. Aldrich. Location was possibly in the lot between the post office and the Legion Hall.

The Regent Theater, also owned by F. W. Aldrich, then by Fred LeMieux, presented the first talking picture February 21, 1931. Before this there were only silent movies. The Regent Theater burned around 1937 or 1938. This theater was located on Main Street near the Legion Hall.

There was another theater in the old Southworth Building on South Main Street, (just up from the bridge on the west side of the street) owned by Mr. LaValley. George DeBoice ran it for Mr. LaValley until it burned around 1949 or 1950.

Chapter 7

LAW ENFORCEMENT

On June 7, 1921, Troop "B" of the New York State Police was officially headquartered in Malone. It consisted of forty-eight troopers. Troop "B" became known as the "Black Horse Troop". The first troop car was a 1923 Model "T" Ford.

The St. Regis Falls outpost was established in 1922 or 1923 and was originally located at the Waverly House. The mounted patrol quartered their horses at the rear of the Waverly in stables operated by William Kidney. It was at this location that persons vandalized the troopers leather saddles, reins, etc., causing then troop commander, Captain Charles J. Broadfield, to relocate the troopers to Mrs. Robeson's residence, a large white house located across from the Catholic Church on North Main Street.

Some of the troopers stationed in St. Regis Falls in 1923 were John Tierney, H. Lavaseur, T. J. Ryan and Donald Martin.

Sometime after 1926, troopers were again relocated to Otto Smith's garage and residence on the Nicholville Road and still later were quartered at Dr. Frank Green's residence on North Main Street.

The State Police outpost was removed from St. Regis Falls in 1960, as part of a consolidation effort by the State Police; however, the area continues to be patrolled by troopers assigned at the Malone barracks.

Chapter 8
ORGANIZATIONS

Durkee Post, G.A.R. #504, was one of the first organized groups. However, it was a very short lived organization with membership steadily decreasing—veterans from the Civil War fast being summoned to their last final roll call.

Lodge #100, I.O.O.F. was organized December 1886, with Hon. William H. Flack, Noble Grand and S. R. Gile, Vice Grand. The first building housing the lodge was destroyed by fire. The second building was then constructed at a cost of about $8,000.

The upper floor occupied by the lodge room and rented other rooms to the masons and a number of local organizations. Ground floor occupied two business places, one of which was used for a post office.

Blue Mountain Lodge #874, F.&A.M. was organized June 29, 1909. Jerry LaPoint was Worshipful Master and J. L. Blood, Senior Warden.

The St. Ann's Society was organized in 1919 with Mrs. Margaret Breyer as President.

The Oneita Rebekah Lodge #264 was instituted in 1902 with Mrs. Anna D. Falusha as Noble Grand.

The Order of the Eastern Stars #455 was organized in 1909 with Lena Wardner as Matron.

SANITARIUM

A sanitarium for the treatment of alcoholics and drug abusers was transferred to St. Regis Falls from Tupper Lake in 1893. There were a considerable number of patients for two or three years. Many cures actually "stuck" in many decidedly tough cases. Other ailments were also treated here. The establishment closed due to business failure. Known as the "Kill or Cure" Sanitarium, it burned in 1913 and was located at the lower end of St. Ann Street.

Odd Fellow's Hall

Lodge #100, I.O.O.F. was located where the American Legion Hall and Senior Citizen Center is now

The ruins of the I.O.O.F. building, looking north
This was before the school and Methodist Church burned in 1926.

Waverly Band, 1892—Stand in front of Webb's Block, Main Street Side

The Third Waverly Town Band
Left to right, top row: Mel Reed, Robert Carlin, Pat Clookey, Fred Raymo, Arthur Bouckard, Ed Bero. Front row: William Owens, Thomas Marcus, Perry Bishop, William DeShaw, Phillip Prior, Louis Bouckard.

Photos of some of St. Regis Fall's Civil War veterans

CIVIL WAR VETERANS

Civil War (1861–1865) Veterans taken from St. Regis Falls Cemetery Records.

NAME	DATES	RANK	UNIT
Besa, Alex	1846-1929 ('63–'65)		Co. F, 193rd N.Y. Inf.
Brabon, Oliver F.			Co. F, 16th N.Y. Cav.
Brown, Alexander	Feb. 28, 1835–July 3, 1923	Pvt.	Co. F, 142nd Reg., N.Y. Inf.
Bruce, Jonah C.	d. Mar. 17, 1908, age 62 yrs.		Co. D, 142nd Reg., N.Y.V. N.Y.S.
Caskinett, Richard	d. Apr. 21, 1909, age 62 yrs.	Prin.	
Clooky, William B.	d. Oct. 20, 1917, age 74 yrs.	Pvt.	Co. G, 142nd Reg., N.Y.S.V.
Cuturia, Joseph	1842-1899		Co. E, 8th Reg., Vt. Vet. Vol.
Debien, Francis	d. May 18, 1896, age 60 yrs.		Co. I, 118th Reg., N.Y.I.V.
DeLania, John D.	d. June 24, 1900, age 59 yrs.		N.H.V.
Dubuque, Thomas	1838-1928		Co. I, 60th Reg., N.Y.V.
Dugall, Joseph	1843-1909	Pvt.	22nd Reg., N.Y. Vol.
Gardner, Joseph	d. Nov. 5, 1890, age 64 yrs.		Co. K, 1st Reg., Vt. A
Haley, Clark	d. Feb. 7, 1901, age 70 yrs.		142nd Reg., N.Y.V.
Harvey, William H.	1840-1921	Pvt.	LD F, 16th Brig., N.Y.V.
Hill, James S.	d. Aug. 14, 1890, age 50 yrs. 10 mos.		Co. F, 193rd Reg., N.Y.V.
Hunkins, Harrison	1839-1919		12th N.Y. Cal. Vol.
Johnson, Adnor	1842-1933		Co. F, 14th Reg.
King, Theodore	d. May 30, 1910, age 83 yrs.	Pvt.	Co. C, 5th Reg., N.Y. Vol.
LaBounty, Simeon	1845-1920	Pvt.	Co. K, 118th N.Y.V. Inf., UFF
LaCroix, Jacob	d. Feb. 1889, age 53 yrs.		Co. D, 98th N.Y.S.
Mashtar, John	d. Mar. 10, 1904, age 67 yrs.		Co. A, 95th Reg., N.Y.V.

CIVIL WAR VETERANS (cont.)

Name	Dates	Rank	Unit
Palmer, Henry S.	1833-1905	Corp.	Co. A, 14th N.Y.H. Art.
Peck, Otis W.	d. Feb. 2, 1909, age 66 yrs.		Co. F, 92nd Reg., N.Y. Vol.
Perry, Martin	d. July 5, 1906, age 80 yrs.		Co. A, 98th Reg., N.Y.S. Inf.
Phipps, John	d. Jan. 26, 1908, age 75 Yrs.	Pvt.	10th Reg., N.Y. Ca.
Pierce, Henry M.	d. June 8, 1902, age 57 yrs. 10 mos. 5 days		
Richards, Francis R.	1837-1916	Pvt.	Co. D, 11th Reg., N.Y. Cal. Vol.
Ross, John G.	d. Feb. 16, 1901, age 76 yrs.		Co. H, 106th Reg., N.Y. Inf.
Shampine, Charles	d. Dec. 13, 1913, age 67 yrs.		Co. F, 142nd Reg., N.Y.V.
Somers, G. Arba	1845–1917		Co. C, 6th Reg., N.Y.V.
Stone, Joseph	d. July 25, 1899, age 78 yrs.		Co. F, 142nd Reg., N.Y.V.
Thomas, Matthias E.	d. May 4, 1907, age 67 yrs.		Co. K, 17th Reg., Vt. Vol.
Wardner, L. M., M.D.	d. Jan. 12, 1896, age 54 yrs.		Co. D, 7th Reg. N.Y.H. Art.
Wards, William E.	d. Jan. 29, 1898, age 79 yrs.		Co. C, 1st Vt. Cav. Vol.
			Co. A, 142nd Reg., N.Y.V.

Additional Civil War Veterans

Ezeckel Hewitt	Columbus Farr	Nelson Ramsdell	Allan Bastin
Edward Day	Cyrus Redear	Allan Farr	Adams Haynes
John Ramsdell	Sydney Irish	Colson Somers	Harvey Waste
Ezra Joanette	Isaac Farr	Antione Young	Philemon Wood
Ogilvy S. Southworth	Guy Hollister	David Rivers	John Gibbs
James Gibbs	Martin Giffin		

ORGANIZATIONS • 69

SPANISH-AMERICAN WAR

Spanish-American War (1898) Veterans taken from St. Regis Falls Cemetery Records.

NAME RANK	DATES UNIT
DeShaw, Albert C. Pvt.	Sept. 5, 1870-July 18, 1911 TRPE 3rd N.Y. Reg. Calvary
Soetemon, Peter W. 1st Sgt.	June 15, 1867-Oct. 20, 1950, N.Y. Co. B 203rd N.Y. Inf.
Surprise, Frank B of Rt.	1856- 183rd of O.N.Y.

Spanish-American War veterans of St. Regis Falls
front: Aloney, Babcock, Carl Drew, unknown, Phil Prior, Sr.
back row: Henry Allen, _____ Jewler, Alfred Currier, Pvt. Clookey, Mert McGovern

WORLD WAR I VETERANS

Aldrich, Cherol, St. Regis Falls
father—Edwin Aldrich, St. Regis Falls
In June 1918, went to New York University-Auto Mechanic

Austin, Wesley C., Private, St. Regis Falls
father—Charles W. Austin, St. Regis Falls
Co. H, 59th Pioneer Inf.
July 21, 1918 went to Camp Dix, Wrightstown, N.J.
Aug. 31, 1918 sailed for France on "Leviathan" embarking at Hoboken, N.J.
July 15, 1919 returned to U.S.A. on "Leviathan", landing at Hoboken, N.J.
discharged-July 9, 1919.

Baker, Henry Joseph, Private, St. Regis Falls
wife—Mrs. Fannie Baker, Dickinson Center
301st Ambulance Co., 301st Sanitary Train 4th Corps. 3rd Army.
Oct. 5, 1917 went to Camp Devens, Ayer, Mass.
July 12, 1918 sailed for France on "Durham Castle" embarking at Montreal, P.Q. June 1919 returned to U.S.A. on "Calamares" landing at Boston Harbor
discharged June 18, 1919.

Barnes, Wayne D., Private, St. Regis Falls
father—Charles A. Barnes, St. Regis Falls
Co. A, 108th M.G. Battalion, 28th Div
May 10, 1918 went to Camp Hancock, Ga., sailed for France, embarking at Newport News, Va.
Oct. 3, 1918 gassed
Returned to U.S.A. on "Peerless", landing at Philadelphia, Pa.
discharged Apr. 30, 1918

Bean, Harvey F., Private, St. Regis Falls
Parents—Mr. & Mrs. Peter Bean, St. Regis Falls
Co. H, 59th Pioneer Inf.

ORGANIZATIONS • 71

July 21, 1918 sailed for France on "Leviathan", embarking at Hoboken, N.J.
July 5, 1919 returned to U.S.A. on "Leviathan"
discharged July 9, 1919.

Blade, Fay E. E., Private 1st Cl, St. Regis Falls
Parents—Mr. & Mrs. B. E. Blade, St. Regis Falls
Battery A, 308th Field Art., 153rd Field Art. Brigade, 78th Div.
Apr. 30, 1918—went to Camp Dix, Wrightstown, N.J.
May 26, 1918—sailed for France on the "Cedric", embarking at New York.
Returned to U.S.A. on "Pesaro" landing at New York.
Discharged May 26, 1919.

Blade, Leo J., Private, St. Regis Falls
Parents—Mr. & Mrs. B. E. Blade, St. Regis Falls
Co. J., Fighting Mechanics
July 1, 1918—went to Buffalo Tech., thence to Camp Upton, L. I.
Discharged Sept. 4, 1918

Brown, Judson, St. Regis Falls
Co. B, 306th Field Battalion, Signal Corps.
Went to Camp Jackson, S.C.

Campbell, Benjamin L., Private, St. Regis Falls
reference—Mrs. Inez Campbell, Moira
Co. F, 312th Engineers, 87th Div.
July 25, 1918—went to Camp Dix, Wrightstown, N.J.
Aug. 24, 1918—sailed for France on the "Corona", embarking at Hoboken, N.J.
June 25, 1919—returned to U.S.A. on "Dakotian"
Discharged June 27, 1919.

Carlin, Charles H., Corporal, St. Regis Falls
parents—Mr. & Mrs. Charles Carlin, St. Regis Falls
Co. G and Headquarters Co., 7th Inf. 3rd Div.
Nov. 21, 1917—went to Camp Green, N.C.

Apr. 6, 1918—sailed for France on "America", embarking at Hoboken, N.J.
Participated in all the battles that were credited to 3rd Div.
Aug 21, 1919 returned to U.S.A. on "Kaiserine Augusta Vicoria" landing at Brooklyn, N.Y.
Discharged Aug. 27, 1919.

Caskinett, Alfred, Buck Private, St. Regis Falls
Parents—Mr. & Mrs. Hays Caskinett, St. Regis Falls
Co. D, 347th Inf. 87th Div.
July 21, 1918—Went to Camp Dix, Wrightstown, N.J.
Aug. 26, 1918—sailed for France, retuned to U.S.A. on "Mauritania"
Discharged Jan. 18, 1919.

Caskinett, George, St. Regis Falls
May 27, 1918—went to Camp Devens, Ayer, Mass. thence to Camp Gordon, Ga.

Caskinett, Mose, St. Regis Falls
mother—Mrs. Emma Caskinett, St. Regis Falls
Sept. 9, 1918—went to Camp Jackson, S.C.

Cheney, Harold W., Private, St. Regis Falls
Parents—Mr. & Mrs. Fred Cheney, St. Regis Falls
Co. B, 309th Inf. 78th "Lightning" Div.
Apr. 1, 1918—Went to Camp Dix, Wrightstown, N.J.
May 20, 1918—Sailed for France on "Morvada", embarking at Hoboken, N.J.
Served as Runner or Message Carrier.
June 1, 1919—returned to U.S.A. on "Lancaster"
Discharged June 7, 1919.

Christian, William P., St. Regis Falls
wife—Mrs. Eva Christian, St. Regis Falls
Sept. 9, 1918—Went to Camp Jackson, S.C.
Discharged Dec. 1918.

Clothier, Marshall, St. Regis Falls
Oct. 6, 1917—Went to Camp Wheeler, Ga.

Conger, Ernest, St. Regis Falls
Father—Ernest Conger
Went to Camp Wadsworth, Spartanburg, S.C.

Cummings, Martin B.,Corporal, St. Regis Falls
Parents—Mr. & Mrs. James Cummings, St. Regis Falls
15th Canadian Battalion, 48th Highlanders of Canada
No. 4 Co. 13th Platoon 3rd Canadian Brigade, 1st Canadian Div.
Mar. 21, 1916—Enlisted in 53rd Battalion of Cornwall, Ontario
June 10, 1916—Went to Barry Field Camp, Kingston, Ontario.
Oct. 14, 1916—Sailed for France on embarking at Halifax, N.S.
Served as Lewis Gun Corporal, wounded twice; also slightly gassed.
Aug. 8, 1918—received gunshot, wounding thumb and fingers.
Served in France and England. Received one gold stripe.
May 7, 1919 returned to Halifax on "Baltic"
Discharged May 29, 1919.

Dabiew, George C., Private, St. Regis Falls
Parents—Mr. & Mrs. Frank Dabiew, St. Regis Falls
Co. D, 347th Inf. U.S.A., 87th Div.
July 21, 1918—Went to Camp Dix, Wrightstown, N.J.
Aug. 26, 1918—Sailed for France, embarking at New York
Jan. 1, 1919 returned to U.S.A. on "Mauritania", landing at New York
Discharged Jan. 18, 1919.

DeCarr, Samuel, Private, St. Regis Falls
Reference, Louise DeCarr, St. Regis Falls
Co. C, 311th Reg. of Inf. 78th Div.
Apr. 29, 1918—Went to Camp Dix, Wrightstown, N.J.

May 29, 1918—Sailed for France, embarking at Hoboken, N.J.
Acted as Scout. Returned to U.S.A. on "Mexican" landing at New York
Discharged Mar. 18, 1919.

Delaire, Fred G., Private, St. Regis Falls
Reference—James Delaire, St. Regis Falls
Co. E, 2nd Reg. 77th Div.
Apr. 5, 1917—Went to Camp Devens, Ayer, Mass.
July 4, (no year stated) sailed for France, embarking at Hoboken, N.J.
Participated in battle of Argonne Forest.
May 5, 1919 returned to U.S.A. on "Mount Vernon", landing at New York.
Discharged May 9, 1919.

Delaire, Thomas H., 2nd Lieut., St. Regis Falls
Father—David Delaire, St. Regis Falls
10th Co. 20th Engineers
Feb. 7, 1918—Went to American University, Washington, D.C.
Feb. 27, 1918—Sailed for France on "Mount Vernon" embarking at Hoboken, N.J.
June 1, 1919—Returned to U.S.A. on "Luckenbuck" landing in Hoboken, N.J.
Discharged June 10, 1919.

Donovan, Daniel H., St. Regis Falls
Mother—Mrs. Phoebe Donovan, St. Regis Falls
Sept. 9, 1918—Went to Camp Jackson, S.C., thence to Camp Gordon, Ga.

Dow, Floyd, 1st Lieut., St. Regis Falls
Father—Frank B. Dow, St. Regis Falls
Quartermaster's Dept.
Sept. 22, 1917—Went to Camp Devens, Ayer, Mass., thence to Camp Meade, Md.
Discharged Dec. 1918.

ORGANIZATIONS • 75

Dupre, Bayard T., 1st Sergeant, St. Regis Falls
Co. A, 310th Inf. 78th Div.
Went to Camp Dix, Wrightstown, N.J.

Duprey, Henry, St. Regis Falls
Aug. 23, 1918—Went to Camp Gordon, Ga. (deceased)

Fadden, Arthur H., Private, St. Regis Falls
Parents—Mr. & Mrs. James Fadden, St. Regis Falls
Battery A, 35th Reg. 12th Div. Field Art.
Aug. 6, 1918—Went to Fort Slocum, N.Y., thence to Camp McClellan, Alabama and Camp Upton, L. I.
Discharged Feb. 6, 1919.

Farmer, Clarence, Sailor, St. Regis Falls
U.S. Navy, stationed at Newport, R.I.

Farmer, Floyd, St. Regis Falls
Reference—John Farmer, St. Regis Falls
Went to Camp Upton, L.I., thence to Fort Slocum, N.Y.

Fortier, Joseph A., Seaman 2-C, St. Regis Falls
Parents—Mr. & Mrs. E. J. Fortier, formerly of S.R.F. (then resided in Bury, Ontario, Canada)
July 9, 1918—Went to U.S. Naval Training Station, Newport, R.I.
Transferred to Receiving Ship at Boston, Mass. At Newport, R.I. was with 8th Reg. 18th Co. at Boston, Mass. with 11th Div. Was made a yeoman in Dec. 1918 and released as such on Apr. 1, 1919.

Fullerton, Willis, Sergeant, St. Regis Falls
Sister—Miss Muriel Fullerton, South Glens Falls, N.Y.
Battery F, 52nd Art. RAR with 4th French Army
Enlisted Aug. 1, 1914.
Aug. 25, 1917—Sailed for overseas on "Panonia", an English Ship. Was first with Battery K, 8th Reg. of Art. RAR 1st Div. On July 5, 1918 at the second Battle of Marne, was under German shell fire for four days and nights, "My first

engagement was on May 3, 1918; was in sixteen different engagements."

Jan. 3, 1919—Returned to U.S.A. on USS "Antigone", landing at Newport News, Va.

Discharged Jan. 30, 1919, furloughed to the Regular Army Reserves.

Galyen, Lonnie G., Chief Cook, St. Regis Falls
Reference—Mollie Jane Galyen Hewlett, Va.
327th Fire and Guard Co. Quartermaster's Corps.
Aug. 5, 1918 went to Syracuse, N.Y., thence to Camp Stuart, Va. and Camp Lee, Va.
Discharged Dec. 26, 1918.

Guthrie, E. Julian, Seaman 2nd C, St. Regis Falls
U.S. Naval Air Forces.

Hawkins, Clarence F., Private 1st C, St. Regis Falls
Reference—Mrs. Henry Hawkins, St. Regis Falls
Co. H., Headquarters Troop 3rd Div. 8th U.S. Inf.
July 3, 1917—Went to Syracuse, N.Y., thence to Camp Greene, N.C.
In Apr. 1918, sailed for France on the "George Washington" landing at Hoboken, N.J.
Discharged July 22, 1920.

Hawkins, Warren H., Wagoner, St. Regis Falls
Parents—Mr. & Mrs. Henry Hawkins, St. Regis Falls
Supply Co., 50th U.S. Inf. 20th Div.
July 3, 1917—went to Syracuse, N.Y., thence to Camp Dix, Wrightstown, N.J. and to Camp Merritt, N.J.
Discharged Mar. 29, 1918.

Hazen, Kyle, St. Regis Falls
Father—Fred Hazen, St. Regis Falls
Sept. 22, 1918—Went to Camp Devens, Ayer, Mass. Came back home on furlough, and rather than go back into service, was supposed to have drowned himself in Baker Pond,

near St. Regis Falls. His coat and hat were found on the bank of the pond—he has never been heard from since.

Hewitt, John, St. Regis Falls
May 27, 1918—Went to Camp Wadsworth, Spartanburg, S.C.

Johnston, Frederick W., Private, St. Regis Falls
Reference—Alexander H. Johnston, Canada
66th Co., 17th Bat. 153rd Dept. Brigade
Oct. 23, 1918—Went to Camp Wheeler, Ga., thence to Camp Dix, Wrightstown, N.J.
Discharged Dec. 23, 1918.

LaFave, Andrew, Navy, St. Regis Falls
Mother—Mrs. Clara Defore, St. Regis Falls
May 1, 1918—Went to Pelham Bay, N.Y., thence to Key West, Fla. Was in the Signal Corps. Naval Reserves
Released Feb. 26, 1919.

LaFave, Francis H., Seaman, 2nd C, St. Regis Falls
Co. B, 309th Reg.
Went to Camp Dix, Wrightstown, N.J.

LaFrance, Joseph, Private, St. Regis Falls
Parents—Mr. & Mrs. Samuel LaFrance, St. Regis Falls
Co. A, 2nd Div. ARF
Sept. 9, 1919—Went to Camp Jackson, S.C., thence to Camp Upton, L.I.
Discharged Dec. 31, 1919.

LaGray, Henry, St. Regis Falls
Wife—Mrs. Helen LaGray, St. Regis Falls
Sept. 9, 1918—Went to Camp Jackson, S.C.

Lang, Fred W., Private, St. Regis Falls
Wife—Mrs. Elizabeth M. Lang, St. Regis Falls
Headquarters Co. 13th Reg.

Sept. 9, 1918—Went to Camp Jackson, S.C., thence to Camp Dix, Wrightstown, N.J.
Was first with Battery B 13th Reg. 5th Brigade FARD
Discharged Dec. 30, 1918.

LaRose, Louis H., Private, St. Regis Falls
Parents—Mr. & Mrs. Nelson LaRose, St. Regis Falls
Co. D, 310th Inf. 78th Div.
Aug. 25, 1918—Went to Camp Gordon, Atlanta, Ga.
Sept. 16, 1918 sailed for France, embarking at Hoboken, N.J.
Returned to U.S.A. on the "Luckenburg", landing at Hoboken, N.J.
Discharged June 6, 1919.

LaRouche, Earl A., Private 1st C, St. Regis Falls
Parents—Mr. & Mrs. Henry LaRouche, St. Regis Falls
Co. D, 301st Engineers 76th Div. transferred to the 4th Army Corps.
Mar. 2, 1918—Went to Camp Devens, Ayer, Mass.
July 14, 1918—Sailed for France on "Katoomba", embarking at South Brooklyn, N.Y.
June 3, 1919—Returned to U.S.A. on "Calamares", landing at Boston, Mass.
Discharged June 20, 1919.

LaRouche, George, Navy, St. Regis Falls
USS "Fanning"
Sept. 29, 1920—Still in service on USS "Fanning" during the War. Then in active service in European waters, on "Smith Thompson".

LeMieux, Fred W., Private, St. Regis Falls
Wife—Mrs. Mayme Beyette LeMieux, St. Regis Falls
Co. C, 6th Replacement Inf. Reg.
Aug. 26, 1918 went to Camp Gordon, Atlanta, Ga.
Discharged Jan. 11, 1919.

ORGANIZATIONS • 79

Ludic, Clarence E., St. Regis Falls
Troop E, 6th Cavalry

Ludrick, Otis H., Corporal, St. Regis Falls
Mother—Mrs. Mary Ludrick, St. Regis Falls
15th Ordnance, Guard Co.
Sept. 3, 1918—Went to Syracuse, N.Y., thence to Charleston, S.C. and Camp Hancock, Ga.
Discharged Mar. 22, 1919.

Ludrick Walter A., Private, St. Regis Falls
Wife—Mrs. Edith Ludrick, St. Regis Falls
34th Field Art., Bat. B
Aug. 8, 1918—Went to Fort Slocum, N.Y., thence to Camp McClellan, Alabama,
Discharged Feb. 5, 1919.

Merrick, Bert, born 1889, St. Regis Falls
Troop G, 6th Cal., US Army
Discharged from service on Mexican border, on account of tuberculosis, on Sept. 11, 1917
Died in the year 1919.

Mulholland, Ralph R., Fireman, US Navy, St. Regis Falls
Reference—Henry Mulholland, St. Regis Falls
Nov. 19, 1917—Went to U.S. Naval Training Station, Newport, R.I.
Sailed on USS "Des Moines" in convoy duty, embarking at Brooklyn, N.Y. Convoy was turned over to destroyers
Returned to U.S. on "Des Moines", landing at New York.
Released Apr. 19, 1919.

Murphy, Glenn B., Sergeant, St. Regis Falls
Parents—Mr. & Mrs. John D. Murphy, St. Regis Falls
Co. E, 403rd Telegraph Bat. and independent organization under Chief Signal Officers of AEF
Oct. 16, 1917—Went to Camp Sherman, Ohio, thence to Camp Mill, L.I.

80 • WATER OVER THE FALLS

June 10, 1918—Sailed for France, Alsace-Lorraine and Luxembourg, building telephone lines
Returned to U.S.A. on Italian Steamer "Belvedere", landing at Hoboken, N.J.
Discharged July 11, 1919.

O'Neil, Arthur S., Sergeant, St. Regis Falls
Mother—Mrs. Ophelia O'Neil, St. Regis Falls
First with Headquarters Detachment 41st Engineers, then with Headquarters Detachment 13th Bat,. 20th Engineers
Dec. 14, 1917—Went to Fort Slocum, N.Y., thence to American University, Washington, D.C. and to Camp Belvair, Va.
Feb. 26, 1918—Sailed for France on S.S. "Olympia", embarking at New York.
July 6, 1919—Returned to U.S.A. on "Great Northern", landing at Hoboken, N.J.
Discharged July 14, 1919.

Page, Eugene F., Private, St. Regis Falls
Parents—Mr. & Mrs. Peter Page, St. Regis Falls
271st Aero Squadron Air Service
Jan. 28, 1918—Went to Fort Slocum, N.Y., thence to Ellington, Texas and to Aberdeen Proving Grounds, Maryland.
Discharged June 12, 1919.

Page, Fred A., Private, St. Regis Falls
Parents—Mr. & Mrs. Peter Page, St. Regis Falls
Co. C, 328th Inf., 82nd Div.
Sept. 21, 1917—Went to Camp Devens, Ayer, Mass., thence to Camp Gordon, Ga. and Camp Houston, Texas.
May 11, 1918—Sailed for France on "Great Northern" embarking at Boston, Mass.
Oct. 9, 1918—Was wounded by machine gun bullet; as a result had left arm amputated about four inches from shoulder.
Feb. 27, 1919—Returned to U.S.A.
Discharged May 31 , 1919.

ORGANIZATIONS • 81

Palmer, Ernest G., St. Regis Falls
Mother—Mrs. Sophia Palmer, St. Regis Falls
May 27, 1918—Went to Camp Wadsworth, Spartanburg, S.C.

Parks, Walter L., Mechanic, St. Regis Falls
Parents—Mr. & Mrs. John Parks, St. Regis Falls
Co. A, 69th Engineers, 14th Grand Div.
July 22, 1918—Went to Camp Dix, Wrightstown, N.J., thence to Fort Benjamin Harrison, Indiana and Fort Meyer, Va.
Sept. 21, 1918—Sailed for France on "Wilhelmina", embarking at Hoboken, N.J.
Served as locomotive Engineer on a French Railway.
Aug. 13, 1919—Returned to U.S.A. on "Mercury", landing at Norfolk, Va.
Discharged Aug. 19, 1919.

Patraw, Clyde R., US Navy Fireman, St. Regis Falls
Mother—Mrs. Lois Patraw, St. Regis Falls
July 20, 1917—Went to Naval Training Station, Newport, R.I.
Later transferred to Receiving Ship, Boston, Mass., thence to City Park Barracks, Brooklyn, N.Y.
Served on USS "South Dakota"
Lost right arm through accident
Confined to hospital eight months.
Released Jan. 23, 1919.

Patraw, Preston P., Army Field Clerk, St. Regis Falls
Mother—Mrs. Lois A. Patraw, St. Regis Falls
Headquarters Co., 26th Div.
Mar. 16, 1916—Appointed Headquarters Clerk, U.S. Army
Aug. 29, 1916 made Army Field Clerk by Act of Congress
Sept. 26, 1917—Sailed for France on SS "New York", embarking at New York.
Served as Secretary to Major-General C. R. Edwards, Commanding 26th Div.
Nov. 14, 1918—Returned to U.S.A. on SS "Plattsburgh", landing at New York

July 26, 1921—still in service as Army Field Clerk, Headquarters 3rd Corps. area, Fort Howard, Maryland.

Patraw, Ray H., Seaman 2nd C, St. Regis Falls
Mother—Mrs. Lois Patraw, St. Regis Falls
Engineer's Corps.
Aug. 6, 1918—Went to Pelham Bay Park, N.Y., thence to Wissahickon Barracks.

Prespare, George, Jr., St. Regis Falls
Father—George Prespare, St. Regis Falls
Co. C, 107th Inf., A.P.O. #748; Formerly with Co. K, 1st Reg. N.Y.N.G.
Went to Camp Wadsworth, Spartanburg, S.C.
Badly wounded in leg and hip.
Confined to hospital in France, also in England.
Returned to Camp Upton, L.I.

Rafter, George A., Private 1st C, St. Regis Falls
Parents—Mr. & Mrs. David Rafter, St. Regis Falls
Co. G, 59th Pioneer Inf.
July 31, 1918—Went to Camp Dix, Wrightstown, N.J.
Aug. 31, 1918—Sailed for France on "Leviathan", landing in New York
Discharged July 8, 1919.

Radloff, Earl C., Navy, Seaman 1st C, St. Regis Falls
Father—Charles Radloff, St. Regis Falls
Enrolled at Syracuse, N.Y.
May 1, 1918—Went to Pelham Bay Naval Training Station, where he remained for seven months, then transferred to USS "Northern Pacific" and USS "El San", a troop ship. "On this ship I was a third class painter". Made two trips overseas.
Released Sept. 17, 1919.

Regis, Arthur J., St. Regis Falls
Parents—Mr. & Mrs. Joseph Regis, St. Regis Falls
Co. 7, 153rd Depot Brigade, Div. No. 2

July 2, 1918—Went to Camp Dix, Wrightstown, N.J. discharged July 27, 1918.

Reid, Robert A., Seaman 2nd C, St. Regis Falls
Mother—Mrs. Mary Reid, Schenectady, N.Y.
Went to Helms Island.

Rowell, Lynn A., Sergeant, St. Regis Falls
Parents—Mr. & Mrs. M. A. Rowell, St. Regis Falls
290th Aero Squadron in U.S.A. and General Headquarters, France.
Mar. 15, 1918—Went to Kelly Field, Texas, thence to Rockwell Field, Calif. and Camp Kearney, Calif.
Aug. 22, 1918—Appointed Army Field Clerk.
Jan. 7, 1919—Sailed for France on "Mongolia", embarking at Hoboken, N.J.
Sept. 7, 1919—Returned to U.S.A. on "Leviathan", landing at Hoboken, N.J.
Discharged Oct. 6, 1919.

Rowell, Percival L., Sergeant, St. Regis Falls
Parents—Mr. & Mrs. M. A. Rowell, St. Regis Falls
Quartermaster Corps. at Large.
Sept. 25, 1917—Went to Camp Meade, Maryland, thence to Overseas Casual Camp, Fort Jay, N.Y. Governor's Island, N.Y.
Dec. 4, 1917—Sailed for France on "George Washington", embarking at Hoboken, N.J.
Aug. 10, 1919—Returned to U.S.A. on "Imperator", landing at Hoboken, N.J.
Discharged Aug. 18,1919.

Sampson, Jerry J., Private 1st C, St. Regis Falls
Reference—Mrs. Addle Dwyer, Nashua, N.H.
309th Inf., 78th Div.
Apr. 11, 1918—Went to Camp Dix, Wrightstown, N.J., thence to 422 Post Bakery, Bush Terminal, Brooklyn, N.Y.
Discharged June, 19, 1919.

Sawyer, Douglas J., Private 1st C, St. Regis Falls
Parents—Mr. & Mrs. Richard Sawyer, St. Regis Falls
Co. C, 48th Bat., U.S. Guards
Aug. 28, 1918—Went to Camp Dix, Wrightstown, N.J., thence to Fort Niagara, N.Y. and to Camp Morgan, N.J.
Discharged Dec. 17, 1918.

Schuyler, Patrick P., Private, St. Regis Falls
Uncle—John Ford, St. Regis Falls
63rd Pioneer Inf., Headquarters Co.
Apr. 28, 1918—Went to Camp Devens, Ayer, Mass., thence to Camp Dix, Wrightstown, N.J.
Discharged Dec. 18, 1918.

Shattuck, George L., Ensign, Navy, St. Regis Falls
Mother—Mrs. C. G. Clark, St. Regis Falls
Enlisted May 6, 1917, New York, called in one month later.
Went to Brooklyn, N.Y., thence overseas several times.
Served in U.S. Naval Reserve Forces, as M.M. 1, C.M.M., C.M. and Ensign E.
May 18, 1918—Torpedoed on U.S.S. "William Rockefeller".
Sent home casual in H.M.S. "Megantic", and re-shipped
Discharged Dec. 22, 1918.

Surprise, Frank H., St. Regis Falls
Mother—Mrs. Mary Surprise, St. Regis Falls
87th Div.; entrained July 23, 1918.
Jan. 25, 1919—returned to U.S.A.

White, Verne, Buck Private, St. Regis Falls
Brother—Walter White, St. Regis Falls
Co. D, 23rd Inf., 2nd Div.
July 14, 1917—Went to Syracuse, N.Y.
Sept. 7, 1917—Sailed for France.
Discharged July 11, 1919.

Woods, Milfred, Private, St. Regis Falls
parents—Mr. & Mrs. Antoine Woods, St. Regis Falls
Co. C, 166th Inf., 42nd "Rainbow" Div.

Jan. 5, (no year stated)—Went to Camp Devens, Ayer, Mass., thence to Camp Merritt, N.J.
Jan. 20, (no year stated)—Sailed for France on "Great Northern", embarking at Hoboken, N.J.
Wounded in left shoulder. Returned to U.S.A. on "Madawaska" landing Norfolk, Va.
Discharged Feb. 28, (no year stated).

Young, George M., Seaman 2nd C, St. Regis Falls
Grandmother—Mrs. Ellen Bredrow, St. Regis Falls
Enlisted in Navy Dist. 2, No. 45.

List of men whose names appeared in draft as having gone out from the town of Waverly, but concerning whose military service information can't be had.

Joseph Baker	Lovell Day
Warren Norton	Leo Parks
Vernon Parks	Glenford P. Patraw
John Paul	Arthur F. Perry
Millard H. Prespare	Julius Rusaw
Roy Russell	George Sausville
Morris Taylor	Thomas P. Wood
Nelson D. Woods	Ernest E. Young
Frank A. Young	

Additional information about World War I (1914-1918) Veterans in St. Regis Palle Cemetery records:

Name	Dates	Rank	Unit
Austin, Wesley C.	Aug. 30, 1894-Sept. 2, 1977	Pvt.	U.S. Army
Baker, Henry J.	Dec. 27, 1892-Feb. 27, 1975	Pvt.	U.S. Army
Bean, Harvey F.	June 23, 1894-Dec. 28, 1970, N.Y.	Pvt.	Co. H, 59th Pioneer Inf.
Belmore, Lewis D.	1896-1918 Co. B 504th Eng's. Bat.		
Bickford, Edward	Nov. 7, 1890-Apr. 1, 1967, N.Y.	Sgt.	Co. C, 346th Inf.
Biggers, Beverly A.	May 9, 1887-Nov. 7, 1974	Pvt.	U.S. Army
Brown, Claude	May 5, 1895-May 29, 1921, N.Y.	Pvt.	Btry. F, 13th Reg., Fard
Christian, William R.	Apr. 21, 1892-Jan. 28, 1970, N.Y.	Pvt.	75th Inf. Reg.
DeLaire, Fred G.	May 1, 1896-Feb. 27, 1957 N.Y.	Pvt.	Co. E, 306th Inf.
Files, George E.	Jan. 20, 1899-July 14, 1945, N.Y.	CPL.	30th Inf., 3rd Div.
LaChance, Fred G.	June 27, 1894-Nov. 1, 1972, N.Y.	Pvt.	U. S. Army
LaFrance, Joseph	Mar, 27, 1892-Aug. 19, 1969, N.Y.	Pvt.	Co. A, 1st Prov. Div. Brig.
Lang, Fred W.	July 2, 1891-Dec. 14, 1975	Wagr.	U.S. Army
LaPoint, Earl J.	Mar. 25, 1890-Mar. 4, 1971, N.Y.	Pvt.	Co. B, 304th Ammo Train
LeMieux, Fred W.	1890-Mar. 28, 1958, N.Y.	Pvt.	Co. K, 3 Casual Reg.
Page, Frederick A.	Jan. 18, 1894-Dec. 20, 1964, N.Y.	Cpl.	Co. C, 328th Inf. Reg. WWI PH
Parks, Leo S.	Aug. 17, 1890-Sept. 14, 1968, N.Y.	PFC	548th Co., MTC
Parks, Vernon D.	May 10, 1893-Oct. 6, 1959, N.Y.	PFC	Quarter Master Corps.
Rafter George Alex	Apr. 15, 1895-Sept. 8, 1958, N.Y.	QM Sgt.	Co. G, 59th Pioneer Inf.
Rowell, Percival L.	Mar. 19, 1892-Jan. 30, 1969, N.Y.		U.S. Army
Smith, William J.	1897-1931		U.S. Navy
Taylor, Frank L.	May 29, 1897-Nov. 20, 1959, N.Y.	PFC	320th Bakery Co., QMC

Additional information about World War I (1914-1918) Veterans in St. Regis Palle Cemetery records (cont.):

Thompson, Henry H.	May 29, 1891-May 10, 1964, N.Y.	2nd Lt.	Infantry
Votra, John L.	Feb. 28, 1895-May 6, 1960, N.Y.	Pvt.	U.S. Army
White, Vernon J.	1892-1954		Vet. WW I
Wilkins, Roy L.	Apr. 10, 1894-Oct. 18, 1944, N.Y.	Pvt.	105th Inf., 27th Div.

World War II (1939-1945) Veterans

*Researched and listed by Ralph Farmer, St. Regis Falls 1984
Assisted by Howard Haynes and the local American Legion.
Also, taken from the cemetery records.*

Aiken, Robert E.   Mar. 24, 1920-July 9, 1945, N.Y.   Cpl.   402 Bomb Sq. AAF WW II PH
Allen, Ernest B.   Oct. 1, 1901-June 1, 1979   MABT U.S. Army
Austin, Raymond
Bailey, Bernard
Baker, Daniel
Bellmore, David
Betterley, Audrey
Brabon, Marshall
Brabon, Robert
Bray, Harold
Brown, Edward
Brown, Elwood
Brown, Laurice
Brown, Robert

World War II (1939-1945) Veterans (cont.)

Name	Dates	Rank	Unit
Brown, Ronald			
Brown, William			
Bump, Goldie			
Burdo, Harold Albert	Feb 23, 1925-Nov. 21, 1970, N.Y.	PFC	Co. C, 155th Engr. CBT BN
Butler, Ralph			
Camp, Eugene			
Camp, Lyman (Jim)			
Camp, Maurice			
Caron, Ernest L.	Nov. 5, 1914-Nov. 11, 1974	Cpl.	U.S. Army
Cascanette, Bernard			
Cascanette, Floyd			
Cascanette, Harold			
Caskinette, Leslie			
Chesbrough, Thurston			
Clark, Edward			
Clark, Lester			
Conger, Hubert			
Courtney, John T.	Oct. 28, 1904-May 29, 1967, N.Y.	M. Sgt.	Scv. Co., 318 Infantry
Cronk, William			
Cummings, Arthur			
Cummings, Earl			
Cummings, Kenneth			
Cummings, Sheldon			
Debuque, Floyd			

World War II (1939-1945) Veterans (cont.)

Name	Dates	Rank	Unit
Debuque, Glenford			
Debuque, Howard			
DeCarr, Prescott			
DeCarr, Seymour	1920-1945, died in France	Sgt.	14th Armored Div. 3rd Army
DeLaire, Bernard			
DeLaire, Dewey			
DeLaire, George Morton			
Delosh, Donald			
Delosh, Harold			
Delosh, Robert			
Dresye, Gerald			
Drew, Donald D.	June 2, 1919-Jan. 18, 1974, N.Y.	Pvt.	U.S. Army
Dupree, Eileen			
Fadden, Bernard			
Fadden, Lyman			
Falvey, (no name)	Jan. 19, 1907-July 30, 1957, N.Y.	SK1	U.S. Navy
Falvey, Bernard			
Farmer, Carlton A.	Nov. 26, 1922—Oct. 8, 1967, N.Y.	S1	U.S.
Farmer, Daniel			
Farmer, Ralph			
Farmer, Royal			
Farmer, William			
Foley, Kenneth			
Ford, Allie			

World War II (1939-1945) Veterans (cont.)

Ford, Floyd			
Ford, Harold			
Fournier, Roy Leonard	1913-1956, N.Y.	MM3	U.S.N.R.
Frey, Melvin J.			
Gage, Rollin			
Garrow, Bert			
Gokey, Fred Jr.			
Gokey, Lawrence			
Goodrow, Clarence			
Goodrow, Clifford			
Goodrow, Dwight			
Goodrow, Ernest H.	Mar. 4, 1900-Oct. 5, 1957, N.Y.	Pvt.	Army Air Forces
Goodrow, Harold			
Goodrow, Howard			
Goodrow, Thomas			
Goodrow, Lawrence			
Green, Frank Morton			
Hadlock, Waren			
Hall, Donald			
Hall, Maurice			
Hall, Vila			
Hart, Elmer			
Haynes, Alton			
Haynes, Howard			

World War II (1939-1945) Veterans (cont.)

Name	Dates	Rank	Unit
Hewitt, Forest			
Hewitt, Whiter			
Johnson, Orton			
Jones, Ronald H.	June 10, 1920-Sept. 22, 1947, N.Y.	Sgt.	180th Inf. 45th Inf. Div.
Jones, Vranous A.	1914-1976	Pvt.	U.S. Army
Kelley, Darwin			
Kelley, Orvil			
LaBarr, Buddy (Peck)			
LaBarr, Merrill			
LaBounty, Elwin P.	Nov. 21, 1925-Dec. 12, 1977	QMS	U.S. Navy
LaBounty, Floyd			
LaBounty, Harold E.	Nov. 2, 1908-Apr. 12, 1975	PFC	U.S. Army
LaFrance, Kenneth			
LeMieux, Joseph			
LeMieux, William			
LaPoint, Donald			
LaPoint, E. Douglas			
LaPoint, Halcyon			
LaRose, Charles W.	Oct. 1, 1909-July 29, 1974		U.S. Army
LaVare, Arthur			
LaVoy, Carl H.	June 19, 1923–July 22, 1994		U.S. Navy
LaVoy, Effard	July 2, 1917		
Martin, Albert			
Mayville, Francis			

World War II (1939-1945) Veterans (cont.)

Mayville, Lloyd			
McGarvey, Harold			
McGarvey, Kenneth G.	Mar. 13, 1924–Oct. 7, 1969, N.Y.	TEC 5	920th TECH SVC Unit
McGarvey, Willard			
Meacham, Everett			
Meacham, Frederick			
Meacham, Gilbert			
Mourick, Edward			
Mourick, Frederick			
Mulholland, Albert			
Mulholland, Floyd			
Mushtare, Henry	Feb. 27, 1898-Nov. 3, 1961, N.Y.	Pvt.	HQ Btry., 8 Coast Arty.
Nelson, Charles Bernard			
Nichols, Gerald			
Nichols, Winifred			
Niles, Glenford			
O'Neil, Bernard P.	Mar. 17, 1904-Sept. 23, 1979	Pvt.	U.S. Army
O'Neil, Rexford			
Palmer, Erwin			
Palmer, Lloyd			
Palmer, Percy			
Paradise, Gerald E.	Nov. 1, 1915-Apr. 24, 1961, N.Y.	Sgt.	9th Air Force
Parks, Frank			
Parka, John Jr.			

World War II (1939-1945) Veterans (cont.)

Name	Dates	Rank	Unit
Parks, Kenneth			
Parks, Robert			
Parks, Roy			
Peck, Robert			
Ploof, Edward			
Ploof, Donald L.	Sept. 13, 1922-Feb. 1, 1966, N.Y.	PFC	U.S. Army
Ploof, Gerald L.	Mar. 8, 1916-Aug. 13, 1957, N.Y.	Pvt.	Medical Dept.
Prespar, Madge			
Price, Charles			
Prior, Philip			
Raymond, Frederick L.	Oct. 12, 1909-May 28, 1979	Cpl.	U.S. Army
Reed, Otto			
Reed, Robert			
Rivito, Frank			
Rivito, James			
Richards, James			
Rivers, Ray John	July 23, 1907-Dec. 17, 1964, N.Y.	TEC	4 Hq. & Hq. Btry. 49th Ca. Brig.
Russell, Bernard			
Scharf, Vern A.	Aug. 10, 1905-Sept. 25, 1975	Pvt.	U.S. Army
Schenk, Ira			
Schenk, William			
Servant, Henry			
Smith, Wendell			

World War II (1939-1945) Veterans (cont.)

Smith, William			
Sochia, Howard			
Sochia, Eli			
Sochia, Stanley			
Sochia, Wilfred			
Socia, Theodore			
Sovay, Oleta			
Stewart, Howard			
Story, Wallace			
Susice, Richard A.	Feb. 28, 1926-May 18, 1945, N.Y. 1972	Pvt. 7th	Marines 1st Marine Div.
Waldman, Joseph			
Wardner, Joseph Jr.			
Winters, Stanley			
Winters, Walter L.	Aug. 28, 1915-Apr. 28, N.Y.	Cpl.	Hq. & Svc. Co. 85th Inf. WW II BSM
Wood, John E.	Apr. 11, 1916-Dec. 2, 1967, N.Y.	Pvt.	Co. B, 23rd BN 6th Regt. 1st RTC
Wood, Lye Joseph	Aug. 31, 1922-Jan. 19, 1945, N.Y.	TEC 5th	Co. C, 19th Armo Inf. BN WW II BSM-PH
Votra, Harold			
Young, J. Stanley			

This list is believed to be 98–99 % complete.

Chapter 9
POINTS OF INTEREST

The Town Lock-Up—There was an "over-night lock-up" located behind the Legion Hall. Also 1906-1915 there was another "lock-up" on River St. probably across from where Ross's Store is now.

The village was incorporated at one time in 1887 and subsequently rescinded such action. Mr. H. E. O'Neil was the first supervisor. Other supervisors were: Charles H. Young, Leroy M. Wardner, Alexander MacDonald, and M. B. Ramsdell.

August 13, 1887—The telephone line is nearing completion. We expect to soon be able to talk to our distant neighbors without any difficulty. (Reported by the *Adirondack News*)

In 1918 it is reported that there were 15 stores, 3 churches, a public and parochial school, a bank, and 4 hotels in St. Regis Falls.

Adirondack News reports—May 28, 1887, There should be some way provided for extinguishing fire in our village. If any building on Main St. should take fire the whole street on both sides would be very likely to be destroyed, as we have not the first essential for extinguishing fire, should it once start in any part of town. We should look to this matter immediately. The cost of some kind of fire protection would be trifling compared with the cost of a fire which is liable to occur any time.

The first store was a Hammond concern, run by Mr. Babcock. The second—Samuel W. Gillett's and third—William T. O'Neil. The Fleming Store, which was a continuation of the first mercantile venture of William O'Neil, was bought later and run by the Shaws in connection with their tannery.

June 4, 1887—The nineteenth *American Newspaper Directory*, published by George P. Rowell & Co., has just appeared. It shows that there are 14,706 newspapers printed in the United States, an increase of 546 over the last year. There are 95 more daily publications than in the preceding year, 500 more weekly, and 52 more monthlies. Pennsylvania shows the greatest increase in dailies, Kansas leads the growth in weeklies, and New York State stands first as to monthlies.

The township of Waverly was erected from Dickinson in 1880, before this division started the entire area was all the township of Dickinson, which encompassed over 146,666 assessed acres.

A list of medical doctors practicing in St. Regis Falls:

Dr. L. M. Wardner, M.D.	1883
Dr. M. E. Flenning	1891
Dr. Clarlen	
Dr. S. Dandorand Ph.D. Sur.	1890
Dr. A. W. Atwater	1890 (then went to Santa Clara)
Dr. A. Rocchi	1891 (from Italy)
Dr. Markey, M.D.	1893
Dr. M. E. Flenning	1895 (Physician to Adirondack Sanatorium)
Dr. R. F. Cunnion	1896 (only 2 months, then went to Hogansburg)
Dr. D. W. Powers, M.D.	1896
Dr. H. H. Atwater, M.D.	1902
Dr. W. A. Wardner, M.D.	1899 (son of L. M. Wardner, relocated in Saranac Lake—1925)
Dr. Fred Flanagan Gremore	1905
Dr. Blake Bigelow, M.D.	1906 (was also an attorney)
Dr. Frank M. Green, Dentist	1907
Dr. D. E. Moody	1909
Dr. Spapiro	1927
Dr. William Tanner	1929

98 • WATER OVER THE FALLS

Dr. Gasper					ca. 1932-1934
						(relocated in Malone)
Dr. Klein
Dr. Leon C. Bernadot			(relocated in Malone)

At present there are several doctors that come to St. Regis Falls from Saranac Lake, with an office shared in the Town Hall in the Firehouse building.

Dr. George Cook, M.D.
Dr. Josh Schwartzberg, D.O.
Dr. W. Roy Slaunwhite, M.D.
Dr. Jay S. Federman, M.D.
Dr. Barry Kilbourne, M.D.

Large Forest Fires in surrounding St. Regis Falls area

Lake Ozonia—May 1903 burned 10,000 acres from Daniels to Rice Mountains
Blue (Azure) Mt.—1908
Santa Clara area—May 1921
Three miles south of Blue (Azure) Mt.—June 1923

Clayton and Lottie Southworth, inside the Southworth Store

POINTS OF INTEREST • 99

The Southworth Store, located on South Main Street

The J. LaPoint Store, located on Main Street

Earl LaPoint, inside the LaPoint Store

View From Upper Main St, St. Regis Falls, NY
Taken about 1910 in front of the Catholic Church on North Main Street, looking north. Note the old Baptist Church, located in the lot up from where the Methodist parsonage is now.

Upper Main Street

Old Bridge Going Toward Nicholville, Facing East

A plaque erected in the park in 1936 reads:

*This park and fountain
commemorate the
construction of the first
comprehensive water supply
for the village of
St. Regis Falls by the people
of the town of Waverly
and the Federal Government
1936*

Town Board
*Joseph E. Wardner, Supervisor
Malcolm Tweed
Peter W. Soetemon
John Proulx
William Kidney
Maurice W. Plumb, Engineer*

Contractors
*Frazza Construction Company
Pittsburgh Desmoines Steel Co.*

The Electric Trolley: Recollection of a story told to Keith Ploof by his father, Joe.

The trolley was used to haul logs from an area on the south side of the present St. Regis Falls-Nicholville Road. The tracks were behind the Rollin Giffin home and the Poquette residence, and went several miles southward toward Lake Ozonia. It came out to the road, down Mica Hill and on to the Brooklyn Cooperage mill.

The trolley itself was not a large contraption, but pulled several log buggies or rail-cars which carried logs.

The track was built similar to a railroad, but the rails were of lighter steel.

The hill was quite steep and when wet because of rain or snow, was slippery. On such occasions the engineer or driver often had a wild ride.

> A local boy, who was noted for his practical jokes, greased the rails on the hill one day. No one noticed what he had done. The trolley started down, picking up speed rapidly. The brakes were applied to no avail. Finally, in desperation, the trolley was reversed. Amid a shower of sparks and squalling like the banshees of hell, it came to a stop a few short yards of total disaster. The local lad was sad but was hard to find for several days.

Electric Railway Between St. Regis Falls and Lake Ozonia
The Electric Trolley was owned by the Cascade Chair Company and was used to haul logs to the mill from Lake Ozonia area.

There was a taxi business started in the spring of 1914 and ran until the winter of 1915. This was operated by James D. Bean of Dickinson Center.

With the logging done for the winter, the bed blankets were brought by the basketload to be deloused.
This was taken in front of the old Methodist Church and school before 1926 when these buildings burned; looking west from Duane Street.

Dave DeLair had a barber shop where the liquor store is now. There was a cabinet with shelves and glass doors and each man that went for a shave or hair cut had his own shaving mug with a bar of shaving soap all his own.

There was a miniature golf course between the Catholic Church and the Fred Ramsdell farm on North Main St. late 1920s and early 1930s.

1907 there was a covered ice skating rink.

Ice-skating Rink, St. Regis Falls

War of 1812—The soldiers marched through this wild, unsettled, harsh area on way from Lake Champlain to Lake Ontario. The troops were lead by Captain William L. Marcy. There was the Northwest Bay Road, the Port Kent Road and the Jennings Road, which was a road that crossed the Northwest Bay Road; the Jennings Road is marked with a

Moules' Store
It was located between the present liquor store and the Prior Building. "A French lumberjack went into the store to buy some pants. He said to Mr. Moules, with a French accent, 'take down your pants and let me see what you have.'" All the pants were hung high up along the wall and had to be taken down with a long pole.

state sign, however, no longer exists. It is told that there was a blockhouse occupied by the British troops which was located approximately where the St. Regis Falls Legion Hall—Senior Citizen Center stands today. This blockhouse was captured by the American troops on their way through the area; quite a few prisoners were taken.

William L. Marcy was born in the 1780s in Massachusetts. The story goes that he was quite the devil in school. However, he was smart in his studies. William attended Lesser Academy, then Brown College; he graduated around 1804. He then went to Troy, N.Y. and studied law, and became a lawyer. He entered into the armed services and became a captain in the War of 1812. Marcy became quite a political figure in New York State.

Ebenezer Emmons climbed mountains in northern New York at the instigation of Marcy to make a survey. Many of these mountains had never been climbed or surveyed by a white man. Emmons ascertained the height of one mountain and he named it Mt. Marcy—which is, of course, the highest mountain in this range.

Where the post office is located now, used to be Bandy's Bakery—owned and operated by Ed and Fanny Bandy.

The St. Regis Paper Company began as a single newsprint mill in a small, upstate New York town (Watertown), in 1899 and became one of the largest industrial corporations in the United States.

Early in 1899 the five partners incorporated the St. Regis Paper Company; David M. Anderson, George C. Sherman, George E. Dodge, Titus B. Meigs, and Ferris J. Meigs formed the partnership. The name was suggested by the river and falls dominating the Santa Clara timberland that was formally deeded to the paper company later that year.

In the 1930s the train master was Paul Smith from the Bombay area, and Archie Niles was in charge of freight and baggage.

There were two village pastures for the townspeople to pasture their cows in. One located on Spring Street across from Kidney Ave. and the other on South Main St. in back of where the newspaper office building was. The men would gather morning and evening to milk their cows, and of course, have a friendly visit with a neighbor.

In the 1930s and 40s Fay Trim had a contract with the town to keep the Trim Road (Long Pond Road) plowed in the winter. Others around town were also contracted to plow other roads in their own area. They were paid $5.00 per day for self and their team of horses—10 hour days.

Mr. Wallace (Wally) Story plowed sidewalks with his bay horse and a sidewalk wing plow until the late 1950s or early 1960s. Mr. Story was a "top-notch" blacksmith.

Chapter 10

SURROUNDING HAMLETS

Small lumbering hamlets surrounding St. Regis Falls now extinct

SHANLEY

Just three miles up river on the south River Road there was once a village. It was known as Shanley, now totally disappeared and forgotten.

In the booming days, this little settlement was noted for its great lumbering project. In 1901, Giles Cheney was foreman over 28 lumberjacks. At this time there was a railroad siding, a station, a store, a post office, a blacksmith shop, two large mills, also five houses and a large barn owned by the lumber company. One of the sawmills located in Shanley produced hardwood flooring. At present, this land is owned by the State of New York. If you haven't figured out this location yet, it is where the red brick pump-house sits on the corner of the Shanley Road and the River Road. This was a short-lived community.

GUIDE BOARD

Congregation in front of the Presbyterian Church, ca. 1920s

A very small hamlet located at the end of the Blue Mountain Road about four miles south of St. Regis Falls, Guide Board was settled by German people and named because of a guide board located there with road directions. Many wealthy summer people spent time here. A mission church of the First Free Will Baptist Church from St. Regis Falls was located here, erected in 1896. Also a Presbyterian Church under charge

Guide Board School, ca. 1910

of the Adirondack Mission, headquartered at Keese's Mills in Brighton, located in Guide Board. A shingle mill about a mile north of the Blue Mountain Road built in 1876 by William T. O'Neil employed some of the residents. There was never a post office at the Guide Board. It was mostly a farming community probably settled about the 1890s.

DEXTER

Orrando P. Dexter, a lawyer from New York City, born about 1855 and murdered Sept. 9, 1903 near Santa Clara, built the Dexter hamlet about four or five miles south-west of St. Regis Falls off the Blue Mountain Road. Dexter was also a Boy's Camp, after the death of Mr. Dexter, for boys from the cities to come and learn to swim, canoe, and other outdoor activities. They made their own canoes. Dexter Lake was later a small lumbering camp, here local lumberjacks worked until the lumbering was exhausted. This property is presently owned by the St. Lawrence University.

Cat Mountain from Dexter Lake

Sunbeam Lodge, Dexter Lake

GILE

Gile was a little town on the Blue Mountain Road about six miles south of St. Regis Falls once known as Goose Pond. It was cradled between Cat Hill, named so because in the early days many wild-cats were known to roam on it; and the other was White Hill.

It is believed that the town got its name from two brothers who were early settlers, Steve and Rich Gile. At one time there were about twenty families living in Gile. There was a post office kept by Jennie Conklin. After her death, it was run by her son, Isaac, and his wife Mary. Later the post office was run by Franklin and Ada Peck.

The school was on the old Dexter Lake Road, which was between Blue Mountain Road and Santa Clara. It was called the Brown Tract School and was situated on the right side of the road at the foot of the first hill. Neva Allen and Floy Bruce taught school here.

A little farther down the road was the Brown Tract Sawmill and several houses where the people who worked in the sawmill and on the landing lived. There was also a store and a boarding house.

Some of the residents of this little town attended church located at Guide Board, which was about two miles toward St. Regis Falls from Gile. Most of the ministers who preached there were students from college. One of them was Harry Emerson Fosdick, who later became pastor of the Riverside

Church in New York City, and a very prominent religious figure throughout the United States.

With the decline of lumbering, people moved away. Through the years, what was a busy little community, has all but disappeared into a ghost town. There are only a few houses, and only one family of those early days remain.

LAKE OZONIA

Log Hotel at Lake Ozonia

A settlement at Lake Ozonia? Yes! First called Big Pond, then Trout Lake until about the late 1890s Frederic M. Heath gave it the name Lake Ozonia. Located about four miles west of St. Regis Falls toward Nicholville. A charming body of water about three miles in length and from a quarter to a half mile in width. While most of the land was owned by large lumber companies and speculators, like Mr. Dexter; there were at one time twenty-one houses located on the lake road, between the state road and the lake. Mr. Heath owned a fine hotel which sat upon the northerly bluff, over-looking the lake, with several cottages hidden in the timbers. There was the Red School House, District #5, which some of the teachers that taught were; Mary Hughes, Sarah Raymo, Pauline Boyer, Martha Levine, and Sarah Koch. In 1919 teachers at this school were paid $15.00 per week. Today, the old cellars are marked out by lilac bushes, vines and broken down fences.

EVERTON

Everton was located in the township of Santa Clara on the south end of the Eddie Road, at its intersection with the Port Kent Road, now called the Duane Road (Red Tavern Road). The railroad bed used to cross the road at Flynn Crossing, then around Trim Hill, and on through to St. Regis Falls. The Red Tavern Hotel, located on the old Port Kent Road used to be a stagecoach stop and was used by Civil War soldiers.

SURROUNDING HAMLETS • 111

This road started at Port Kent, running west, cutting down over Trim Hill (Trim's Crossing) through the swamp, over Pothook Hill and through to where the Haynes Road is, coming out in Nicholville.

In 1886, the partnership of W. J. Ross, Peter C. Macfarland and H. W. Stearns acquired sixteen thousand acres of timber lands in Santa Clara, Waverly and Duane; and built a lumber railroad six miles in length from St. Regis Falls to a point that they called Everton. (In this same location, Mr. Jonah Sanford had a mill in 1831.) Henry and David Patton of Albany, incorporated as the Everton Lumber Company, which failed a few years later. The tract had then been pretty well stripped of merchantable timber, and no further business was done at Everton. The property was then owned by the Brooklyn Cooperage Company, and the railroad was extended eight miles further east, over the lands of Reynolds Brothers in Brandon, from which the Cooperage Company obtained large lots of hardwood timber for its mills at St. Regis Falls. However, the hardwood had been mostly cut, and within a year or two the railroad became useless except for old iron.

For many years, the clapboard, shingle and circular mill was operated by Robert and Jerry Sampson of Dickinson, occupying the old Sanford Millhouse as a traveler's house and bar. In 1883, Robert Douglas also built a store in Everton.

The mills and houses have utterly disappeared and even the streets are grown up to bushes and briars.

SPRING COVE

Spring Cove was a lumbering settlement just southwest of Santa Clara off the Blue Mountain Road, at a cove in the river. This was at one time in the mid 1870s a busy little community, with two hotels, a post office, and a railroad siding close by. There were Catholic Church services held here by the priest from St. Regis Falls. There was also much hunting and fishing done in this area, such as most other little settlements along the river.

Bingo Town

Bingo Town was never a town! There were a few small homes located to the south-west, off the Wait Road. The residents named this area Bingo Town only as a means of identifying the location.

Typical scenes at a lumber camp getting ready for the day

The man on the far front left is John Bray

Chapter 11
NATURE'S SWEETNESS

"Sugaring Off"

The maple syrup season, or "sugaring off" comes with the winds of spring. According to legend, the practice of gathering maple sap began with the Indians. Early settlers also turned to the large forests of maples when they were in need of sugar. With spring planting not yet begun, they were free from farming chores and the practice of sugaring grew rapidly.

Early farmers knew that when the sap began to run, the snow was beginning to melt, and spring had finally arrived. It was important to know the right time to tap the big maples and start the process. Six weeks of freezing nights and mild, sunny days were considered a good season. Another important part of syrup making is the evaporator, this is the long open pan in the sugarhouse used to boil off the water from the sap. Fueled by wood, this is watched very closely to maintain the proper heat.

With a team of horses hitched to the sap sled, around the sugarbush they labored through the deep snow collecting the sap from the heavy buckets. Then back to the sugarhouse to deposit the sap into the pan, already steaming with boiling sap. It takes many of these trips and many hours of boiling to make the amber colored syrup. Surprisingly, it takes forty gallons of sap to make one gallon of syrup.

The next time you pour that REAL maple syrup over those pancakes, waffles, or french toast, remember how the "old-timers" used to have to do it.

Chapter 12

"CRY WOLF"

The Wolf Ring

In the 1820s there was such a problem with wolves in the area that the county placed a bounty on them. Anyone killing a wolf would present the head, skin and ears to a justice of the peace of the county and make oath of the time and the place where such wolf (or whelp) was taken and killed. At this time the judge would cut off the ears and burn them. The amount of bounty paid on a wolf in 1821 and 1822 was $60.00 in Franklin County.

With the passing of this bounty law a number of persons formed a plan to defraud the towns of large sums of money by fraudulent wolf-bounty certificates. The amount of these certificates granted in 1821 and 1822, exceeded forty thousand dollars. If the certificates were honestly and legally issued, at least 500 full grown wolves had been killed in Franklin County during the two years. The actual number killed was estimated at probably less than one hundred. The result was that the county expenses of Franklin County increased from $1,720.51 in 1820 to $12,038.49 in 1821 and to $9,130.02 in 1822.

The so-called "wolf ring" to carry out their plans used many devices. One of these was to find a dishonest applicant to swear to the killing, and an equally dishonest justice to grant the certificate. Both were found within the "ring". Other devices adopted by the "wolf ring" to secure the certificates included sending emissaries into Vermont and Canada to purchase the heads of wolves killed there. Wolves were caught in Canada, brought across the border and put into the traps of hunters. Dogs were bought from the Indians at Caughnawaga and Vermont in large numbers and certificates granted upon the production of their heads to the certifying magistrate. The skins of the heads of wolves killed several years before were drawn over the skulls of other animals and stitched with thread. Certificates were frequently granted to one person for ten, thirteen and sometimes fifteen wolves, and a dozen or more certificates were granted for the same head. In these cases the Justice would examine the head, and finding "its skin and ears entire there on" would throw it behind him, and become deeply engaged in writing an affidavit "of the time and place when and where the wolf was taken and killed" intending unquestionably, after having prepared the papers, "to cut off and burn the ears" required by law. While thus engaged in writing, another person would slyly throw the head out the window where another would pick it up and bring it back into the room, ready to be presented and sworn as soon as the first papers were completed. Thus the same head, with "skin and ears entire" would pass in at the door and out at the window, until the justice had a dozen heads, in fancy, piled up behind him waiting for their ears to be cut off.

The hunters frequently paid as high as twenty dollars for a wolf's head, as they could well afford to do as the state, county and town bounties combined amounted to the $60.00 in Franklin County.

Many taxpayers ascertained that nearly $12,000 had been assessed upon towns to pay the town and county bounty. They concluded it was better to let the wolves run among their flock and therefore petitioned the legislature to repeal or modify the bounty law. To pacify their townsmen, "the ring" placed one thousand dollars in the hands of the supervisor toward paying the resident taxes. The result of the application to the legislature was the passage of a law limiting the aggregate amount of state and county bounty in Franklin County in any one year to one thousand dollars, which was not to be paid until the board of supervisors had examined and passed upon the regularity and fairness of the certificates issued by the justice. This disposed effectively of the "wolf ring" in the county.

The following bounties were paid in the town of Dickinson:

wolves	$10	in 1809, '10, '11, '12, '17, '18, '19, '20, '28
wolves	15	in 1811, '12, '13, '21
wolves	20	in 1815
panthers	10	in 1820
panthers	20	in 1821
panthers	25	in 1818
foxes	2	in 1816 & 1821
bears	3	in 1820
bears	5	in 1819 & 1821
crows	37½¢	in 1816
squirrels	12½¢	in 1817
chipmunks	12½¢	in 1816

During these years, Dickinson included all the land that encompass what is now Bangor, Brandon, Moira, Santa Clara, Waverly, Altamont, and part of Harrietstown. It was approximately twelve miles wide and fifty some miles long and contained nearly a half-million acres. Residing on this huge tract of land in 1810 were 411 persons, all or nearly all of them living in what are now the townships of Bangor and Moira.

Chapter 13
NEWSPAPER CLIPPINGS

The following clipping was a listing of enterprises in St. Regis Falls in the year 1887.

BUSINESS DIRECTORY
Of St. Regis Falls Twenty-Five Years Ago.

Of Special Interest to Our Older Inhabitants Who Resided Here Then.

[ADIRONDACK NEWS, MARCH 12, 1887.] The St. Regis Lumber Co., who own and operate an extensive saw, employing about fifty men. A. Kingsley, foreman. A box factory that gets out a carload of boxes a day; furnishing work for upwards of thirty men. Azro Giles, foreman. A broom handle factory, W. E. King, manager. Also a store on Main St., where they carry a heavy line of general merchandise.

The St. Regis Leather Co., being one of the largest tanneries in Northern New York, at present upwards of fifty men; but when running to full capacity doubtless double that amount will be employed.

W. T. O'Neil carries a stock of general merchandise. Store on Main St. A. J. Norton & Co.; dealers in general merchandise. Store on River street.

J. LaRocque, dealer in dry goods, etc. He also has a branch store at Brandon.

H. A. Goldstone carries a full line of clothing, hats, caps, boots and shoes, jewelry, watches, etc.

N. M. Parks carries a full line of fresh and salt meats, staple and fancy groceries, flour and provisions. Store on Spring street.

Henry Foster, dealer in fresh and salt meats, flour, provisions, etc.

Calvin Graves, proprietor of meat market on River street.

F. L. Chandler, dealer in furniture, crockery, glassware, table cutlery, lamps. etc.

Dr. L. M. Wardner carries a full line of drugs. patent medicines, Yankee notions, etc. Store on Spring street.

R. P. Lindsay, dealer in drugs, patent medicines, fancy articles, etc. Store in Webb's block.

J. W. Webb, attorney and counsellor-at-law., also postmaster and carries a full line of books, stationery, etc.

I. L. Green, jeweler, carries a full line of watches and jewelry.

D. M. Agnew, dealer in groceries and provisions.

George Robarge, warm meals at all hours.

J. J. A. Murphy, merchant tailor. Shop on Main street.

C. A. Fisk, dealer in hardware. Tin shop in connection. Store on River street.

Charles LaVoy, proprietor of harness shop on River street.

L. C. Goodrich, proprietor of the Waverly House.

K. W. Kinnear, proprietor of the Frontier House.

Warren Cook, proprietor of the livery and feed stable on River street.

George Berdrow, blacksmith shop on River street.

A. A. Cladin, blacksmith shop back of Goldstone's store.

E. M. Russell, barber shop on Main street, opposite Webb's block.

Frank Londerville, barber shop on Main street.

Dr. A. W. Atwater, physician and surgeon. Office in Webb's block.

We also have a millinery store operated by Mrs. J. J. Murphy. A dressmaker, Miss Nora Sullivan. Shop in Mrs. Green's building.

The following clippings were listed in the March 9, 1912 issue of the Adirondack News, celebrating its 25th anniversary.

Edwin S. Aldrich

Edwin S. Aldrich was born in Went Boylston, Mass., on February 10, 1862, and came to Moira, Franklin Co., N. Y., when about seven years of age and continued to reside there until 1877 when he went to Lawrenceville, St. Lawrence County, where he clerked in stores and the post office and operated a job printing office until March 1887, when he came to St. Regis Falls as a partner of the writer to establish this paper and has continued to reside here most of the time since.

He was married to Miss Jennie Dupee in the fall of 1888.

Mr. Aldrich was for years engaged in the hardware business, and recently formed a partnership with F. L. Tryon to conduct a garage and sell automobiles.

During his residence here he has served the town about ten years as town clerk and three years as an assessor.

Prin. J. L. Blood

John L. Blood was born in Heuvelton, St. Lawrence County, March, 1875. He received his early education in Heuvelton Union Free School and later attended Potsdam Normal School from which he was graduated in 1887. In February 1901, he received the degree of Ph.D. from Central University. He was married in January 1906 to Miss Maude L. Merrill, of Nicholville. Since his graduation he has taught at Nicholville, Burke, Lake Placid and St. Regis Falls.

Mr. Blood entered upon his duties as principal of our high school in January 1906. Since his coming, the school has steadily increased in number of pupils both resident and non-resident. The school records show that in January 1906 there were 17 academic pupils attending school and in January 1912, there were 50 academic pupils. This marvelous growth has been due largely to the interest which the principal has shown in his work, as well as respect for his scholarship and teaching ability.

Mr. Blood is not only interested in the school, but he is interested and gives his hearty support to all movements for the advancement of the community.

Rev. Norman A. Darling—Pastor of the Methodist Episcopal Church, of St. Regis Falls.

Norman Addison Darling, oldest son of John and Mary Darling, was born in the town of Salisbury, Herkimer County, N.Y., January 30, 1867. Mr. Darling's early years were spent on the farm, his parents being farmers. Owing to the fact that when but a small boy he had to work on the farm and in the

lumber woods, his opportunity for study in school was limited. However, even after he had worked all day at manual labor on the farm or in the woods, he spent his evenings, when he could, in reading some good book or studying some subject taught in the public school. One winter he went for a few weeks to the Salisbury Village School. To do this he had to walk each day a distance of six miles. When he became "his own boss" he managed to attend Fairfield Seminary, which he did, graduating from that school in 1886. Then for a period of six years he taught school. He held the principalship of Knoxboro Union School and Little Valley Union School during this time. He was also vice principal of Ives Seminary for one year. In 1891 he entered Hamilton College, expecting to prepare himself for a teacher. During this time in college Mr. Darling felt called to the work of the ministry. So after studying one year and two terms in Hamilton College, he went to Allegheny College, where he graduated in 1896 with the degree of A. B. The following year, he was elected to the principalship of the Canaserago High School, where he stayed only one year. (This year's work was to secure the money to pay debts contracted while in college) He then entered Drew Theological Seminary at Madison, New Jersey, in 1887, and from this institution he graduated in 1900, with the degree of B.D. the same year the degree of A.M. was conferred upon him by Allegheny College. In 1901 he received the degree of Doctor of Philosophy from Taylor University.

Mr. Darling was licensed to preach Feb. 18, 1898. In April, 1900 he was admitted to the Wyoming conference and ordained deacon by Bishop Foss. In April, 1902, he was ordained elder by Bishop Merrill, and admitted in fall connection to the Wyoming conference.

His appointments have been as follows: 1898–1900, supply, stationed at Rockaway Valley, Newark Conference: 1900–01, stationed at Hawleyton, N Y.. Wyoming conference: 1901, transferred to Northern New York Conference and was stationed as follows: 1902–3, Taberg: 1904–5, Westmoreland; 1907–10. Plessis and Redwood: 1911, St. Regis Falls and Dickinson Center.

Dr. Frank M. Green

Dr. Frank M. Green was born in Chateaugay. N.Y., attended the high school at that place and graduated from that institution in 1901: also graduated from the Chateaugay training class. Later he attended the Philadelphia Dental College, graduating with the class of 1907.

Four years ago Mr. Green hung out his shingle as a dentist in this village, and during this time he has built up a fine practice. His office is equipped with all the latest tools and electric appliances. His practice has increased to such an extent that much of the time engagements have to be made some time in advance.

Hon. Alexander Macdonald

Alexander Macdonald was born in Nova Scotia, September 13, 1867. He came with his parents to Boston, Mass., when ten years of age, where he was prepared for college. He entered Middlebury College, and graduated from that school in 1892 with the degree of A.B. In 1900 the degree of M.A. was conferred upon him

Mr. Macdonald came to St. Regis Falls in 1892 and accepted the position of principal of St. Regis Falls Union School which position he continued to hold until he was elected school commissioner of the second district of Franklin County in the fall of 1899.

He continued in this office for nine vents when he relinquished it to assume the duties of a legislator in the state assembly, having been elected on the Republican ticket in the fall of 1909. He was re-elected in 1910 and 1911, and is making a record at Albany that is highly satisfactory to his constituency. He is a member of some of the most important committees in the lower house.

In 1908 Mr. Macdonald was chairman of the Franklin County Republican Committee. He is now and has been for several years, cashier of St. Regis Falls National Bank.

Robert R. McLane

Robert R. McLane. the subject of this sketch, was born in Waterloo, P. Q., November 23, 1838. He moved with his parents to this county when 11 years of age, residing here ever since. When he came here, the town of Waverly was still a part of the town of Dickinson.

Mr. McLane was a stone mason by trade, and followed that avocation for some years.

During his long residence here he has served the town as constable, collector of taxes, town clerk and justice of the peace.

He has always been a strong Republican politically, and in 1905, through his own efforts and the influence of his staunch friend, the late Congressman Wm. H. Flack, he was appointed postmaster at St. Regis Falls, which position he still holds. He with the able assistance of his wife has given the patrons of the office highly satisfactory service during these years.

Dr. Adelbert E. Moody

Adelbert E. Moody was born on June 11, 1857, at Saranac Lake, N.Y. His early life was spent in the grammar and high schools of that village.

In March, 1885 he graduated from the Albany Medical College, having been associated for three years while there with Dr. John Swinburne in the Swinburne Dispensary.

In October, 1886, he was united in marriage to Miss Jessie M. Churchill, of Mooers, Clinton County, and resided there for a number of years in the practice of his chosen profession. From there, he came to Dickinson in March 1898. In the fall of 1899, he was elected coroner on the Republican ticket, and continued to hold the office for four terms, 12 years, his final term ending the first of January. During his long service as coroner, he performed the duties of the position faithfully and well.

In the spring of 1905, he took a post-graduate course in the New York Homeopathic Medical College and Hospital.

In May, 1919, he moved to St. Regis Falls when he has succeeded in building up a splendid practice.

H. E. O'Neil

H. E. O'Neil, son of the late Senator W. T. O'Neil, was born in St. Regis Falls, N.Y., March 19, 1876. He attended school in this village and Franklin Academy, and was one of the members of the first graduating class of St. Regis Falls Union school, which occurred in June, 1894.

Even before he graduated, a business career appealed to him and he has been engaged in some branch of the lumber business practically all his life.

He realized that a national bank was needed at this place, and that it could be made to pay a fair dividend, so he proceeded to organize the St. Regis Falls National Bank, which opened its doors for business on May 17, 1905. He was elected as the first president of the institution, and the position has been accorded him without question ever since, and a large measure of credit is due him for the success it has attained.

Mr. O'Neil is also connected with the St. Regis Light and Power Co., the Cascade Wood Products Co., and the St. Regis Creamery Co., each one of which responds to his personality.

The subject of this brief sketch is one of St. Regis Falls' foremost business men: a man of ideas, who thinks for himself and has the courage to act upon his convictions. And to judge the future by the past he is sure to succeed in all his undertakings.

Rev. F. J. Ouellet

Rev. Father Ouellet was born at Sandwich, Ont., April 14. 1842. He studied for the priesthood, first at Sandwich College, then at St. Hyacinthe and later at the Grand Seminary of Montreal. He was ordained priest by the Rt. Rev. Bishop Welsh on Dec. 29. 1867. From that time until 1884, when he came to St. Regis Falls, he had charge of different parishes in the province of Ontario. The territory assigned him when he came here included St. Regis Falls, Santa Clara, Spring Cove, Brandon and Everton, besides the numerous lumber camps near these towns. Of course there were no churches in any of these places and Father Ouellet informs me he celebrated his first mass in what is now the McLeod Hotel. The first duty then was to provide places of worship, and with characteristic energy and ability he proceeded to bring his people together and interest them in the matter. It was his custom to travel from camp to camp during the logging season, ministering to his people and soliciting their aid in building the necessary churches. A church at Brandon and the beautiful church and home at St. Regis Falls were the result of his perseverance and hard labor. Today two-hundred and thirty families are members of this parish.

Nelson Ramsdell

Nelson Ramsdell, the subject of this brief sketch, was born in the town of Dickinson, Franklin County, N.Y., in 1833. He followed the occupation of farming during his early life. In May, 1861, he married Miss Eliza C. Smith, who has been a worthy helpmate during all these years.

In September 1862, he enlisted in Company F, 192d Regiment, N. Y. V., and served his country in the great Civil War, until its close—about three years.

On September 12, 1891, Mr. Ramsdell was licensed to preach by the Free Will Baptist Society, and was ordained September 11, 1892. During his ministry he has served the following churches: Dickinson Center, Pierrepont, West Parishville, North Lawrence and St. Regis Falls.

He moved to this village in April, 1900, and has served the local church at various periods during his residence here. Alhough he earned his retirement long ago, he has continued to preach for his people, when for any cause they happened to be without a minister. Upon these occasions he could always be depended upon to fill the vacancy until such time as a new pastor could be secured, even if his physical powers were taxed to the full limit.

Attorney Leslie M. Saunders

Leslie H. Saunders was born in the town of Dickinson, December 8, 1871. He is the son of Willard J. and Ellen E. Saunders. He attended the public schools of Dickinson, and in the fall of 1886 he entered Franklin Academy and graduated from that school in the spring of 1889. He taught school until he entered the University of Vermont in the fall of 1891, he graduated from this institution in the spring of 1895 with the degree of Ph.D. Mr. Saunders, after graduating from the university, taught school for several years, including the village schools at Nicholville and Moira, and met with marked success.

In the summer of 1899 he studied law in the office of Weeds, Smith & Conway at Plattsburgh, entering the Albany Law School the same fall. He completed the prescribed course and graduated in May, 1901 with the degree of LL.B. He was admitted to the bar of the State of New York in June, 1901. A little later he formed a law partnership with his father, W. J. Saunders, at Dickinson Center, under the firm name of Saunders & Saunders. In 1906 this partnership was dissolved when Leslie M. Saunders decided to start out for himself and opened a law office in this village, and he has succeeded in securing a long list of clients.

On June 8, 1910, he was married to Miss Bessie Davidson, of this village. They have one son about one year of age.

Mr. Saunders was appointed transfer tax commissioner by State Comptroller William Sohmer early last year, but resigned the position last August. He is a commissioner of elections for Franklin County, having been appointed by the board of supervisors last fall upon the recommendation of the chairman of the Democratic County Committee, and he, together with A. H. Proctor, of Malone, the Republican commissioner, constitute the board of elections of Franklin County.

Dr. W. A. Wardner

W. Allen Wardner was born in Brushton, N. Y. in 1873. He is the son of Dr. and Mrs. LeRoy M. Wardner; Mrs. Wardner's maiden name being Mary Jane Fleming.

He came with his parents to St. Regis Falls in 1883. He graduated from our Union School receiving the first diploma granted by the school. A little later he attended the Albany Business College, then accepted a position with the J. & J. Rogers Co., of Ausable Forks, manufacturers of sulphite fibre. Upon the death of his father he came home to look after his affairs. Soon after this, he decided to study medicine and entered the Albany Medical College, graduating from that institution in 1893. since which time he has been actively engaged in the practice of his profession at St. Regis Falls, and now has a practice that might well be envied by a much older practitioner.

In 1901, he was married to Miss Lena E. Palmer, of Upper Jay, N.Y., and has one son, two years old.

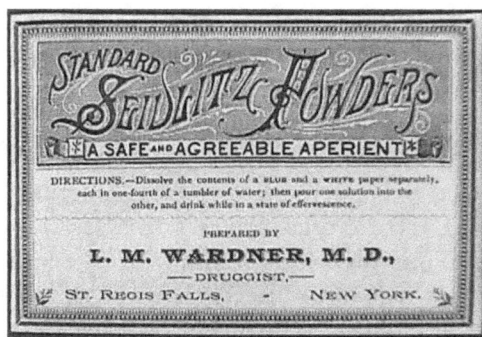

Pharmacy label from Leroy M. Wardner, father of Dr. W. Allen Wardner

Mr. Wardner was appointed health officer of the town of Waverly soon after he commenced the practice of medicine, and has faithfully served in that capacity ever since.

Orin L. Wilson

Orin L. Wilson was born at North Bangor, N. Y., June 27, 1834, was married to Miss Lucina Foster, August 24, 1879. He came to St. Regis Falls in the fall of 1883 and in company with his father-in-law, Henry Foster, built the store building he now occupies and put in a stock of groceries. In the spring of 1887, he moved to Lawrence, Mass., where he remained until 1894, when he moved back to St. Regis Falls and opened up a grocery and meat market in the same building he helped to construct eleven years before, and has continued to conduct the same with various other lines added until the present time.

In the fall of 1903, he was elected supervisor of the Town of Waverly, and has continued to hold the office uninterruptedly ever since.

At a special session of the Franklin County Board of Supervisors held June 6, 1911, he was selected for chairman of the board, which honorable position he still holds. He has also served the Town of Waverly as constable, town clerk and assessor at different periods of his residence here.

Chapter 14
FAMILY GENEALOGIES

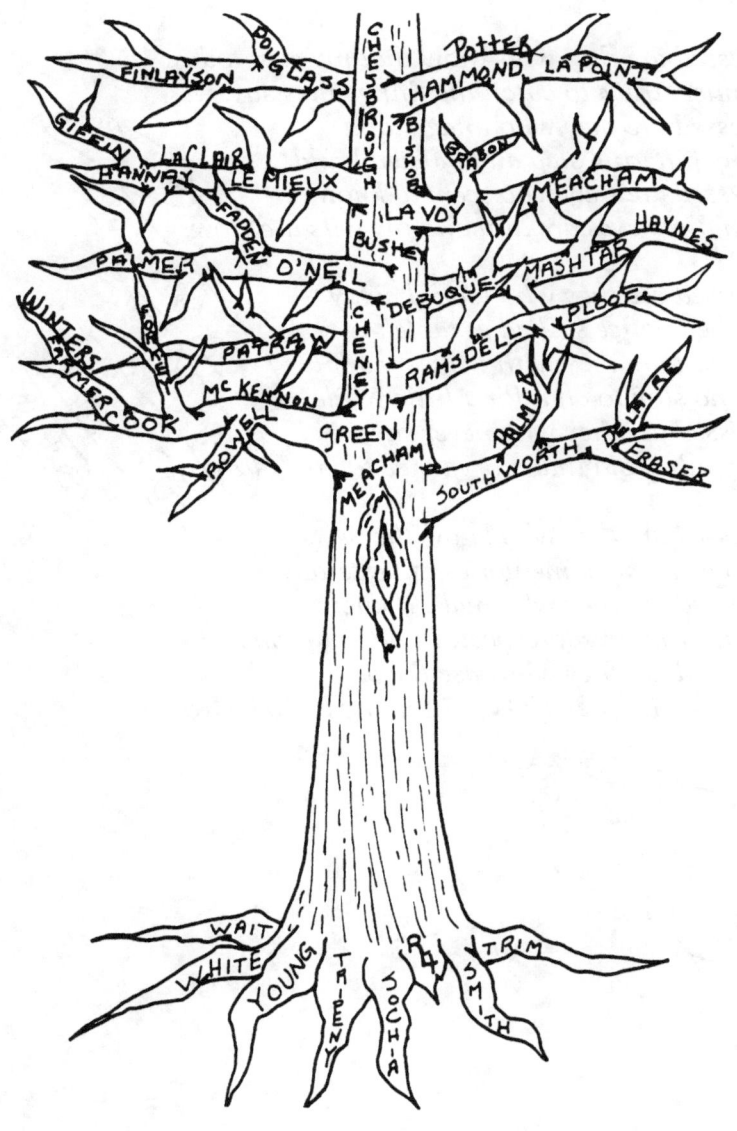

FRIENDS OF THE AGED

by Esther Mary Walker

Blessed are they who know that my ears today
  must strain to catch the things they say.
Blessed are they who understand
  my faltering step and palsied hand.
Blessed are they who seem to know
  that my eyes are dim and my wits are slow.

Blessed are they who looked away
  when coffee spilled at table today.
Blessed are they with a cheery smile
  who stop to chat for a little while.
Blessed are they who never say
  "you've told that story twice today."

Blessed are they who know the ways
  to bring back memories of yesterdays.
Blessed are they who make it known
  that I'm loved, respected and not alone.
Blessed are they who ease the day
  on my journey HOME in many loving ways.

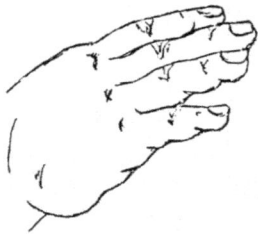

FAMILY GENEALOGIES • 131

THE BISHOP FAMILY

Charles Eugene Bishop/Levesque (Lavac) was born 1907 on the island of L'Verte, P.Q., Canada, the son of Andrew and Orellia Levesque. Andrew Levesque, who apparently had a reputation for not wanting to stay very long in one place, came to the U.S. on a boat (as a stowaway) down the St. Lawrence River, leaving his family behind temporarily. He traveled over to Nashua, New Hampshire, and upon finding employment in a mill, went back for his family. At the time Charles came to the States, he was 7 years old.

Around 1921, Andrew and Orellia Levesque moved from New Hampshire to the town of Santa Clara as he was an avid hunter. The rest of the family remained in New Hampshire as they all worked, including Charles who was then 14 years old and had quit school to go to work.

In 1923 when Charles was 16, he came alone from New Hampshire to Santa Clara and thereafter worked as a lumberjack.

The children of Andrew and Orellia Levesque were: Alfred, John, Paul, Charles, Caroline Levesque Gilbeault, Mary Ann, Anna Levesque St. Germain, Ida Levesque Delude, and Blanche Levesque Delude.

In 1927, Charles Levesque married Ida Mary Susice, the daughter of John and Katherine (Cayea) Susice. Charles was thereafter naturalized at the age of 33 years in 1940 and at that time changed the name "Levesque" to the supposedly english version "Bishop".

In Santa Clara there was a company called the Brooklyn-Cooperage Lumber Company who thereafter sold to the St. Regis Paper Company. Also, there was the Santa Clara Lumber Company. Apparently, the railroad (at that time known as New York Central) went right through the middle of town. They had a turntable, one of the few in the State of New York, which enabled the station operator to completely turn a train around and head it in the other direction.

The children of John and Katherine (Cayea) Susice, who originally lived at "Goose Pond" in the Town of Santa Clara, were: Ida Mary, John, Julius, Bert, Stella Susice Boucher,

Thomas Soucy, Ernest, Vina Susice Lontagne, Alfred, Alfreda Susice Judware, Joseph and Peter.

The children of Charles and Ida (Susice) Bishop are: Rose Marie (married to Rexford George O'Neil), Gloria (married to David Mosier), Violet (married to and subsequently divorced, Alton Haynes), Elsie (married to Bernard Bailey), Charles Andrew (married to Arlene Philips), Yvonne Marie (married to Ernest Nowicki), Delores Genevieve (married to Amos Dufore, now deceased—no children), William (Billy) Eugene (married to Joan Poole), and Linda Ida (married to Reginald Holmes).

Rex and Rose O'Neil's children are: Rexford Charles George O'Neil (married to Ann Susice Boyce—4 children), and Patricia Ann O'Neil Susice (married to Daniel Susice—3 children).

Gloria and David Mosier's children are: Joseph (married to Debra—4 children), Charles (married to Donna—1 child), Merry Ellen (recently married—no children), Jeffrey and Stephen.

Violet and Alton Haynes' children are: Alton Charles (married to Jacqueline—no children), and Gisele Marie (married to Stanley Harris—1 child).

Elsie and Bernard Bailey's children are: Bruce (married to Sheila—4 children), Michael (married to Lynn—5 children), Sharon (unmarried), Sheila (unmarried), Donna (unmarried), Cynthia (married to Gar Smith—no children), Susan (married to Sam Bradford—2 children), Barbara (married—2 children), and Wilbur (married to Rose—3 children).

Charles and Arlene Bishop's children are: Debbie (married to David Murray—4 children), Tammy (married to William Haynes—3 children), Susan (married to Peter Arcadi—4 children), Charles Eugene (married to Valerie Richards) and John Paul (unmarried).

Yvonne and Ernest Nowicki's children are: Laura Ann (married to Michael Richards—no children) and Joseph (unmarried).

William (Billy) Eugene and Joan Bishop's children are: Shawn, Darien, and Aaron.

Linda and Reginald Holmes' children are Reginald Jr. and Melissa Mary.

Bishop information obtained from Linda Bishop Holmes now living in Malone, N.Y.

THE BRABON FAMILY

The earliest knowledge of the Brabon/Brabont family is that they came from France to Quebec, Canada. Oliver F. Brabont was born 1846 in Beauhanois, Canada. The family then moved to Malone, N.Y., where he got his schooling. Oliver was very young when he enlisted in Co. F, 16th N.Y. Calvary, 1862, and was discharged in 1865. Shortly after his discharge, Oliver moved to Waverly where he met and married Mariam Ross, in 1867.

Since the Civil War the "t" has been omitted from the name making it Brabon. When Oliver Brabon first moved to Waverly, he lived at Shanley. He worked at a sawmill here and bought lumber from the mill to build a house and barn on the main road between St. Regis Falls and Santa Clara. This house is over 100 years old and is now occupied by Eugene Brabon, Oliver's grandson. Oliver Brabon died in 1929.

The children of Oliver and Mariam (Ross) Brabon were, 1) William born 1869, never married, and died Jan. 10, 1918, 2) Frank born 1883, married Martha Sochia and died Jan. 13, 1943, they had two children, Ethel born 1901 married Wesley C. Austin (1894–1977) and Bernard who died in 1948, 3) Marry Brabon Fisk died on May 8, 1954 age 80 years. After the death of Oliver's wife, Mariam, he remarried in 1883 to Katherine Pickham Johnson (1851–1935). To this union there were three sons; 1) Ernest, 2) Harry born 1891, never married and died Nov. 3, 1948 at the age of 57 years, and 3) George E. born 1893, married Nov. 1, 1915 to Emma Martin. Emma was born 1897 and died Nov. 26, 1975. They had one son, Eldred, who died Sept. 11, 1980. Eldred married Ruth Spinner and had two sons—Keith and Lyndon. George remarried in 1977 to Agatha Wood Hollister, and is still living—age 90 years.

Ernest O. Brabon (1884–Mar. 14, 1967) married Dora S. Austin (1888–1964), they had eight children—1) Eugene W. born 1908 married Arietta Cummings born 1911. They had seven sons, Austin died 1932, Hayden died 1942, Barclay, Harry, John, Harley, and Alton. 2) Pearl married George Ward, deceased 1983, and had four children; Emerson (married Eleanor Fairchilds), Beverly (married James Gadway), Richard (married Dorothy Pritchard), and Sharon (married Kenneth Disotelle). 3) Robert never married, 4) Laura married Gerald Martin, died 1981 and had four children; Gerald Jr. (married Nancy Greene), Geraldine (married Robert Godreau), Leon (married Ruth Wilson), and Marion (married Robert Preston). 5) Marshall married Florence Clary and had two children; James and Judy (married Michael LaFrance), 6) Reginald married Graceann Fadden and had; Daniel, Susan and Mickey. 7) Carroll born 1907 and 8) Wesley born 1916 and died 1926.

Brabon information obtained from Eugene Brabon—SRF.

THE BUSHEY FAMILY

Joseph W. Bushey was born Jan. 22, 1887, the son of David Bushey (1847–1907) from Vermont. Joseph had two brothers—Leo and John (born 1870 and married Ellie _____ (1872–1918), and six sisters—Jennie (1879–1967) married Amos Forkey (see *Forkey Family*), Maude married _____ Dauray, Mary married _____ Rivard, Addie (1872–1963) married Eugene Goodrow (1865–1959), Lucy married _____ Chagnon, and Annie married _____ Perry. All are deceased.

David Bushey had a brother, Joseph. This is the Joseph Bushey who deeded the land to the Catholic Church in St. Regis Falls. He had a son, George, who was a priest and a daughter (unknown name) who was a nun. Both are deceased.

Joseph W. (Joe) Bushey (born 1887) married Nov. 18, 1912 in Rockland, Ontario to Rose Brisbois, born April 18, 1888 in Clarence Creek, Ontario. Rose came to St. Regis Falls with the mica factory. Joe and Rose had six daughters—1) Vivian married Fred Tyler, they had seven children; Frederick, Robert, Richard, Kathleen, Jimmy, Eddie, and John. 2) Mary married Robert Plunkett and had five children; Robert, John, Larry, David, and Gary. 3) Irene married John Listovitch, they had two children; David and Denise. 4) Beatrice married Paul Jones and had four children; Theresa, Phillippe, Michael, and Stephen. 5) Helen married Charles Listovitch and had two children; Mark and Carol. 6) Louise B. born 1928, married Grant J. Wilcox, no children.

Joe Bushey died July 15, 1976 and is buried in St. Ann's Cemetery in St. Regis Falls. His wife, Rose, at the very active age of 96 years, stays with her daughter in Norwich, N.Y. for the winter months and comes to her St. Regis Falls home on South Main Street for the summer months.

Bushey information obtained from Mrs. Rose Bushey and Earl Forkey.

THE CHENEY FAMILY

Giles Cheney born April 19, 1854 and died Mar. 4, 1930, the son of Laurenzo and Lucena (Moffett) Cheney. (Lucena was the daughter of John and Clara Smith Moffett.) There were twelve children of this union—Wyotte, Gilbert, Ann, Ellen (married _____ Gorman), Josephine (married Henry Bruce), Giles, Arlene (married Antoine Sawyer), George (married Ella Stevens), Silas (married Clara Carpenter), Bertha (married John Parks), Lillian (married Alphonzo Rollins) and Fred (married Lillian Chapman).

Giles Cheney married Harriet Daggett born Oct. 10, 1862 and died June 13, 1937, the daughter of Willard and Ruth (Parks) Daggett. Willard's parents were Darius and Anna (Kenny) Daggett. Ruth's father was Even Parks. The children of Willard and Ruth Daggett were: Lucien (married Lydia Witcher), Harriet (married Giles Cheney), George (married Katherine Shatraw) and William (married Carrie La Rock).

The children of Giles and Harriet Cheney are: 1) Loren born Jan. 19, 1884 and died Feb. 1884. 2) Eva Ann born Feb. 20, 1886 and died Jan. 16, 1978. She married Charles Smith (see *Smith family*). 3) Gilbert born July 20, 1888 and died

Apr. 20, 1941. 4) Watson L. born Sept. 11, 1890 and died Apr. 8, 1929. He married Matilda Visneau and had four children—Loren, Merchant, Alletah and Harriet (1922–1923). 5) Ruth born Mar. 9, 1894 and died May 24, 1965, married Fred Desaw and had three children—Fred Jr., Andrew and Betty. Ruth then remarried to Tracy Bickford and they had three children—Ruth, Minnie and Tracy Jr. 6) Leon born Jan 29, 1897 and died Sept. 1900. 7) Willard G. born Oct. 26, 1898 and married Buelah Hicks born 1906. They had three children—Helen married Bernard Cascanette, Norma and Evelyn. 8) Glenn H. born Dec. 10, 1901 and died Jan. 27, 1966. He first married Violet Luck and had two sons—Glenn and Ivan. He then married Joyce Ploof (see *Ploof family*) and had Wayne R. (1942–1947), Nancy, Laurence, Eileen, Lois, and Deborah. 9) Velma born Aug. 2, 1904 and married Marshall Robert. They had three children—Marshall Jr., Leon and Paul. 10) Nora born Mar. 2, 1907 married Edward Moose and had three children—Kathleen (Kay) married Ralph Conger, Edward Jr. married Betty Morrick and Carol married Nelson (Bubby) Farmer, Jr.

Cheney information obtained from Willard Cheney and Nora Cheney Moose, St. Regis Falls.

THE CHESBROUGH FAMILY

Herbert L. Chesbrough was born in Plattsburgh, N.Y. 1865 and died 1950, the son of John B. Chesbrough (1845–1928). There was a sister, Louise, (1874–1925)

Herbert Chesbrough married Mary LaMay born 1867 in Malone, N.Y. and died 1939. Both Herbert and Mary Chesbrough are buried in the Fairview Cemetery in Dickinson Center, N.Y. There were five children in this union. 1) George Fred born July 14, 1895, married July 22, 1919 to Lowessa M. Finlayson (see *Finlayson family*). Fred, as he was called, died in Massena in 1974. Both Fred and Lowessa are buried in Dickinson Center. They had four children; Thurston McCrae, Verlie, Haven Grant, and Eula Autumn. 2) Clara born May 12, 1901, never married. 3) Walter E. born Oct. 21, 1902 and died 1973, married Jessie R. (born 1923). 4) Roy J.

born 1904, his second wife was Ethel P. (born 1906). and 5) Lesley married Leila _____.

Thurston McCrae Chesbrough was born Feb. 24, 1922 in Dickinson Center. He married Oct. 24, 1942 in St. Regis Falls to Genevieve Meacham born July 12, 1923 in St. Regis Falls and died Aug. 25, 1975 in Saranac Lake, the daughter of Vern and Philinda (Sochia) Meacham. Thurston and Gen had three children; 1) Wayne Morris born Mar. 17, 1943 in Malone and married July 15, 1967 to Glenda M. LaVoy (see *LaVoy family*). They have two daughters, Julie and Kathleen. 2) Gary Thurston born Dec 19, 1947 in Malone, married Ethel Chapman and have two daughters, Starr and Sandra. 3) Cynthia Ann (Cindy) born July 22, 1955 married David Austin and have two sons; Mathew and Heath.

Verlie Chesbrough married Charles LaBounty and they have four children; Paula, Dawn, Vance and Lorraine.

Haven Grant Chesbrough married Grace Gadoua, the daughter of Ernest and Velma (Griffin) Gadoua. They had six children; Michael, James, Thomas, Mary Ann, Lynn (deceased), and Kimberly; there was also a twin girl that died at birth.

Eula Autumn Chesbrough married Max Sawyer. They have two sons; Max Jr. and Cameron.

Chesbrough information obtained from Wayne Chesbrough, Lisbon, N.Y.

Kobbe Mansion, owned by the Cobby/Kobbe family

Kobbe Mansion (Dickinson) ca. 1944, showing a view of the back wall built to keep neighbor from viewing her house

Cobby or Kobbe Mansion (Dickinson) ca. 1944
In the hexagonal (6-sided) dressing room, all sides were mirrored.

THE COOK FAMILY

Hiram Cook, was born Dec. 1821, in Colchester, Vermont; the son of Jesmer and Hettie Cook. Both of his parents were born in New Hampshire. Hiram first settled in Dickinson when he moved from Clinton County with his new wife, Myhitible (Hitty) Rising; the daughter of Samuel and Phoebe (Howard) Rising. Hitty was born in Saranac Hollow, Clinton County, N.Y. Sept. 1832 and died May 6, 1900 in St. Regis Falls.

Hiram and Myhatible Rising Cook

Hiram and Hitty Cook had five children; Hail, Orin H., Ethel, Warren and Oliver. Orin Cook was born 1869 and died 1952. He married Carrie Sochia, the daughter of Theodore and Angelina (Young) Sochia. They had nine children; Nora, Ella M., Dora Mae, Gertrude M., Hiram, Theodore, Emma, Florence and Bessie.

Hiram Cook, one of the first to make permanent residence in St. Regis Falls, helped cut through the wilderness from Dickinson to make the road. He was also part of the crew that built the Hammonds Mill in 1860; others on that crew were Julius Rising, (Hiram's brother-in-law) Amos Harvey, and Kirby and Josephus Titus. At that time, there was only one-half acre of timber cut down on the present site of the village.

THE ORIN COOK FAMILY

Row 1—Orin Cook, Bessie (child), Bert Allen (husband to Nora), Bert Hart (husband to Ella), Elmer LaVoy (husband to Dora), Donald Finlayson (husband to Gertie), Hiram and Theodore.
Row 2—Carrie (Sochia) Cook, Florence (child), Nora, Ella, Dora, Gertie, and Emma.

Hiram's obituary read, "Mr. Cook was a kind-hearted and neighborly man and while he was not connected with any church, he always endeavored to do what he thought was right and was well spoken of by everyone." He died Sept. 30, 1894, and is buried in the Forest Cemetery with his wife in St. Regis Falls.

Nora Cook, the eldest child of Orin and Carrie Cook, was born in June 1892. She married Bert Allen, and had five children; Lawrence, Beatrice, Vergie, Dorothy and Gertrude. Ella M. was born May 1893, and married Bert A. Hart; they had no children. Dora Mae was born June 1896 and married Elmer LaVoy; they had five children, Abraham and Harold, both died in infancy, Alton, Efford and Carl H. Gertrude M. was born May 1897 and married Donald Finlayson; they had three children—Isabel, Arnold and Fern. Gertie and Donald Finlayson were Mr. and Mrs. Santa Claus for many years and made their home at the North Pole, New York. Hiram Jr. was born April 1898; he never married. Theodore was born Nov.

1901 and married Lillian Pratt; they had three children—Lawrence, Margaret and Fulton. Emma was born Oct. 1904 and married Albert Densmore, they had three children—Ruth, Percy and Wilfred. Florence was born Mar. 1908 and married a man named Goff. Bessie was born Sept. 1914 and married (Doe) Barlow.

THE DU BUQUE FAMILY

Thomas DuBuque/DeBuque from Canada (1838–1928) was a Civil War veteran, Co. I 60th Reg. N.Y. Vol. His wife was Louise Center from Vermont (1846–1931). Both are buried in St. Anne's Cemetery in St, Regis Falls. Also on the same grave stone appears—Julia Center (1814–1909); this is probably Louise's mother.

Thomas and Louise had six children:

A) Thomas DeBuque (1877–1955), his wife Flenda R. born 1876. They had one son, Joseph T. (1897–1959), he married Rose M. Rumley born 1903. Joseph and Rose DeBuque had six children; 1) Howard born Nov. 29, 1921, married July 4, 1942 to Eleanor (Tootie) Garrow born July 14, 1923. They had six children—Howard, Ralph, Kenny, Ronnie, Dorothy (Fay) and David (died young). 2) Floyd born Sept. 3, 1935, never married. 3) Glenford born May 30, 1927, never married. 4) Loren born Aug. 10, 1933 married Aug. 6, 1955 to Muriel Powell born May 28, 1939 and they have four children—Jeanne married Duane Mac Donald with two children, Jessica and Dallas; Greg married Beth Morey; Tammy married Terrance Fitzgerald and has a son, Loren Richard; and Larna, not married. 5) Jimmy born Sept. 3, 1925 married Alice Morick with three children—Stacie Jo, Windy and Jimmy. 6) Donnie born June 16, 1937, never married. and 7) Evelyn born 1924 and died 1950; married Bert Garrow, and had three children—Shirley 1944–1973, married first to Phil Prior Jr. and had four children; Shirley then married Harry Arcadi. She died in a car accident. Billy Garrow is married and has no children; Larry Garrow was adopted after Evelyn's death.

B) Steve DeBuque married and had one son who died as a teenager, and a daughter. He lived in Ogdensburg.

C) Charles DuBuque (Mar. 3, 1884–Dec. 16, 1966) married Flossie Winters (Dec. 10, 1892–Feb. 10, 1935) and had a daughter Gladis, who married Lloyd Roscoe. Gladis and Lloyd Roscoe had three children; 1) Lloyd who is married and has no children, 2) Lee married Darlene Arcadi and have two children, and 3) Wanda who is married and has three children. Charles and Flossie DuBuque also had a son, Loren C., who died Mar. 7, 1972; he married Anna Snell (Sept. 15, 1913–Nov. 11, 1972), they had Bonnie, who is married and has two children, and Gary.

D) Racheal DuBuque married and had two sons, Edward and William.

E) Mary DuBuque married _____ Compo and had eight children—Louise, Annabel, Darin, Leli, George, Edward, and Donald. They lived in Massena.

F) Julia DuBuque (1869–1948) married Ferdinand Hewitt (1861–1950) and had five children—William, Steve, Sadie, Dollie and Violet.

DuBuque information obtained from Loren and Muriel DuBuque, St. Regis Falls.

THE DE LAIRE FAMILY

David DeLaire/DeLair-DeLlaire, was born at Riviere-du-Moulin on March 21, 1852 and was baptized at Chicoutimi, Quebec, Canada. The son of Etienne (Eilenne) (1827–1890) and Marie (1818–1888) DeLaire. He was married May 6, 1873 to Florestine Tremblay (1854–1902), the daughter of Joseph and Josephine (Raynot) Tremblay, of the parish of Sainte-Anne of Chicoutimi. David and Florestine immigrated to the United States with six children who were born in Canada. They lived in Tupper Lake and eventually came to St. Regis Falls. Of this marriage there were eight children altogether. Six boys and two girls, the two youngest being born in New York State.

1) George J. born 1874 and died 1938. He never married and worked in the pulp mill in St. Regis Falls. He died in Beacon, N.Y. of a heart attack.

2) Peter J. born 1876 and died 1931. He never married and was a railroader. He died in an accident in Seattle, Washington.

3) David J. Jr. was born 1878 and died 1938. He was a barber. His first wife was Valina Raymond/Raymo (1882–1914). They had one daughter, Doris, who married Dr. Bury in Tupper Lake. After his death, Doris married Howard Martin and resides in Clearwater, Florida and Tupper Lake. David's second wife was Violet Perry (1878–1929). They had no children.

4) Paul was born 1880 and died 1951. He married May 1900 to Clara Dewey. The had seven children—Alfreda, Paul Jr., Frances, Bernice, Bernard, George (Morton), and Dewey. 1) Alfreda married Felix Regenie in New York City. They had one daughter, who is married and lives in Odessa, Texas. 2) Paul Jr. married Dorothy Mannix of Moira and they have three children—Carol, Roger, and Linda. Both Paul and Dorothy are deceased. 3) Frances born Oct. 19, 1906 and died Aug. 19, 1979; she was a registered nurse, graduated from Long Island College Hospital in 1929 and was married in 1935 to William A. Baxter (Dec. 30, 1897—Oct. 25, 1970), a New York City policeman. They had one son, William P. (Billy). 4) Bernice married Clarence Ward of Brasher Falls. They had three children—Thomas, a sergeant with the New York State Police; Paula, a secretary with the Malone village; and Jane, who married Donald Achcroft. They live in Medford, Mass. and have three children—Donald, Michelle and Thomas. 5) Bernard, a World War II veteran, served in the South Pacific theater and was a retired accountant from the Alice Hyde Hospital in Malone; he married Helen Sullivan of Pittsburgh, Pa. They had one son, Dennis, a disabled Vietnam veteran. 6) George (Morton) married Elinor Harris of Norwood, N.Y. They had one daughter, Ellen, who married Wayne Newman and reside in Rochester, N.Y. Ellen and Wayne have one daughter, Sarah. Morton retired from the New York State Dept. of Transportation as an engineer, Watertown and now resides in Clearwater, Florida. 7) Dewey, the youngest, died of a heart attack in 1976 at the age of 53 years. He was married to Patricia Cunningham of Nanuet, N.Y. They had four

children—Paul, Ann Marie, Peter, and Mark. Dewey was a graduate from Cortland College and received his Masters from Columbia University. He was principal of Cocoa Beach Elementary School in Florida. His wife graduated from Plattsburgh State University and is a school teacher.

5) Laura born 1882 and died 1968. She married Jay Bennett and had two children—Joyce, married Pete Lunderman of Potsdam and Kenneth who lived in Beacon, N.Y., now deceased. Married and had two boys—John was killed in Vietnam and David is a policeman in Poughkeepsie, N.Y.

6) Louis born 1884 and died 1949. Never married. He was a station agent at various towns on the New York Central line.

7) Thomas born in Tupper Lake, died in 1952, was married to Jane Murray of Brasher Falls, a school teacher. Tom was a World War I veteran, serving as a lieutenant and was a French interpreter. He then was a banker and served as secretary of the New York State Bankers Association, and was President of the Fishkill National Bank in Beacon, N.Y. He was also mayor of that city.

8) Alice J. (1890–1973) was married to Angus A. Partlow (1887–1971) and had four children—Kenneth (1909–1913), Thomas, Dorothy, and Mary. They lived in Tupper Lake and the moved to Canton, N.Y. Thomas is residing in Florida. Mary is deceased. Dorothy married Robert and resides in Delmar, N.Y.

DeLaire information obtained from Bernard DeLaire, St. Regis Falls.

THE DOUGLASS FAMILY

Henry Bancroft Douglass born 1867, the son of John and Harriet (Bancroft) Douglass, came to St. Regis Falls early in the 1890s from Louisville, N.Y. Henry had three brothers; 1) John (unmarried and lived in Worchester, Mass.), 2) George (a lawyer, married and had two children and moved to California), and William (married, had three children and lived in Scranton, Pennsylvania). There was one sister,

Bertha, who married William Douglass (no relation). They had three children; Harold (a flyer in World War I was killed and buried in France), Claire (unmarried), and Thera (a graduate of Syracuse University, married Charles Wood, a minister, and they had seven children and lived in Fredonia, N.Y.).

Henry Douglas married Gertrude J. Southworth (1871–1906), the daughter of Ogilvy S. and Martha (Carpenter) Southworth. Henry worked in the tannery, he had learned the job in Worchester, Mass. He later worked for Ogilvy Southworth in the grocery store located on South Main Street. This business later became Douglass & Southworth. The children of Henry and Gertrude Douglass were Marion Dorothy born 1896 and married Earl J. LaPoint, and Ruth, who died in childbirth with her mother, Gertrude. After the death of his wife, Gertrude, Henry married Helen Augusta Riggs (1877–1938). Henry and Helen had Donald born Jan. 29, 1909 (now living in California) and Lawrence R. born 1910 and died 1914.

Both Henry and Helen were active in civic affairs of the town. Henry was a director in the local bank and belonged to the Odd Fellows lodge. Helen was a music teacher and gave lessons. They were both active in the church and choir.

Douglass information obtained from Mrs. Marion Douglass LaPoint, Mrs. Halcyon LaPoint Davies, both of St. Regis Falls, and Mr. Donald Douglass of San Diego, California.

THE FADDEN FAMILY

James A. Fadden was born in Alburg, Vermont, Feb. 19, 1863, and died 1933; he was the son of Mr. and Mrs. James Fadden. He married Oct. 5, 1890 in Boston, Mass., to Ida Iby, the daughter of Henry and Phoebe (Sweet) Iby. Ida was also born in Alburg, Vermont, Oct. 5, 1873 and died 1958. After residing in Boston about a year, they moved near Dickinson. In 1910 they then moved to St. Regis Falls. They were members of the Methodist Church. Mrs. Fadden was a member of the "Calendar Club"—a group organized to raise money while building the new church after fire destroyed the first one in 1926, the same time the school burned.

They had eleven children, including a pair of twins.

Arthur, the oldest, was born in Dickinson in 1892. He worked for the Brooklyn Cooperage Company and paper mill in his early years. He was also a World War I veteran and a member of the American Legion. Later he was custodian at St. Regis Falls Central School until he retired. Arthur Fadden married Florence LaChance in 1921 and they had three children; Theda (Mrs. Basil Wells, Potsdam), Beatrice (Mrs. Lee Votra, Newark, N.Y.), and Bernard—he and his wife, Betty, live in New Castle, Pennsylvania.

Ray was born in Dickinson in 1894. He, too, worked in paper mills, and was in World War I, seeing active service in France. He belonged to the American Legion, Ray Fadden married Gladys Merrick of Rochester in 1932. They had five daughters, Carol (married Glenford Niles and later remarried Jack Hall), Ida (Mrs. Harry Brabon), Graceanne (Mrs. Reginald Brabon), Doris (Mrs. Jefferson Haywood), and Evelyn (Mrs. Tim Hartman). Gladys died in 1971 and Ray died in 1976.

George, Leroy, Layman and Claude Fadden, 1910, Reynoldston

Basil E. was born in Dickinson in 1896. He married Anna Beaudry in Canton. Anna died in 1941 and Basil then married Alice Brown in 1946. Basil died in 1965.

George I. born in 1898 and died with pneumonia in 1917 (1919).

Lymon W. was born in Dickinson in 1900. He worked for the railroad, then for Alcoa in Massena until he retired in 1967. He was a World War I veteran and a member of the American Legion. Lymon died in 1974.

Claude was born in Dickinson in 1902, and married Margaret Swamp in 1924. He farmed in this area and then moved to Hicksville, Long Island in 1944, where he worked on a dairy farm. They both died there in 1963—Margaret in January and Claude in October.

Leroy was born in Dickinson in 1907 and married Daisy Barkley (born 1909) in 1927. He worked on construction and later became custodian at St. Regis Falls Central School until his retirement in 1969. They have two children—Joy (Mrs. Richard Hazen) and Nelson (Mike).

Daisy Barkley and John Heywood at Ezra Barkley's cabinet shop, ca. 1927

Joyce and Nelson Fadden, ca. 1935

A daughter, Pearl, was born in Dickinson in 1909 and died in 1928. She was a student nurse at St. Lawrence State Hospital.

Pansey was born in St. Regis Falls in 1912, attended school there and was active in the church. She married Lauriston Hazen in 1933.

Nelson Fadden (Methodist Church in background, ca. 1936, and wearing SRF band uniform, ca. 1948)

The twins, Orie (Peter) and Oral (Marie) were born in St. Regis Falls on Feb. 14, 1916. She married Francis Wells in 1936. They lived in the Plattsburgh area, and had five children, Lucille (Mrs. Bruce Bowes), Gerald, Harold, Geraldine (Mrs. Holly McClung), and John. Oral died January 18, 1982.

Orie (Peter) was married in 1943 in Trenton N.J. He had three children; Arthur, Philip (deceased), and Della (Mrs. Coriea Guyton). Orie lived in New Jersey most of his adult life. He worked in a chemical plant and later became custodian in a college. He retired in 1978 and died January 19, 1982.

Fadden information obtained from Mrs. Pansey Fadden Hazen, Winthrop, New York

Arnold Barkley's print shop in Dickinson, ca. 1948

Ezra Barkley digging a well on LaFayette Street, ca. 1935

THE FARMER FAMILY

James Farmer was born 1847 in Canada, the son of John (born in France) and Mary Ingland (born 1815 in England, died Mar. 26, 1896) Farmer. John and Mary (Ingland) Farmer were married in Canada. Besides James, there were four other children in this union; Lucy, Betsey, John (married Elzira Palmer) and Robert.

James Farmer married in 1868 to Laura Perry, who was born 1846 in Malone. As a family unit they lived both in Canada and the United States, thus could speak both French and English. In 1886 James and Laura purchased land in the St. Regis Falls area and settled here. This land was virgin timberland and it was natural that they went into the lumbering industry.

As these forest lands disappeared it was converted into a farm. Thus the family became farmers. In the winter months the family would go into the lumber camps. Laura to cook and James to drive a team of horses which he always took with him. In the spring they would return bringing with them lumberjacks and relation to work the farm. They later ran a hotel in the area that was always filled with lumberjacks. Laura was the dominate figure in the family. James Farmer became a United States citizen July 5, 1904.

There were nine children of this union; 1) Commodore A. born 1867 married Sophia M. (1870–1901), 2) John, 3) William Wallace born 1878 in North Burke and married Frances Lindsay on Apr. 13, 1897, 4) Fred (lived in Tupper Lake), 5) Elizabeth married _____ Roscoe, 6) Maude married Jack Garrity, 7) May (died in Tupper Lake) married _____ Ploof, 8) Arthur J. 1877–1965 married in 1905 to Libby Collins (1886–1961). Arthur and Libby had nine children; 1) Nelma born 1906 and died 1964, married Mathew Sexton of Tupper Lake, 2) Evelyn born 1907 married Edward Santerre of Tupper Lake, 3) Ethel born 1909 (deceased) married Charles Morbito, 4) Alice born 1914 married Gerald Chapman of Saranac Lake, 5) Francis born 1916 died 1973 married Michael Cimbric of Bloomingdale, N.Y., 6) Royal born 1918, 7) Ralph born Oct. 1920 married Malina Nelson, 8) Carlton A. born 1922 died 1967, was a World War II veteran, and 9) Belva Jean born 1924 married Ralph Darrah of Bloomingdale, N.Y.

9) Lindon James Farmer born Nov. 12, 1882 and died Feb. 2, 1954. He married Aug. 3, 1907 to Natilie (Nettie) LaPage born Sept. 17, 1884 and died Feb. 15 1967, the daughter of Alphonse and Philena (Gardner) LaPage. Alphonse died 1917 and Philena died May 1, 1922, age 77 years. Lindon and Nettie Farmer had ten children; 1) Flora Gertrude born Apr. 8, 1909 and died July 24, 1943, married Roy Chesbrough; they had a son, Richard 1930–1936. 2) Albert Alexander born July 22, 1911 and died Aug. 22, 1973, married Earldean Blade born 1918; they had a daughter Judith P. 1942–1964.

3) James Lindon born Mar. 2, 1914 and died Jan. 2, 1957. 4) Margaret Violet born Aug. 29, 1915, deceased. 5) Thelma Louise born Dec. 4, 1916, drowned Aug. 11, 1935. 6) Beatrice Eva married _____ Daney, and was born May 3, 1919. 7) Elizabeth Philena born Apr. 16, 1922 married Percy Keith Ploof (see *Ploof family*). 8) William Harold born Nov. 25, 1923. 9) Daniel Oliver born May 29, 1926, and 10) Walter Leo born Oct. 31, 1928.

Farmer information obtained from Ralph Farmer and Mrs. Elizabeth Farmer Ploof, St. Regis Falls.

THE FINLAYSON FAMILY

John Finlayson was born May 17, 1840 on way from Scotland on board ship to Canada. He took Canadian citizenship in the town of Ormstown. His first wife was Dona L. Hall (1863–June 26, 1884) and is buried in the Palmer Cemetery in Dickinson Center, N.Y. His second wife was _____ McKenna of St. Regis Falls. His third wife was Cammie Smith (Apr. 7, 1867–Aug. 1942) and is buried in Sandhill Cemetery, area known as Alburg, N.Y. (between Harwood Corners and Moira).

There were ten children born to the third marriage; 1) Lulu Lenora born May 24, 1886, married May 24, 1905 to William R. Trim (see *Trim family*) and died June 18, 1981, 2) Isabel Mae born Jan. 14, 1889 in Dickinson Center, married July 22, 1914 to Ronald Lee, and died Mar. 24, 1958, 3)

Donald McRae born Oct. 23, 1892, married Dec. 23, 1913 to Gertrude Cook (see *Cook family*), and died 1959 and is buried in the Mountain View Cemetery in Gabriels, N.Y., 4) Katie Jennifer, born Dec. 1, 1894 in Dickinson Center, married Clifford Gale and died June 28, 1963, buried in Sunnyside Cemetery in Brushton, N.Y., 5) Bessie Denise born May 3, 1898 and never married, 6) Lowessa Myrtle born Apr. 12, 1900, married July 22, 1919 to George F. Chesbrough (see *Chesbrough family*) and died May 9, 1952, buried in Dickinson Center, 7) John Clayton born Feb. 25, 1903, married Clara Surprise and died Apr. 3, 1983, 8) Arliegh Lynn born Dec. 4, 1907, first married June 9, 1933 to May Cummings and second married Mary Finnell, 9) Jennie B. born Apr. 9, 1908, married Rodney Hanley, and 10) Carmen Fern born Apr. 8, 1912, married Ray Sourwine.

Ronald and Isabel Finlayson Lee had four children; Arliegh, Allen, Phyllis and Alice.

George and Lowessa Finlayson Chesbrough had four children; Thurston, Verlie, Haven and Eula.

John and Clarabelle Surprise Finlayson had six children; Audrey, Darrell, Patsy, Stanley, LeRoy, and Janis Mae.

Rodney and Jennie Finlayson Hanley had eight children; Rodney, Ronald, Peggy, Helen, Carmen, Robert, Kathleen, and Kay.

THE FORKEY FAMILY

Amos Forkey was born May 4, 1876 in Moores Fork, N.Y., the son of Adolphus Forkey (born Aug. 26, 1843 and died Sept. 13, 1896 at Brandon, N.Y.) As a boy, Amos lived in Brandon (the Brandon located where Ross' Park is), where his father owned a shingle mill. Amos worked in the mill during the summer and went to school through the winter, to the fourth grade.

Amos married Jennie Bushey—born May 4, 1879 in Dickinson, the daughter of David and Janet (King) Bushey. They lived in Derrick, N.Y., where they owned and operated a general store with Amos' brother and brother-in-law. After a few years they lost the business and moved to St. Regis Falls. Here they started a clothing store with one of his brothers. Amos operated this establishment for 37 years until his retirement. He was also town clerk for St. Regis Falls for 16 years.

There were five brothers to Amos—Frank, William, Jerry, Charles and Frederick; also three sisters—Cora, Ellen and Libby.

Amos and Jennie had six children, 1) Antoinette, 2) Lillian, 3) Dorothy, 4) Lenore, 5) Irene, and 6) Earl. Amos died in Malone Hospital June 4, 1951 and Jennie died at Moira May 22, 1967.

1) Antoinette married Sibley (Buck) Palmer and had two daughters, Patricia and Elizabeth (Betty).

2) Lillian married Paul Nash and had two boys, Charles Amos born March 1944 and Paul Edward born 1945.

3) Lenore married Edward Ploof (Bud) and had four boys, 1) Frank born Apr. 26, 1946 2) twins—David and Dennis born Mar. 15, 1951, 3) James died at age 4 years.

4) Dorothy married Floyd Caskinette and had one son, Harry J. born Dec. 26, 1946.

5) Earl married Jane R. Morin, Aug. 12, 1936 and had seven children—Gail, Nancy, Diane, Sherry, Terisa, Jerry and Charles.

6) Irene married Joe Strauss and had two children, Margaret born 1944 and died Nov. 27, 1983 and Paul born Oct. 26, 1948.

Information on the Forkey family obtained from Earl and Jane Forkey of St. Regis Falls.

THE FRASER FAMILY

J. A. Fraser in his early years lived in the town of Stockholm, N.Y., St. Lawrence County on a farm. He became Superintendent of Lumbering and Reforestation for the Brooklyn Cooperage Company and located in St. Regis Falls, living on North Main Street. Located at his home was a large barn that housed many teams used in these operations.

The reforestation plantation was located on Duane Street near the cemetery. The old arches marking the area are still standing.

The stave mill was located by the railroad tracks on both sides of the river on Main Street in St. Regis Falls.

The St. Regis Paper Company later bought the holdings from the Brooklyn Cooperage Company.

Old Jack Fraser, as he was always known, was fond of police dogs, He owned a large tan and black police dog called, "Wolf", who was always with him and carried mail and packages in his mouth home from down street.

His wife, Louise, was blind from cataracts, but was able to cook and do many household chores.

John W. and Bessie were born to this family. They also had two other children that lived with them many years. The girl was named Rita, who was a child from the Ogdensburg Orphanage in Ogdensburg, N.Y. Later on, she worked as a waitress in a summer guest house in Saranac Lake and met and married Charles Bruce. They lived on a farm in that area and two sons, Charles and John, were born to them. Another boy that lived at the Fraser house was Arthur Starks. He and Rita took the Fraser name.

Bessie married John Little and they settled in Springfield, Vermont, as he was employed in the Lamson Machine Shop. A son, Donald, and daughter, Louise, were born to this couple.

John, called Johnny to everyone, was superintendent of the Brooklyn Cooperage Company's stave mill at St. Regis Falls. Later he was transferred to Georgetown, South Carolina to build and operate a stave mill there and Johnny, having married Emma McKennon, and their daughter, Helen, moved to Georgetown. While living there a son, Harold, was born. He operated the stave mill there several years and also set up another mill in Tennessee. When the International Paper Company bought out these mills, he returned to St. Regis Falls.

Later he built and operated the jackworks on the south side of the river near the railroad bridge, named the Black Bridge. Pulp was put in Meacham Lake and floated down to the mill here. Bark was peeled and then the wood was sent to mills by rail. The present picnic area above the dam is in that spot now. When logs could no longer be put in the river, he built a shingle mill at Millbrook on the Everton Road. To operate this shingle mill he used a motor from a Lynn tractor which the Brooklyn Cooperage Company had owned previously.

At one time Johnny was a Republican supervisor of our town. At the next election, the Democratic Party won the election by one vote. At this time there were two polling places in St. Regis Falls.

Helen married Morton Parks and they have three children: Betty, Roger and Jack.

Harold married Mildred Woodward of Dickinson Center and they have eight children: Harold (Jack), Howard (Jim), Hal (Jeff), Joanne, Jean, Haven (Jerry), Hugh (John), and Jennifer. Several of Harold's sons are engaged in logging operations on land owned by the St. Regis Paper Company as did their great-grandfather.

Fraser information written by and obtained from Mrs. Helen Fraser Parks, St. Regis Falls.

THE GIBBS FAMILY

John C. and Mary Race Gibbs

John Gibbs residence, l to r: Mary Race Gibbs, Mary's daughter Elsie Gibbs Johnson, Elsie's daughter Myrtle

Flossie Mae Gibbs, born April 28, 1892; she was 16 in this photo

THE GIFFIN FAMILY

Martin E. Giffin was born in St. Albans, Vermont, Jan. 15, 1836 and died 1898. Buried in St. Regis Falls, Forest Cemetery. He married Mary Bruce who died March 1931, the daughter of Abner Bruce of Bloomingdale, N.Y., one-time pioneer guide on the Saranac River. At the age of 17 years, Martin Giffin came from Vermont with his parents, Calvin and Rhoda (Hewett) Giffin, and settled near Pierrepont, N.Y., around 1853. He served during the Civil War in the Union Army with Co. G 98th Reg. N.Y. Vol. Inf. His wife, who survived him, received a widow's pension. Children of Martin and Mary Giffin were, 1) Frank M. 1870–1946, 2) Nona 1874–1943, married Samuel W. Crandall 1870–1905, both are buried in St. Regis Falls, 3) Rollin Glenville, 4) Helen Abbie May, 1878–1885, age 7 years and buried in the St. Regis Falls, Forest Cemetery.

Rollin Glenville Giffin was born in Hopkinton, N.Y., Aug. 24, 1874 and died in St. Regis Falls, 1947. He married in 1908 to Mary (Mamie) Maher, the daughter of Martin and Johanna (Kirby) Maher. Of Irish decent, she came from the area of Moira called "The Patch". Mary Maher Giffin was born Dec. 7, 1878 and died in Ogdensburg, N.Y., Jan. 4, 1965. The children of Rollin and Mary Giffin were, 1) Rollin George, 2) son (unknown name, a twin) born Oct. 12, 1909, died at birth, 3) Helen born Dec. 15, 1910, married in 1932 to Wendell O. Covell, who became an insurance agent. They had four boys—Jack, Tim, Bruce and Jeff.

Rollin Glenville Giffin was a woodsman who worked in the west for a time, but when he married, came back to this area and in 1909 built a house in St. Regis Falls, in which the Giffin family still lives. However, he became involved in the lumbering business and rented their house. His wife, Mary,

R. G. GIFFIN & SON
ST. REGIS FALLS, NEW YORK

LUMBER   **BUILDING SUPPLIES**

This letterhead was used by the Giffin business for many years.

followed him and was the cook in the lumber camps. He conducted a lumber business in Deferiet, N.Y. and was known as a lumber conservationist in the Adirondack Mountains, and he erected numerous lumber mills throughout the North Country. When their children were ready for high school, in 1924, he moved back to their house in St. Regis Falls and opened a coal business. He became postmaster with his wife as his assistant. Building supplies were added to his coal business—then the oil business was added later. Coal was sold by the train-carload and the Giffins had a siding where the car was put and unloaded into the coal shed. Frank Giffin with his trusty horse, "Cub", delivered the coal to the customers.

Rollin George Giffin was born in St. Regis Falls, Oct. 12, 1909 and died Aug. 13, 1982. He married in Boonville, N.Y., Aug. 8, 1934, Bertha Scharbach, born there Sept. 29, 1911, the daughter of John and Sarah (Oberriter) Scharbach. After graduating from high school, Rollin went to work in the St. Regis Falls National Bank and was there for eight years, with "Bert" Dupree and Percy Rowell. Then he joined his father in the business. Mrs. Bertha Giffin taught school in St. Regis Falls for forty years. In 1947, when Rollin's father died, he became owner and operator of the business until his retirement in 1975. The children of Rollin and Bertha Giffin are, 1) Rollin George, born May 14, 1935, and married in Cincinnati, Ohio, Apr. 4,1959 to Shirley Rakish and 2) Jeanne Terese, born May 12, 1938, and married Richard H. Wright, June 24, 1961.

Note—Giffin information obtained from Mrs. Bertha Giffin, of St. Regis Falls.

THE GREEN FAMILY

Ira C. Green born April 22, 1834, I believe, in St. Lawrence County. Mr. Green located in the St. Regis Falls area around the 1870s. He was a pettifogger, a justice of the peace, and an active worker in local politics.

Ira Green married Jan. 1, 1858 to Harriet J. Smith born July 13, 1842, the daughter of Willard and Betsey (Boyce) Smith. There were nine children of this union; 1) infant son died July 4, 1858, 2) infant son died Dec. 25, 1859, 3) Nettie born Mar. 7, 1861, died Dec. 11, 1879, 4) Silas born Dec. 17, 1863, died Jan. 14, 1864, 5) Rosa born Oct. 7, 1866, died Feb. 13, 1880, 6) Bessie born July 30, 1868, died Sept. 28, 1888, 7) I. Clayton born Feb. 27, 1871, died June 8, 1893, 8) Thomas born Mar. 5, 1874, died July 24, 1881 and 9) Willard born Feb. 13, 1876, died July 19, 1881.

Ira Green had brothers living in West Stockholm, St. Lawrence County in 1887, E. E. Green and Silas Green.

St. Regis Falls at one time in 1880 went by the name of Greenville, named in compliment of Ira C. Green. Mr. Green died Dec. 28, 1886.

THE HAMMOND FAMILY

The Hammond brothers, Charles F. and John, the first large landowners in the area, were originally from Pittsford, Vermont, and then relocated to Crown Point, Essex County, New York. The sons of the Honorable Thomas Hammond, esquire; and grandsons of Daniel Hammond, who participated in the old French and English War. Thomas Hammond was an attendant upon an officer in the Revolutionary War and was present at the execution of Major Andre.

Charles' son, Thomas, his wife and their children died on the ill-fated steamer, "Ville du Harve", which went to the bottom of the Atlantic, November 22, 1873. Charles Hammond died December 12, 1873, the immediate cause being the shock of his son's death. Charles' wife died August 28, 1882. Charles Hammond had ten children.

The Hammonds were active in civic affairs and a very resourceful family.

THE HANNAY FAMILY

Gordon Hannay (1865–1942) came to the United States and St. Regis Falls in 1907 from Glasgow, Scotland. In 1898 he married Anna Baird born in Killala, County Mayo, Ireland; Feb. 6, 1868. The third daughter of William and Anna (Sharp) Baird, Grandma Hannay, as she was lovingly called by many of the townspeople, died Dec. 9, 1964 at the age of 96 years. She was the oldest resident in St. Regis Falls.

The children of Gordon and Anna (Baird) Hannay were born in Glasgow, Scotland. 1) Mary A. 1899–1968 (married Vernon D. (Dutch) Parks (1893–1959), 2) Gordon Jr. 1901–1971 (first married Agnes Maloney 1907–1942) and second married Margaret Reynolds 1906– , 3) Elizabeth (Liz) born 1903 (married Lymond R. (Jim) Camp, born 1908), 4) Jessie (married Percy Everett and lived in Tacoma, Washington).

The February 1964 *St. Regis Falls Newsletter* best sums up the 96th birthday anniversary of Anna (Grandma) Hannay as follows:

> Feb. 6, 1964, Mrs. Gordon Hannay of St. Regis Falls, will observe her 96th birthday. She was born Anna Maria Baird in 1868 in Killala, County Mayo, Ireland, the third daughter of William and Anna Sharp Baird. Her mother died when she was a week old, and she and her sisters were brought up by her grandmother Sharp and her aunts. Her father remarried two years later and, soon afterwards, moved to Glasgow, Scotland.
>
> She remained in Ireland until she was seventeen and then she also went to Scotland to be near her father and married sister.
>
> The Ireland of her childhood was a rugged but beautiful country, still reeling from the impact of the famine in which both of her father's parents died.
>
> She loves America but Ireland and Scotland are, to her, beyond comparison.
>
> Soon after she went to Scotland, her father and his younger family came to America. She stayed behind and, in 1898, married Gordon Hannay who was born in 1865 at Gatehouse of Fleet, Kirkcudbright, Scotland. Their four children were born in Glasgow, Scotland.
>
> In 1907, she persuaded her husband to come to America for the sake of their children, so again, she followed her father, only to have him die, four years later. She said it always seemed to her that she just got to know him when he left her.
>
> The Hannay's ship docked at Boston and they came directly to St. Regis Falls, arriving on the hottest July day she can remember with their clothing suitable for Scotland. The brother who was to meet them, somehow didn't, so they set out to walk the five miles to her father's farm with their burden of hand luggage and four small children, one

only 5 months old. They got on the wrong road once, adding two miles to their trip, but they finally reached their destination.

Mr. Hannay found employment with the Highway Dept. and later, with the Brooklyn Cooperage Company at St. Regis Falls.

There were the usual *contretemps* connected with settling in a new country. Such as the morning she kicked the black pussy cat away from the henhouse door. Skunks were new to her.

Mr. Hannay died in 1942. Since then, Mrs. Hannay has made her home with her daughter, Mrs. Vernon Parks of St. Regis Falls. Her other children are; Gordon Hannay of Groton-on-Hudson, Mrs. James Camp of St. Regis Falls and Mrs. Percy Everett of Tacoma, Washington.

Mrs. Hannay is keen and fairly active and, until recently, has been an avid reader. Her beautiful braided rugs grace her children's homes.

We wish her many happy returns of the day.

Hannay information obtained from Mrs. Halcyon LaPoint Davies of St. Regis Falls.

THE HAYNES FAMILY

The Haynes family originally came from down South. They settled in the Waddington area. John Henry Haynes went to the Civil War from St. Lawrence County and when he came home he settled in St. Regis Falls. He was wounded in the battle of Fort Harrison in Virginia. He came home in 1864 and died in 1875. He is buried in Nicholville.

John's son, Levi Haynes, lived on the Howe Road in St. Regis Falls all his life. He worked for the Olmsteads of Nicholville in the woods and farmed a small farm.

Howard C. Haynes, son of Levi, was born 1885 in St. Regis Falls. He had three sisters and a brother who died at a young age. Howard was very successful in the lumbering business. He employed as many as 150 men at one time, and did over $1,000,000 business in one year in the early 1930s. He died in 1957.

He had four boys and two girls. All the children served honorably in the service, except Theresa Haynes Curran.

Harry retired with the rank of Master Sergeant after twenty years. Walter has served as judge and supervisor in the town of Dickinson Center. Alton is fleet captain for the American Steamship Company on the Great Lakes.

Howard C. Haynes (1885–1957) married Eva Paradise (1900–1944). Their children;

1) Howard L. married Marlene LaChance and have two daughters; Helen and Claire.

2) Alton married first to Violet Bishop and have two children by that marriage; Gisele and Alton, Alton then married second to Rose Patlin.

3) Theresa married Thomas Curran and have one daughter, Candace.

4) Walter married Rita Ploof and have five children: Walter, Eva, Debbie, William, and Robbie.

5) Harry married Audrey Radcliffe and have three children; Harry Jr., Susan and David.

6) Marietta married Robert Ham, they have no children.

Haynes information written by and obtained from Howard Haynes, St. Regis Falls.

THE LA POINT FAMILY

_____ LaPoint married Mary Bushy, they had two children, Jerry and a daughter (unknown name). _____ LaPoint left for parts unknown. Jerry LaPoint (1862 [68]–1920) came to St. Regis Falls in 1880, with his mother, Mary. Jerry married Mattie Baird (1865–1945), they had five children; 1) Roy W. born 1888, 2) Guy A. 1884–1886, 3) Halcyon L. born 1892, married John H. Rusterholtz and died in 1951, 4) Elizabeth born 1885, married Guy Gould and died 1973. They had four children; Earl born 1920, Baird born 1922, and died 1940, Chester born 1924, and John born 1926. 5) Earl Jerry born Mar. 25, 1890 and died Mar. 4, 1971.

Earl LaPoint took over his father's fruit and grocery business in 1920 after his father's death.

The store was located on Main Street first near Spring Street, then across the street. Earl later built a garage on the corner of River Street in 1924. In 1941, he started a bus business and ran buses to Massena and Malone from St. Regis Falls, and from Bangor to Massena. The bus station was on the corner of Main and River Streets. This business was run successfully for thirteen years.

Picture taken on River St.—to the left—the LaPoint home before it was remodeled to its present beauty

Earl was a World War I Veteran, Commander of the American Legion, Past Master of the Blue Mt. Lodge F.&A.M., and District Deputy Grand Master. He also served as town clerk in 1920 and as school board member in 1927.

Earl LaPoint married Marion Dorothy Douglass, the daughter of Henry and Gertrude (Southworth) Douglass. Marion was a registered nurse. Earl and Marion had four children; 1) Halcyon born 1923 (first married in 1947 to Raymond Pondysh and had three children, Carol born 1948, Dale born 1950 and Tom born 1957. Halcyon then married in 1960 to Elmer Davies. Carol Pondysh married Marvin Rust and have two children, Tonya born 1975 and Ryan born 1978. Dale Pondysh (married Jonathan Gott) and Tom Pondysh (married Karen Goodrow). 2) Douglass born 1925 (married in 1950 to Phyllis Boulds and have two children, James born 1951 and Jeanne born 1952—married John O'Connor). 3) James born 1926 and died 1926. 4) Donald born 1927 (married 1949 to Betty Snickles and have five children; Gary born 1950, Halcyon, born 1952, Michelle, born 1953 (married 1980 to Robert McCann and has one child, Michael, born 1984), Douglas, born 1956 and Jeffery, born 1966.

LaPoint information obtained from—Mrs. Marion Douglass LaPoint and Mrs. Halcyon LaPoint Davies, both from St. Regis Falls.

THE LA VOY FAMILY

Charles LaVoy was born 1839 in Ohio, the son of Antione and Mary LaVoy (both born in Canada). Charles married Emily E. Mitchell, the daughter of John and Mary (Sherkey) Mitchell. Emily was born 1840 in Plattsburgh, N.Y. Charles was a harness maker, and served in the Civil War. They moved to St. Regis Falls about 1880 and made their home there. He died in 1892 and is buried in the Forest Cemetery. Emily died in 1927 and is also buried in the Forest Cemetery.

Emily Mitchell LaVoy

Clemence LaVoy

They had eight children. 1) Clemence, married first John Mashtare and second married Bert Howe. A daughter, Anna, was born to the first marriage, and there were two children born to the second marriage; Bert and Violet. Violet died young and was the first child to be cremated in New York State. 2) Lewis, their first son, was born in 1860. He married Margaret (Maggie) Mashtare, the daughter of John and Matilda (Stone) Mashtare, born in 1862 in Vermont. Lewis and Maggie had six children; Margaret (Mamie), Frank F., Effie, Elmer L., Sadie and Mabel. 3) Laura, was born March 1, 1864 in St. Louis, Missouri. She was first married to Albert Bailey and second married to Phil Demar. There were two children; George, who died at the age of 10 years, and Grace. 4) Charles Jr. born in 1869 in Redford, N.Y. Charles Jr. married Della _____ and they had four children; Minnie, Roy D., Eva and Edith. Edith was killed in New York City in the early

Lewis and Maggie Mashtare LaVoy

Lewis and Maggie LaVoy with their first four children, Mamie, Frank, Effie, and Elmer

1920s. Charles Jr. died in 1929 in Tupper Lake, N.Y. 5) Freddie B. born Sept. 1871 and died May 24, 1875 and is buried in the Forest Cemetery with his parents. 6) Emma born May 24, 1873 and married April 4, 1891 in Nicholville to Elmer Wolcott and died Nov. 18, 1915. 7) Arthur born 1882 and died July 7, 1886 and is also buried in the Forest Cemetery. 8) Herman born in 1886 and was first married to Philomena Lancto (born 1886 in Canton, N.Y. and died 1927), children by this marriage were; Gladys E. born 1903 and married David F. Nisoff and died Nov. 19, 1928, Lawrence H. born Dec. 31, 1909 and died May 19, 1983, Ruth, Robert, and Arnold. Herman's second marriage was to Frieda _____ and they had three children; Jerry, Raymond and Gloria.

The children of Lewis and Maggie (Mashtare) LaVoy were; 1) Margaret (Mamie) born 1883 and died 1949; she first married Frederick Deno and second married Edward Hanley. There were three children by the first marriage; Fredrick A. born 1901 and married July 25, 1921 to Margaret LaGray, Alfred E. born 1903 and died 1967, married Lila E. Supernault and Floyd. 2) Frank F. born June 5, 1885 and died 1962, married Lydia Debiew and had two children—Walter

Archie and Mabel LaVoy Caturia; Elmer and Dora Cook LaVoy

J. born 1905 and died 1951 and married Anna Dufrene, and a daughter who in 1908 accidently drowned in a tub of water in the front yard, at the age of 17 months. 3) Effie born Aug. 7, 1887 and died 1960; her first marriage was to Francis Mashtare; they had two children—Earl L. born 1914 and died 1964 and married Fannie M. (Tilly) Pierce, and Clifford. Effie second married William J. Hewitt and had four children—Marshall, Herbert (who was accidently shot), Madge, who married Peter Arcadi, and Dewey. 4) Elmer born June

9, 1890, married Dora Mae Cook, the daughter of Orin and Carrie (Sochia) Cook, (*see Cook Family*). They had five sons; Abraham, Harold (both died in infancy), Alton born April 4, 1916 and married Sept. 13, 1942 to Eileen Jandrew, Efford born July 2, 1917 and married Nov. 4, 1942 to Eva Smith, and Carl H. born June 19, 1923 and married April 25, 1943 to Glencie Palmer. His second marriage was Sept. 16, 1978 to Eunice Farrington Erbach.

The children of Alton and Eileen (Jandrew) LaVoy are Joyce Marie, born Jan. 11, 1943 and married Emmett St. Hilaire and Rita Ann, born Aug. 10, 1944 and married Hubert Joanette.

The children of Carl and Glencie (Palmer) LaVoy are Carla Ann, born Sept. 11, 1944 and married Albert (Pudge) Hathaway, Glenda Mary, born May 18, 1946 and married Wayne Chesbrough, and Paula Marie, born Aug. 10, 1947 and married Gerald Trim, Jr.

Carla & Albert Hathaway children:
    Andrew Palmer
    Barbara Ann
    Elizabeth Mary
    Nathaniel Joseph
Carla & Albert divorced
Carla remarried Gerald Cahill

Glenda & Wayne Chesbrough children:
    Julie Ann
    Kathleen Mary

Paula & Gerald Trim, Jr. children:
    Angela Jean
    Rebecca Lynn
    Daniel James
Paula & Gerald divorced

THE LEMIEUX FAMILY

Paul and Josephine Morin LeMieux arrived in this country in 1886. Paul LeMieux was born June 25, 1863 in Notre Dame Parish in Lac St. Jean, Roberval, P.Q. He died Nov. 27, 1958 in St. Regis Falls. Josephine Morin was born Dec. 17, 1865 in Murray Bay, Quebec, she died Dec. 30, 1939 in St. Regis Falls. He, at the age of 22 years and she, 20 years old, married but a year, settled in Santa Clara. Born in Canada, they spoke only the French language and had very little education. Overcoming these difficulties, Mr. LeMieux found work with the John Hurd Railroad and later became carshop foreman with the New York Central when they took over the line. He continued in this capacity until 1900. By this time, having five children, three in school, they were able to speak some English and decided to "strike out on their own". They built a general store next to their home in Santa Clara, and through perseverance and hard work, with the help of the older children they successfully operated the store until 1910. At this stage there were nine children. Hearing the F. L. Tryon block in St. Regis Falls was for sale, they purchased the Tryon block and moved to St. Regis Falls. A year later the Santa Clara store burned, along with several other buildings. Located in the Tryon Block, was a grocery store, a drug store, and the post office. The general store which included hardware, feed, cement, and groceries, was known as Paul LeMieux & Sons and was family-operated for twenty-eight years. The year following the purchase of the block, the Tryon residence was also bought and has remained the family residence to this day.

In 1932 Mr. LeMieux purchased the 840-acre tract of land owned by Darwin Day, known as the Blue Mountain property. Later he sold 420 acres, including the Mt. Azure Observatory, to the State of New York. On the remaining land, he built "Camp Cheerio" where the family and friends spent many happy hours.

In 1934, Mr. & Mrs. LeMieux renewed their nuptial vows and with relatives and friends celebrated their fiftieth anniversary at their home on Pleasant Street.

In 1938, Mr. LeMieux retired and a son, William, took over the management of the store.

The death of Mrs. LeMieux in 1939 was the first to sadden the family. Mr. LeMieux died in 1958 at the age of ninety-five.

The family were devout members of the Roman Catholic Church. Mrs. LeMieux was a member of the St. Ann's Society and a devoted mother. Mr. LeMieux was a member of the St. Jean Baptiste Society, the Knights of Columbus, Holy Name Society, and a good community worker. He was a member of the Board of Education and also a trustee of his church. An ardent sportsman, he was awarded the Dr. Trudeau prize for being the oldest deer hunter in New York State, for five consecutive years.

The nine children of Paul and Josephine LeMieux were as follows: 1) Fred W. born in Tupper Lake Dec. 30, 1890, was a private in Co. K casual Regiment in World War I, and married Mayme Beyette on Sept. 12, 1915, Fred died March 28, 1958. There were no children of this marriage. A born salesman, he owned a dry goods store, a liquor store, and a theater. He was educated at the local school and went to the University of Ottawa. 2) Mamie F. was born in Tupper Lake, Nov. 1, 1893 and first married Nov. 21, to Benjamin Flanagan who died Oct. 17, 1921. There was a daughter, Evelyn born to this marriage. Mamie then married Nov. 25, 1926 to Alfred LeBoeuf, who died Feb. 14, 1935. Mamie died Aug. 11, 1962 and is buried in the St. Ann's Cemetery. 3) Ida Mae was born in Santa Clara, July 6, 1895 and married Aug. 7, 1915 to Henry Fortier who died Jan. 30, 1961. Ida Mae died Dec. 14, 1968 and is buried in Lyon Mountain, N.Y. There were nine children is this union. 4) Joseph Arthur was born in Santa Clara, Aug. 8, 1897 and married Aug. 1920 to Vita Lucas. He died April 13, 1960. There were nine children in this union. 5) William Wilfred was born in Santa Clara, Feb. 6, 1900 and married Aug. 1, 1929 to Genevieve McKenna. William died in Boston, Mass. on July 24, 1952. They had four children. 6) Laura Isabel was born in Santa Clara Jan. 30, 1902 and taught school in St. Regis Falls for forty-two years. She never married. 7) Anabel Ellen was born in Santa Clara, Feb. 2, 1904 and married Dec. 27, 1933 to Bernard Falvey who died July 30, 1957. There were no children in this union.

Anabel taught school for twenty-five years. 8) Charles Paul was born in Santa Clara, Mar. 4, 1906 and married first to Cecilia Wolfe and had three children in this union. Charles second married Anne Tuell and had one child. Charles graduated from St. Lawrence University and coached the "Wonder Five" Basketball team in St. Regis Falls. He was in World War II in the European Theater. He lived in Syracuse, N.Y. and was director of the Red Cross until his retirement in 1971 and then moved to Bradenton, Fla. He lived there until his death on January 17th, 1984. 9) Lionel Oscar was born in Santa Clara, Jan. 6, 1910 and married July 26, 1937 to Margaret McLaughlin. They had two children. He died June 23, 1982 and is buried in St. Ann's Cemetery.

LeMieux information obtained from Miss Laura LeMieux, St. Regis Falls.

THE MASHTAR FAMILY

John Mashtar (Marcheteau, Marcheterre) was born Apr. 1839 in North Hero, Grand Isle, Vermont. The son of Francis Mashtar, (born 1805 in Canada) and Phebe (Duguay—Flavia Dewyear) Mashtar. Phebe died July 1892.

John married Sept. 9, 1858 in South Hero, Vt., to Matilda Stone, who was born Dec. 1837 at Rouses Point, Clinton County, N.Y., the daughter of Antoine and Marguerite (Berno) Stone. After marriage, they moved to Dickinson where they lived for a while before moving and making permanent residence in St. Regis Falls, then just taking its first steps as a town. John was a farmer and a veteran of the Civil War. He was shot in the left wrist and lost partial use of his arm because of the injury.

They had four sons and three daughters. 1) John Jr. born in 1859 married Clemence LaVoy and had one daughter, Anna. They divorced. 2) Margaret (Maggie) born April 28, 1862 and married in 1884 to Lewis LaVoy (see—*LaVoy family*) and died Dec. 2, 1929. 3) Joseph born 1865 in Dickinson married Feb. 9, 1891 to Margaret Debiew (1872–1957) and died 1942. 4) David married Dec. 29, 1890 to Nellie Story and died 1942. 5) Jennie born 1871 married Daniel Antonio and died 1926. 6) William born 1869 married Phebe Deno and died in Tupper Lake Feb. 21, 1931 and 7) Clarica (Clara) born 1867 and married John Cross.

Joseph and Margaret (Debiew) Mashtare had six children, 1) Carrie married Nov. 21,1928 to James Rafter, 2) Rose born 1893 married Frank Rafter, 3) Milon W. born Aug. 24, 1902 married Oct. 19, 1937 to Pearl E. Glover and died May 10, 1982, 4) Edward born Aug. 31, 1907 married Oct. 1928 to Ruth H. Winkle and died 1984, 5) Henry born Feb. 27, 1899, never married and died in Tupper Lake Nov. 2, 1961, and 6) Timothy married Bessie _____.

David and Nellie (1875–1957) (Story) Mashtare had a daughter, Bessie, who married _____ Morgan and died 1980.

William and Phebe (Deno) Mashtare had three children, 1) Floyd, 2) Ray and 3) Alice—married _____ Cassidy.

Jennie and Daniel Antonio (1881–1954) had a son, Edward born Oct. 10, 1908 died the same day. They then adopted a daughter, May.

Edward and Ruth (Winkle) Mashtare (Ruth Winkle was born Sept. 20, 1909 in Rochester, Pennsylvania and died April 17, 1980 in Saranac Lake, N.Y., the daughter of Elmer and Margaret (Shockey) Winkle, had three children: 1) Dorothy Louise born Feb. 22, 1929, first married William Patraw and second married Victor LaMoy, 2) Della Mae born Aug. 8, 1931 and married Darwin Kelly and 3) Harold Edward (Sonny) born Oct. 10, 1933 and married Shirley Susice.

THE McKENNON FAMILY

James and Isabelle McKennon with their young daughter, Emma, traveled from the Province of New Brunswick across the border to settle in Danforth, Maine.

His occupation was a buyer of bark for companies used in the tanning of leather.

Years ago, in-season softwood was cut, peeled and the bark was salvaged and sold to these companies for tanning.

The McKennon family later came to St. Regis Falls, N.Y. from Maine to buy bark for a company. While doing this, he became acquainted with the Cutting Lumber Company of New York City. In a short time he began employment with this company and settled on their land, which were large holdings situated on land surrounding the east end of Lake Ozonia, which was known to many people as the Cutting Tract.

This company had a large lumbering operation and saw mill in the area known in Northern New York as Center Camp Logging. Roads and railroads were used in this operation in traveling to St. Regis Falls and Santa Clara.

Isabelle McKennon, known as Belle, cooked at Center Camp for the Cutting family and their guests. Many of the employee's wives helped at the Big House too.

Emma went to school at St. Regis Falls, boarding during the week at the home of John Murphy (this home is now owned by Leroy Fadden). Friends of Emma enjoyed staying weekends with her at Center Camp as they had to cross the lake each way to get to and fro.

After this operation ceased, the McKennon family moved into St. Regis Falls, living in the Tiesdel House, next to school.

Many families and friends of the Cutting's came by rail from New York City to stay for two week periods at their home. The boarders enjoyed the fresh country air and came for many years.

Later when the Tiesdel House was sold to George Yerrick, the McKennon's moved to the Tryon house on Spring Street, (this house now owned by Royal Phillips) and she boarded school teachers.

Emma married John W. Fraser and they built the bungalow on Main Street, second house from school, and lived there.

McKennon information written by and obtained from Mrs. Helen Fraser Parks, St. Regis Falls.

THE MEACHAM FAMILY

George Meacham born 1852 in Dickinson Center, N.Y. and died May 9, 1893 at age 41 years. He married Mary Clark born 1862 in Dickinson Center and died Feb. 28, 1911 age 49 years. They had four children;

1) George Meacham Jr. born 1881 and died Oct. 4, 1898 at age 17 years, shot accidently while hunting.

2) Milon Meacham born Aug. 8, 1882 and died Jan. 18, 1954. He never married.

3) James J. Meacham born June 13, 1886 (87) and died Mar. 12, 1944(45). He married Mary Ann Mushtare (1887–1945) the daughter of Frank and Elizabeth (Bruly) Mushtare. They had six children; 1) Mildred born Jan. 20. 1906 and died the same day, 2) Ethel born Sept. 29, 1907 married Sept. 16, 1929 to Gordon F. Smith, the son of Frank Smith. They had a son, Ronald, born May 14, 1939. 3) Beatrice born Mar. 12, 1909 died May 30, 1913. 4) Gilbert L. born Nov. 15, 1911 (12) died Mar. 21, 1963, a World War II veteran. He married Edna born 1909. 5) William born Jan. 5, 1920 died 1978 and married Catherine Farmer born 1920. 6) Frederick born June 26, 1922 married and had four children; Robert, Linda, Nancy and Christopher.

4) Vern Meacham born Feb. 13, 1889 died Apr. 1932. He married Oct. 10, 1908 in St. Regis Falls to Philinda Sochia (see *Sochia family*). They had five children; 1) Viola born Apr. 17, 1915 died 1959, never married. 2) Wesley born July 5, 1919 died 1943, never married. 3) Lena M. born July 25, 1917 died Jan. 25, 1975, married Bernard W. Rivers (Sonny) born 1914. They had three children; Elaine married Edson Lindsay, Lawrence (Larry) married Jeanne Patnode and Doris Ann married Joseph Poquette. 4) Genevieve born July 12, 1923 died Aug. 25, 1975 married Thurston Chesbrough (see *Chesbrough family*). 5) Everett married Kay _____ and had two children, Michael and Deborah. They live in Ephrata, Pennsylvania.

THOMAS MEACHAM—One of the Very First Settlers in Waverly

Thomas Meacham, born about 1770 and died May 7, 1849 at the age of 79 years, alone in his chair, noone near to console him. A noted hunter and trapper, perhaps the greatest that ever lived in the county. He kept a running list of all the animals he ever killed. An account of his life was written and published in Dec. of 1849, of which all copies were lost in a fire in 1861.

Thomas Meacham is the man who gave Meacham Lake its name. He had one or two children by his first wife, and two or three by his second union. Stephen Meacham was his son by the marriage. There was also Thomas Jr. and Norman.

STEPHEN MEACHAM—AREA "HERMIT"

Stephen was born sometime around 1820; however, because of his father being a hunter and moving around alot, we can't be sure if Meacham was actually born in the township of Waverly.

Stephen married and had five daughters and two sons. He was a very religious man and he and his family were baptised into the Morman religion.

After this Meacham packed up his family in a prairie schooner wagon and headed west. His brother, Norman and his family, moved with them also. Their destination was Mauvoo, Illinois.

They soon found themselves almost into total slavery. They became sick and decided to return home. Apostasy was said to be a high offense to a Morman and merited death.

However, a small group decided they were going back home. Plans were made and the return trip home was begun. This was soon found out and quickly interupted. Brother Norman was killed, and only a handful of them escaped. Stephen Meacham's wife and family were lost to him forever. For him to go back in search of them would mean certain death for him.

After due time and many hardships, Meacham made his way back to Nicholville area. He decided to become a hunter and trapper like his father and he built a small log cabin on Stony Brook, near the Franklin and St. Lawrence County line. Traveling into town only a couple of times a year for supplies, he rarely saw anyone. Townspeople gave Meacham used clothes which he used in great appreciation. However, his heart and thoughts were always of his lost family, and his dreams of meeting them again in the promised land.

Living to be an old man, for his years, with long pure white hair and full beard, always a sad face, Stephen Meacham died Feb. 27, 1869, on one of his few trips near Parishville. The snow was deep and the kind, gentle, sad man took his last journey.

However, a year or so before his death, Meacham did hear from a son in California and received some help from him. How he wanted to go to his son.

Although the Meachams associated more in the villages of Nicholville and Parishville, they did live in the township of Waverly. Perhaps it's because when they first came to the area those towns were pretty well developed and St. Regis Falls was still just someone's dream.

THE O'NEIL FAMILY

Maurice O'Neil was born in County Kerry, Ireland, about 1800. He came to this country around the age of eighteen, and located at Hogansburg, Franklin County, N.Y. Farming was his life's occupation. Maurice had six children; 1) Cornelius, a farmer and settled in Massena, 2) Michael, moved and settled in Dayton, Ohio, 3) Jeremiah, 4) Mary, married C. P. Lantry, of Hogansburg, 5) Catherine and 6) Thomas.

Jeremiah O'Neil was born in 1832 in Hogansburg. After moving west for a time, returned to New York and took up farming in Massena. He married Charity, born in Brasher, in 1835, the daughter of Joshua and Nellie (Lyons) Lantry. They had eight children; 1) Maurice, married Minnie Haggerty, lived in Rochester, N.Y. and was a real estate broker, 2) Joshua, died at the age of 21 years, 3) Barney Stephen, born in Massena, Dec. 13, 1868, was a lawyer and married in 1900 to Margaret, daughter of Jeremiah and Zilpha (Byron) Traver, of Canton. (They had no children), 4) Nellie, died at the age of 15 years, 5) John, died at 25 years, 6) Rev. Thomas J., a Roman Catholic priest of the Paulist Order, lived in Calif., 7)

Franklin, died at the age of 11 years, and 8) James M., M.D. a physician at the State Hospital at Ogdensburg.

Thomas, the youngest child of Maurice O'Neil, was born in Bombay, N.Y. in 1829, and died at Boonville, N.Y., 1894. Thomas being a "lumberjack" all his active life. He married (first) Lucy Comstock, born 1827, and died July 11, 1869, daughter of Samuel and Annie (Weller) Comstock. He married (second) Margaret Wilson. Thomas fathered four children, two by each marriage. William T. and Fred by his first wife; and Katherine and Jennie by his second wife.

William Thomas O'Neil, the eldest son of Thomas, was born in Brighton, Franklin County, N.Y., Feb 7, 1850. William located at St. Regis Falls in the 1870s, becoming a merchant, building and conducting a hotel, and also dipping into the lumbering industry. He was president of the Cascade Chair Company, a director of the St. Regis Falls National Bank and the St. Regis Light and Power Company. He also owned the St. Regis Creamery and several farms. One of which was located on the Cook Road and was stocked with fine dairy cows and the latest equipment of the period. Mr. O'Neil early became a power in local politics, and served his town as the first supervisor, and was in the Assembly for four years from 1882. He also acted as principal aide and counselor to Theodore Roosevelt.

In 1902, Mr. O'Neil was a candidate for the Republican nomination for Congress. In 1906, he was elected to the State Senate, at once taking high rank in that body, and was reelected in 1908. His health began to fail in the latter year, adhering to his work when he ought to have been at home or in an institution; he died during the third session of his service. Mr. O'Neil was strong with the people as a canvasser, straightforward and upright in all of his personal and public life, and well-balanced. He died May 5, 1909, with a great many accomplishments accredited to him.

William O'Neil married Nov. 19, 1872, Ophelia Young, daughter of James H. Young (see *Young family*). They had five children: 1) Edith C. born in St. Regis Falls, Feb. 9, 1874 and died in 1934; she married Alexander MacDonald of St. Regis Falls, a cashier of the St. Regis Falls National Bank, also a member of the State Assembly, 2) Henry Edward born in St. Regis Falls, Mar. 19, 1876, never married, 3) Florence, born Oct. 25, 1885, 4) Dorothy, born Oct. 5, 1891, 5) Arthur S., born Aug. 27, 1893 and a World War I Veteran.

Fred O'Neil, the second son of Thomas, was born in Brighton, Franklin County, N.Y., Dec. 25, 1852. He engaged in the lumber business in 1875 in Duane, N.Y. and continued there for the next twelve years. In 1880, he moved to Malone, embarking in the insurance business in partnership in the firm of O'Neil and Hale. He was elected County Treasurer in 1887, and reelected for a second term, serving until 1894. President McKinley appointed Fred O'Neil postmaster of Malone; he held this position for several years.

Fred O'Neil married in 1874 to Ella S., born in Essex County, the daughter of Orrin and Harriet (Knowlton) Grimes. They had four children, 1) William born in St. Regis Falls, March 17, 1875, married Ella J. Wright, and moved to Great Barrington, Mass., where he farmed, 2) Frederick E., born in Duane, N.Y. Feb. 14, 1884, 3) Harold G., born in Duane Dec. 1, 1886, was a lawyer in Malone, and 4) Herbert born in Malone July 22, 1893.

THE PALMER FAMILY

Ervin Joseph Palmer

Ervin Palmer was born in Hinesburg, Vermont, Oct. 1, 1836, the son of Joseph Hoyt and Elizabeth (Betsey) Simpson (Dolloff) Palmer, both born in New Hampshire. Joseph Palmer moved his family to Dickinson in the late 1830s. He died June 23, 1847, and his wife, Betsey, remarried Brooks Hudson in the 1850s.

Ervin Palmer was the fifth child of eleven. The other children were, 1) Beniah D., born July 1816 and married Fanny B. Ellis. 2) Elijah A., born Aug. 1824 and married Harriet Bean. 3) Jones J., born 1831, and married Ann _____. 4) Henry S., born 1833; his second wife was Nancy Huse. 5) Ervin J., 6) Hoyt, 7) Sally, 8) Betsey, 9) Ravina, 10) Ziba A. (Zibby), 11) Mary Jane 1834–1836.

Ervin Palmer married Sarah Jane Ramsdell in 1857, in Dickinson. She was the daughter of Nathaniel and Phebe Ramsdell. Jane, as she liked to go by, was born July 1, 1837, in Dickinson, and died Aug. 8, 1900 in St. Regis Falls. They had eleven children: 1) Madora J. born 1858 and married Thomas Somers. 2) Flora U. born 1862 and married Riley Orton. 3) Louise born 1865 and married William Patraw. 4) Eliza A. born 1866 and married Henry Winters. 5) Elzira married John Farmer. 6) Carrie born 1868 and married Bert Chase. 7) Luna born 1869 and married Edward Patraw. 8) Azro I. J. born 1870 and married Hattie Camp. 9) Homer E. born 1873 first married _____ Walker and second married Maude Somers. 10) Milton H. born 1875 and married Eudora Young. and 11) Betty who died young.

Ervin Palmer was a carpenter by trade. He was one of the first settlers in St. Regis Falls, and built one of the first permanent cabins on the south side of the river. He was a Private in Co. E the 19th Regiment in the Civil War.

Ervin Joseph Palmer

After his wife died, Ervin remarried in 1904 to Verie Suits. He died Feb. 25, 1912 in Staten Island, when he came down with an illness on their way to Florida on vacation. His body was sent back and buried in Dickinson beside his first wife.

During his life Ervin purchased a great deal of land, especially in the area between St. Regis Falls and Santa Clara.

Palmer-Azro Family.
Information on back of photo states: "Left to Right; Adults—Milan Meachem, Iva Palmer, Martin (standing), Homer Palmer, Azro Palmer (father), Hattie Palmer (mother), Jesse Hall, Douglass Palmer, Elvia Hall (Jesse's wife); Boys seated—Loyde (big ears) Palmer, Gerald (cross-eyed) Palmer, Arther (peaked head) Palmer, John Palmer. Girl standing by mother, Theo (Tickie) Palmer"

Some of the land is still lived on and worked by Palmer descendents. However, much of the land was sold by his second wife after his death.

Azro Irvin Joseph Palmer, the first son of Ervin, born Dec. 13, 1870, was married July 23, 1892, to Hattie Camp (daughter of Charles and Nancy (Farmer) Camp, born May 3, 1873 in Skerry, N.Y.). Azro and Hattie had ten children, 1) Alva Jane, born 1893 and married Jesse Hull. 2) Sibley J. (Buck) born 1894 and married Antoinette Forkey. 3) Homer E. born 1897 and married Gertrude Demar. 4) Douglas born 1899 and married Lillian Bray. 5) Iva J. born 1902 and married Elmer Martin. 6) John L. born 1905 and married Doris Schillic. 7) Lloyd born 1907 and married Odina Martin. 8) Arthur C. born 1909 and married Helen Best. 9) Gerald L. born 1911 and married Helen Patraw and 10) Theo E. (Ticky) born 1915 and married Eugene Rabitaille.

Azro lived and worked a farm between St. Regis Falls and Santa Clara that his father cleared the land for. The first big house that was built burned in the early part of the century.

Azro Irvin Joseph Palmer, Hattie Palmer with Gary White

The house that now stands is across the road from the original house. There was also a large barn near the first house, which also burned many years ago. Most of the land has now grown back to thick brush and is no longer farmed, as has most of the other surrounding farms and timberland.

Douglas and Lillian Palmer

Douglas and Lillian (Bray) Palmer (my grandparents) had four children, 1) Glencie Helen married first Carl LaVoy and second Alton Kujawsky. 2) Rita Harriet married Carlton White. 3) Douglas (Sonny) married Virginia Hollifield and 4) Darlene Nancy married Roger Rockhill. All of whom live either in Rochester or Hamburg, N.Y.

Grandpa was a lumberjack most of his life, until they moved to Rochester in 1962. In the spring of the year when the woods were closed to "dry-up", Grandpa would work a sugarbush. That was the time I liked. I would spend all my spare time in the sugarbush with him. In those days they still used a team of horses and the sap sled to collect the sap from the trees. The snow would be real deep in some places on the side of the mountain, and the trail would twist its way back and forth around stumps and boulders until it reached back to the sugarhouse; usually located in the middle of the sugarbush. We would always take fresh syrup and some clean snow, which Grandpa chose very carefully, home with us and Grandma would make sugar-on-snow for us. What a treat!

Grandma has told me stories about going into the lumber camps with Grandpa to cook for the lumberjacks. She would get up very early in the morning, long before the sun came up, to make biscuits, johnnycake, and start the homemade bread for the day. With more than twenty hungry men to feed, it would take several dozen eggs and a number of pounds of bacon and sausage for their breakfast. After this early morning chore was done, preparations would begin for the midday meal. In the meantime, all the rest of the daily work around the cabin would have to be done. You must remember, there were none of today's conveniences like running water, electric lights, gas or electric kitchen range, etc. Water was carried from a nearby spring, and heated on the wood cook stove, kerosene lamps were their source of light, and the wash was done on a scrub board.

Grandma told about one day in particular, she had started her berry pies a little late in the morning so she set them outside on the window sill to cool for the men's lunch. (By the way, the berries had all been hand picked the day before.) As the pies were cooling, Grandma went about the rest of her chores. All of a sudden she heard this awful crashing noise, she ran out the door and there in the middle of her pies sat a big racoon with blueberries all over his face. She had to shoo him away with a broom because he wasn't going to leave those pies willingly. Poor Grandma, out of a dozen big pies, only saved one that didn't fall off the sill, and the lumberjacks didn't get their dessert at lunch that day.

PALMER—POTTER FAMILIES

William James Palmer born 1830 in Vermont, the son of James and Sarah (Brown) Palmer. William died Feb. 16, 1910 in Dickinson Center, N.Y. He married Marion S. Smith born 1837 in Essex County, N.Y. and died Dec. 14, 1923. They had six children:

1) Idelle B. born 1860 in Vermont.

2) William James born Apr. 6, 1867 in Dickinson Center and died July 15, 1954. He married Sept. 17, 1892 to Sophia P. Potter born Apr. 14, 1873 in Dickinson Center, the daughter of Ira and Clara Potter. Sophia died Sept. 23, 1931.

3) Ida born 1870 in Dickinson Center, married William Bigelow.

4) Charles Asa born 1872 in Dickinson Center.

5) Eva Marion born 1875 in Dickinson Center.

6) Ardie C. 1879 died 1964, first married Edith G. Root (1883–1919) and second married Susan O. (1883–1969).

William James and Sophia Palmer had fifteen children; 1) Ernest Charles born Sept. 5, 1893 married Irene Buckley and had a son William. 2) Clara Marion born Mar. 26, 1895 and died Nov. 4, 1975, she married June 30, 1919 to Wilbert

Conger (1895–1977). They had three children; Edith married Royal Phillips, Ralph married Kay Moose, and Donald married Phyllis Woods. 3) Dean William born July 3, 1898 (twin) died Mar. 16, 1899. 4) Doris Grace born July 3, 1898 (twin) and died Feb. 1941, she married Buell Mott (1879–1954), 5) James William (1899–1899), 6) Ralph Willie born May 2, 1900 died Jan. 9, 1902, 7) twin girl born and died June 4, 1903, 8) twin girl born June 4, 1903 died June 8, 1903, 9) Rowena Sophia born Aug. 10, 1905 died Nov. 23, 1906, 10) Willie James born Dec. 9. 1907, died Mar. 18, 1908, 11) Eric Potter born July 17, 1909 and married Christena Perkins, 12) Idella Blanche born June 23, 1911 and married Sept. 1, 1934 to Lawrence Nunn, 13) Reginald born Aug. 9. 1913 married Jan. 1, 1937 to Kathleen Manchester, 14) twin girls born and died June 12. 1917.

Ira Potter born July 24, 1829, died May 1, 1896. He married Sarah _____, born Sept. 30, 1837 and died Aug. 27, 1908. They had eight children—l) William S. born May 6, 1865, died Feb. 22, 1920, 2) Mary R. born Mar. 11, 1866, died Jan. 24, 1946 (nickname, Min), married _____ Marks, 3) Lyman A. born Oct. 7, 1867, died June 27, 1885, 4) Henry T. born Dec. 14, 1868, died Jan. 3, 1938, married Bernice A. (1878–1942), had a son, William H. (1907–1909), 5) Ezra I. born June 18, 1870, 6) Elsie C., born Nov. 14, 1871, died June 6, 1935. 7) Sophia F., born Apr. 15, 1873, died Sept. 23, 1931, married William James Palmer, 8) Leon S. born Feb. 19, 1879, died May 13, 1944.

THE PATRAW FAMILY

The Patraw name was changed from the French-Canadian name of Patreau. William A. Patraw (1856–1908) married Louise A. Palmer (1865–1921), the daughter of Ervin and Sarah Jane (Ramsdell) Palmer. (see *Palmer family*) William and Louise lived in Dickinson Center all their lives. They had ten children; 1) Wendell E. (1887–1962) married Harriet Blanche Peck, born 1897, now deceased. 2) Preston P., a World War I veteran, died Jan. 1984. 3) Peter, 4) Clyde Robert born in Dickinson, July, 1898, was in the Navy in World War I and lost an arm in an accident in the war. 5) Ray Homer (1892–1947) also in the Navy in World War I and married

Janet M. born 1899, 6) Blanche married _____ Coffin, 7) Beatrice, 8) Freda, 9) Thelma and 10) Edith.

The family of Wendell and Blanche Patraw consisted of six children—1) Eloise born 1922 married Lawrence Sanford, 2) William Aaron born July 18, 1923, first married Dorothy Mashtare. 3) Helen born June 11, 1925 married Gerald L. Palmer, 4) Edna married Henry Price, 5) Eugene first married Ann Baker, and then married Barbara _____, and 6) Roy married Elaine Dow.

Patraw information obtained from William (Bill) Patraw, Forest Home Road, Saranac Lake, N.Y.

THE PLOOF FAMILY

Joseph Ploof (Plouffe, Blouf) born in Dickinson Center, May 24, 1886, the son of Francis and Maranda (Jesmer) Ploof. The Ploofs came into Vermont from Canada in the mid 1800s. Francis' father, Peter, was killed in the Civil War at the Battle of Shiloh.

There were twelve children born to Peter and Mary (Richards) Ploof, 1) Edith married Ezra Jeanette, 2) Lilah married Frank LaRose, 3) Anice (1891–1957) married Daniel A. Villnave (1889–1962), 4) Alvina first married Thomas Villnave and then married Elzear Sovey, 5) Martha married Clarence Kirkey, 6) Alice died 1899 age 2 weeks, 7) Frank A. (1884–1936) married Mary A. Noonan (1884–1959), 8) Leonard (1890–1959) married Emma LaChance, 9) Joseph married Lavina Morey, 10) Howard died Sept. 8, 1906 age 5 yrs. 3 mos., 11) Earl G. (1906–1947) married Regina Brunette and 12) Mayfred born 1908 first married Lincoln Richards and then married Stephen Peer.

Frank and Mary (Noonan) Ploof had eight children, 1) Donald L. born Sept. 13, 1922, died Feb. 1, 1966 was in World War II, 2) Jerald L. born Mar. 8, 1916, died Aug. 13, 1957 was also in World War II, 3) Edward born 1911 married Lenore Forkey (1911–1965), 4) Frank (moved to California), 5) Royal F. born May 27, 1908 never married, 6) Leona E. (1910–1977) married Walter L. Scott, 7) Margaret married

_____ Noll and 8) Florence (1906–1973) married _____ Braatz.

Leonard and Emma (LaChance) Ploof had seven children, 1) Seymore L. died Aug. 19, 1897 age 4 yrs. 6 mos. 19 days, 2) Shirley, 3) Enola, 4) Nowelle married Walter Clookey, 5) Lois and Leonard Jr., were twins, and 6) Carol.

Joseph (Joe) married Jan. 31, 1909 to Lavina Morey born Apr. 5, 1891 in Dickinson Center, the daughter of Jackson and Della (Wilson) Morey. Joe died Apr. 3, 1965 and Lavina died Mar. 4, 1978, they are buried in Dickinson. Joe Ploof was a "Jack-of-all-trades". He moved many buildings in town. When the school and Methodist Church burned in 1926, he moved the parsonage from the school lot to its present site. It's told that he could move a building without taking pictures off the wall or dishes out of the cupboards. These buildings were moved with a horse and a homemade winch.

The children of Joe and Lavina Ploof were, 1) Lloyd, died at the age of 12 years, 2) son, died at birth, 3) Ruth died at the age of 3 years, 4) Keith born July 19, 1913 in Dickinson, 5) Evelyn born Feb. 15, 1917, 6) Joyce born Feb. 5, 1923, and 7) Jean born June 1, 1929.

(Percy) Keith Ploof married Nov. 22, 1943 to Elizabeth (Liz) Farmer born Apr. 16, 1922, the daughter of Lyndon and Nettie (LaPage) Farmer. They had six children, 1) Michael born Aug. 15, 1944, deceased, 2) Patricia born Oct. 13, 1945, 3) Joan born June 6, 1949, 4) Lloyd born May 20, 1958, 5) Penny born Sept. 9, 1959 and 6) Bryon Richard 1961 died right after birth.

Evelyn Ploof married Nov. 28, 1933 to Harold E. LaBounty (Nov. 2, 1908–Apr. 12, 1975, WW II Veteran). They had five children; Martin (Marty), Marsha, Jackson (Jack), Linda, and Richard (Dick).

Joyce Ploof married Glen H. Cheney (1901–1966). They had six children; Nancy, Wayne (drowned), Lawrence (Larry), Eileen, Lois, and Debbie.

Jean Ploof married Sidney (Sid) Dewey. They had three children—Susan born Feb. 16, 1949, Terrence (Terry) born June 18, 1951, and Timothy born Aug. 3, 1969. Sidney Dewey was born May 16, 1923.

Ploof information obtained from Keith and Elizabeth Ploof, St. Regis Falls.

THE RAMSDELL FAMILY

The Ramsdell family starts in America with Joseph Ramsdell's marriage to Rachel Eaton on Mar. 2, 1645, Rachel the daughter of Francis Eaton, a signer of the Mayflower Compact. (An early spelling of Ramsdell was Ramsden.)

Their son, Daniel, hence a Mayflower descendant, born in Plymouth, Mass., Sept. 14, 1649 and married Hannah Caswell.

Thomas, son of Daniel and Hannah Ramsdell, married Sarah Alverson at Scituate, Mass., Mar. 22, 1703. Thomas died at Hanover, Mass., Sept. 16, 1727.

A son, Gideon, born in Scituate to them on Sept. 13, 1712, married Sarah Farrington, June 24, 1736. Gideon died between Jan. and Mar. 1795.

John, born to Gideon and Sarah in Abington, Mass., Sept. 30, 1738, married Eunice Cobb on Dec. 31, 1761. John died at Abington, Mass., Oct. 29, 1816. They had a son, John Jr. and a son, Farrington, born in Washington, Vermont, May 13, 1769. Farrington married Lois Fitts (Peitz).

The children of Farrington and Lois (Fitts) Ramsdell were, 1) John born May 3, 1801 in Wardsboro, Vt. and married Polly Rice (Roice) June 1, 1825, John died Feb. 1886, 2) Prudence born May 23, 1803, 3) Farrington born June 10, 1805, 4) Robert born Feb. 11, 1807, 5) Lois born July 21, 1809, and 6) Nathaniel born May 13, 1811.

The children of John and Polly (Rice) Ramsdell were, 1) Eunice born May 12, 1829 and married James Littlejohn, 2) Mary (Polly) born 1830 and married Bradley Morrison and 3) Nelson born May 19, 1833 in Dickinson Center, N.Y., and married May 4, 1861 Eliza C. Smith the daughter of Willard and Betsey (Boyce) Smith, born May 6, 1829 in East Roxbury, Vermont (see *Smith family*).

The children of Nelson and Eliza (Smith) Ramsdell were, 1) Carrie born Feb. 25, 1862 and died Feb. 26, 1862, 2) Herbert Nelson born May 11, 1863 and married Nettie Page on Nov. 30, 1886 and he died Apr. 24, 1940, 3) Fred Smith Ramsdell born Aug. 1, 1867 married Elizabeth M. Fleming on Oct. 26, 1897 and he died Sept. 16, 1947, 4) Melvin Blanchard born Oct. 20, 1869 married Elizabeth A. Shaw on June 19, 1895 and he died Feb. 10, 1949.

The Ramsdell family was very much involved with the Baptist religion. Nelson Ramsdell was a Baptist minister for many years, and had great influence in keeping the church organization strong during its existence in St. Regis Falls. His son, Fred, was also very active in the Baptist Church.

Ramsdell information obtained from Winnifred Ramsdell, Potsdam, N.Y.

THE ROWELL FAMILY

M. A. Rowell
Founder and Twenty-five years editor of *The Adirondack News*

Mark A. Rowell, born 1864, came to St. Regis Falls in the 1880's from Michigan. His wife, Jennifer (Jenny) Lennon was born 1864 and died 1944. Mark Rowell was a school teacher and was the principal of St. Regis Falls School from Sept. 1886 through January 1887. The beginning of 1887 he started the *Adirondack News*, a weekly publication. This venture was entered into with his sister-in-law, Grace B. Lennon (1877–1948), as partner. Mark died in 1923.

There were two sons in this union, Lynn Avon 1889–1927, was in World War I, the 290th Aero Squadron, and Percival L. born March 19, 1892 and died January 30, 1969. Percy, as he was affectionately known, was also in World War I, New York QM Sgt. U.S. Army. The *St. Regis Falls Newsletter* of Feb. 1969 puts Mr. Rowell's life best:

January 30, 1969 was a dark day in the history of our village as we suffered the loss of one of our most prominent citizens.

The death of Percival L. Rowell after a short illness, created a great void in our community. His accomplishments in life were not ordinary. He was born March 19, 1892, a son of Mark and Jennifer Lennon Rowell, in St. Regis Falls and received his early education in local grade and high schools.

He received a law degree from Georgetown University and worked seven years in the Treasury Dept. in Washington, D.C. He served in World War I with overseas duty in France.

After a few years with the law firm of Leslie Saunders he was employed by the Ogdensburg Trust Co. and later became manager of the local branch.

To his widow, the former Agnes Pierce, we extend our sincerest sympathy.

Percy married in 1926 to Agnes Pierce born Jan. 28, 1901, the daughter of Morris and Katherine Walsh Pierce. She was a registered nurse working many years at the Alice Hyde Hospital in Malone. There were no children. Agnes Pierce Rowell died Feb. 17, 1984.

THE SMITH FAMILY

Willard Smith born Aug. 28, 1796 in Randolph, Vermont, the son of Jedediah and Esther Fuller Smith. His first marriage was Aug. 28, 1823 in Roxbury, Vermont to Betsey Boyce born 1806 and died Oct. 10, 1845. After Betsey's death, Willard then married on March 15, 1846 to Mrs. Jane Ann Swift born 1831 and died Feb. 1877. Willard died Aug. 28, 1872.

The children of Willard and Betsey Smith were, 1) a son born Aug. 19, 1824, lived only five hours, 2) a daughter born July 17, 1825 and died July 22, 1825, 3) a son born July 24, 1826 and died July 28, 1826, 4) Denison Samuel born Sept. 21, 1827, married June 26, 1853 to Alma Niles (born Fairfax, Vermont and died Apr. 24, 1913) and died May 30, 1916. 5) Eliza C. born May 6, 1829; married May 4, 1861 to Nelson Ramsdell (see *Ramsdell family*) and died Aug. 31, 1916. 6) Julia-Ann Matilda born Oct. 2, 1831, married 1856 to William Chaffee and died Dec. 14, 1909. 7) George B. born July 5, 1834 and died Mar. 9, 1837. 8) George B. born Aug. 10, 1837 and died Jan. 22, 1842. 9) Jedediah born Mar. 24, 1840 and died Mar. 30, 1841, 10) Harriet S. born July 13, 1842, married Jan. 1, 1858 to Ira C. Green (born Apr. 22, 1834 and died Dec. 28, 1886) and died June 26, 1922, and 11) Joseph Perkins born Sept. 13, 1845, married July 4, 1866 to Lucy Barnes (born 1848 and died Oct. 17, 1920) and died Dec. 2, 1930.

Samuel Denison and Alma Niles Smith had a son, Justin D. born May 17, 1855, married Ella Kingsley and died Oct. 17, 1933.

William and Julia-Ann Matilda Smith (Chaffee) had two children, Edwin and William.

Ira C. and Harriet Smith (Green) had nine children, 1) a son died July 4, 1858, 2) a son died Dec. 25, 1859, 3) Nettie born Mar. 7, 1861 and died Dec. 11, 1879, 4) Silas born Dec. 17 1863 and died Jan. 14, 1864, 5) Rosa born Oct. 7, 1866 and died Feb. 13, 1880, 6) Bessie born July 30, 1868 and died Sept. 28, 1888, 7) I. Clayton born Feb. 27, 1871 and died June 8, 1893, 8) Thomas born Mar. 5, 1874 and died July 24, 1881 and 9) Willard born Feb. 13, 1876 and died July 19, 1881.

Joseph Perkins Smith was a Civil War Veteran. He and his wife Lucy had nine children, 1) Cammie born April 7, 1867, married June 5, 1886 to John Finlayson (see *Finlayson family*) and died Aug. 22, 1942, 2) George D. born June 17, 1869, married July 1, 1896 to Rhoda Rollins (1879–1964), 3) Myrtle L. born Oct. 22, 1871, married Nov. 26, 1892 to G. Edward Bristol, 4) Charles P. born Mar. 7, 1874 first married Jan. 12, 1899 to Grace M. Young (1880–1910) second married to Eva A. Cheney and died Jan. 31, 1978, 5) Francis A. (Frank) born June 21, 1876, married July 5, 1901 to Harriet M. Leonard (1872–1915), 6) Fred N. born Sept. 18, 1880, married Oct. 30, 1905 to Emma L. Thomas (1883–1946) and died Aug 25, 1970,

7) Jennie E. born May 20,1883, first married Mar. 28, 1905 to John McCollum (1877–1906), second married to James J. Jones (1889–1957), 8) Alma J. born Nov. 25, 1885,

married Oct. 18, 1902 to Luther H. Cook (1880–1945) and 9) Thomas B. born Jan. 24, 1890, married Gertrude Hill (1880–1957) and died 1961.

Charles P. Smith

Charles P. and Grace, his first wife, lived at Santa Clara around the turn of the century. A son, Clifford was born to them. Grace Smith succumbed to illness and Charles then married Eva Cheney from St. Regis Falls. In 1908, Mr. Smith became bookkeeper in the Santa Clara car shops. When the shops burned in Oct. 1915, Charles studied for the Ministry and was soon ordained, serving several Baptist Churches in the North Country. Their son, Clifford, became a vice-president in one of the Vermont Banks.

Charles P. Smith

Information of Smith family obtained from Winifred Ramsdell of Potsdam and from bible records of Beulah Smith Aiken.

THE SOCHIA FAMILY

Leonard E. (Leon) (Sochia) Saucier (1850–1911) with his brother, Theodore, came to St. Regis Falls from Grand Isle, Vermont. They married sisters, Leon married Chloe M. Young (1852–1913) and Theodore married Angelina Young. There was also a brother, Napoleon.

Leon and Chloe had a large family—some of which were; 1) Frank Joseph born 1878 in Vermont and died 1954. He was a blacksmith and a guide. First he married in 1900 Almeda L. Thomas, born 1881 in Lowell, Mass. and died of shock Nov. 1928. Almeda was the daughter of Wilber and Julian Thomas. Frank and Almeda had five children; a) Everett Lynn born May 8, 1910, married May 8, 1937 to Helen Mary Sather (born Dec. 21, 1914, the daughter of Oscar S. and Ann Viola (Surprise) Sather). (Oscar S. Sather was born 1888 in Trondheim, Norway and died 1977, the son of Peter and

Louise Sather—both born in Norway). Anna Viola Surprise born 1897, the daughter of Frank and Mary Frances (Aubery) Surprise. Frank Surprise's mother was Amelia Monarch.) Everett and Helen Sochia have five children—Everett Jr. born 1938, Roger born 1944, Diana born 1945 married Greg Hill, Bernard born 1946, and Judy born 1957. b) Cecil R. Sochia born 1905 married Emerilda Robitaille born 1910. c) Mildred born 1901 married Lester Farmer, the son of Fred Farmer. They had three children; Kathryn born 1920 married William Meacham, Patricia first married Don Martin and second married Elmer Lohr and Beverly. d) Harold M. 1914–1918, e) Dorothy 1908–1928 (died in childbirth) married Roy L. Wilkins (1894–1944), the child born 1928 was Bernard. After Almeda died, Frank remarried to Beatrice C. (1901–1069). They had two children; Janice and Martha.

2) Rose Sochia married July 4, 1892 to John J. Deno. 3) Mary Sochia (1875–1952) married Joseph M. Regis (1870–1952) from Three Rivers, Canada.

4) Waldo Sochia married Amelia Bean, they had seven children; a) Ethel M., born May 28, 1908 in St. Regis Falls died Feb. 25, 1983, married Louis Radloff (died May 26, 1979), b) Floyd, never married, c) Stanley, d) Lawrence, e) Alice, f) Leo, never married and g) Harvey.

5) Edison E. Sochia 1888–1956, married Hattie Caskinette born 1892. They had—Eldora May born Jan. 22, 1929 and Elsie May born Mar. 5, 1930 and died July 26, 1930 of chicken pox.

6) Philinda Sochia born Oct. 27, 1890 in Waverly died 1970 (69) married Vern Meacham (see *Meacham family*).

7) Exzildia (Zelda) Sochia (1893–1944) married Archie E. Gilber (1892–1960).

8) William Sochia, 9) Martha first married _____ Brabon and second married Edward Bickford. There were two children by the first marriage—Bernard; and Ethel married Wesley Austin.

THE SOUTHWORTH FAMILY

Ogilvy Sylvester Southworth came to St. Regis Falls after the Civil War from Louisville, N.Y. He married Martha M. Carpenter, she died 1902 and he died 1914. Their children were; 1) Clayton C. 1868–1941 (first married Edith Herne, then married Lottie Sharp born 1878 in Madrid, N.Y. They had a son Harold 1905–1965. Harold was a high school teacher and baseball coach at Central High School in Syracuse. He married Dorothy Popp and had a son, Robert.) 2) Gertrude J. 1871–1906 (see *LaPoint family*), 3) Lena M. died Oct. 4, 1885 age 7 mos. 4 days.

Ogilvy Southworth was a Civil War veteran. After arriving in St. Regis Falls, he started a grocery store located on South Main Street. Clayton Southworth took over this business after the death of his father. Clayton and Henry Douglass became partners in the Douglass & Southworth Store. They started a grist mill in back of the store. They sold grain, hay and building materials. Warehouses were behind the store and they shipped grain in by the railroad.

Southworth information obtained from Mrs. Marion LaPoint and Mrs. Halcyon Davies, both of St. Regis Falls.

THE TRIM FAMILY

Frank Trim was born to Alvin and Alvira (Drew) Trim on Dec. 16, 1856 in the settlement of Skerry, N.Y. Alvin Trim was also born in Brandon-Skerry area. His wife, Alvira, was born in Stockholm, St. Lawrence County, N.Y., the daughter of Michael and Nancy (Reynolds) Drew, who were both born in Canada. Alvin's father, William, was born in 1797, in Palmer, Massachusetts. William's father, Benjamin Trim, who was in the Revolutionary War, marched to Canada with Benedict Arnold, and was at Valley Forge with General George Washington.

Frank Trim married Caroline Adelia Barber, the daughter of William and Sally (Owens) Barber, born Oct. 6, 1858 in Brandon, N.Y. They married May 9, 1875 in Brandon.

Frank and Carrie had three children, 1) Fay, 2) Eva Mae and 3) William Rubin. Fay Hubert Trim born 1876, married Rose M. Gravel, the daughter of Michael and Melvina (Campbell) Gravel. Fay and Rose had two sons, Burlan and Gerald. Eva Mae married Charles Flynn and had seven children, two of whom died young. William married Lulu Finlayson and had five children, including twin girls.

In 1877 Alvin Trim gave his son, Frank, his wife Carrie, and their new son, Fay, who was only four months old, a team of oxen, a double wagon, a barrel of salt pork (hogshead, it was called), a feather tick mattress, a kerosene lamp and a kerosene lantern—just enough supplies to last the trip. Then, Frank, with his new family, started their journey into the wilderness. They traveled south on the Eddie Road through Reynoldston, which was a small lumbering settlement on the north end of the Eddie Road. Frank bought some acreage from Henry Levansworth just south of the Duane Road (Red Tavern Road), which use to be call the Port Kent Road, this area is now the Trim Road (Long Pond Road) where the farm was. They built a small log cabin and lived in it about eight years, when they then built a big frame house, which still stands on the left, the first house on the Trim Road. He bought more land at $.50 per acre. They cleared the land and farmed. With hard work and apparently a good businessman, he accumulated over 200 acres of land.

Through the years, most of the land has been sold, but there is still a small portion that belonged to the son, Will, that remains in the Trim family. This is located on the corner where the Trim Road starts, and now owned by Will's daughter, Joyce and her husband Manuel Millares.

The Trim Road leads to Long Pond, where there was probably a bridge across the river that would take you to the little hamlet of Shanley.

THE TRIPENY FAMILY

Raphael W. Tripeny Sr. (1866–1942) married 1888 in Waterbury, Connecticut to Anna Strand (1864–1943) who born in Brunskog, Sweden and came to the United States in 1885.

Raphael had a brother, William, (1856–1897) who died in St. Regis Falls and is buried in St. Anne's Cemetery. His wife, Angelica, (1859–1934) moved to Casper, Wyoming and is buried there. William and Angie Tripeny's children were; John, William, Maude and Marie. Grandchildren still live in Wyoming and California.

The children of Raphael and Anna Tripeny were; 1) Charlotte M. (1891–1978) married Walter White (see *White family*). 2) Ernest C. (1893–1950) married Geraldine Ward born 1900. They had three children; son—died 1928, Rita and John. 3) Raphael Jr. (Budd) 1897–1974 married Mary C. Fargerstrom born 1898. They had five children; Bernard (1919–1932), Raphael W. 3rd (1921–1930), Margaret married Stanley Mosher—one daughter, Rose Marie; Anna married Robert Starks and lives in Texas—they have three daughters: Margaret, Mary (twins), and Linda. Evelyn married Edward Fronzack; they have two children. 4) Evelyn A. (1895–1918) and 5) Harriet (1900–1984) married Henry H. Thompson (1891–1964). They had two sons, Raphael and Donald.

Tripeny information obtained from Miss Rita Tripeny, St. Regis Falls.

THE WAIT FAMILY

Almon Elsworth Wait/Waite (1860–1932) is believed to have come from South Colton, N.Y. Almon married Mary E. Scovil (1861–1932), also from South Colton. It is believed that Almon had at least one sister and a brother, Ernie, from whom he bought some of the original land for the farm on the Waite Road. Almon and Mary moved to the farm on the Waite Road after they were married and remained there until their deaths. They had two sons; 1) Archie born 1902 and died 1926 at the age of 24 years of spinal meningitis and epilepsy, and 2) Myron A. (1899–1971) first married Clara LaFrance, they had a daughter, Margaret born 1917 and married Floyd LaPage; they adopted two boys—Mike (a twin) not married and Paul (a twin) married with two children. Myron and Clara divorced. Myron then remarried Edna Bouchard (also divorced) (1903–1975). In this union there were four children; 1) Odena Mary born 1921, 2) unnamed child born dead 1922, 3) Albert born 1924 and died at the age of 3 years with a growth on his spine, caused him to be crippled from birth as a results of a fall sustained by Edna during pregnancy, and 4) Almon L. born 1925.

Odena Mary Wait married Leo Patnode born 1913, affectionately called Pat, now deceased. They had eight children; 1) Beverly born Sept. 30, 1941, married Donald (Jack) Kimball born Dec. 23, 1939; they have three children—Donald Jr., born Mar. 1, 1960, Kevin born Jan. 5, 1963, and Deanna born July 9, 1966. 2) Nancy born Jan. 26, 1943 married Russell Walker born Apr. 17, 1938; they have two children—Kathy born June 10, 1963 and Jimmy Jo born Aug. 18, 1966. 3) Jeanne born Jan. 6, 1947 married Lawrence (Larry) Rivers born Dec. 28, 1943; they had three children—Larry Jr. born Dec. 30, 1970, Melanie S. born Mar. 24, 1971 and died Mar. 25, 1971 and Chad born Feb. 3, 1975. 4) Thomas born Sept. 16, 1950 married Cindy Guth born Oct. 4, 1947; they have two children—Kierstin Yager born Nov. 27, 1971, adopted daughter of Cindy's and Kory David born Dec. 2, 1976. 5) Barbara born Mar. 4, 1953 married Bruce Ploof born Aug. 31, 1951; they have two children—Amanda born June 3, 1976 and Ian. 6) Anne born Feb. 26, 1954 married Don Roberts born Jan. 30, 1946; they have three children—Nathan, and twins—Jeremy and Joshua. 7) Leo (Corky) born June 18, 1955 married Jan Haskell born Mar. 3, 1957; they have two children—Amber born June 5, 1975 and Jamie born May 16, 1976. and 8) David born Nov. 9, 1959 and died from an accidental shooting at the age of 16 years.

Almon L. Wait born Aug. 28, 1925 married Jennie May Susice born Feb. 29, 1929; they have four children—1) Veronica Ann born Aug. 18, 1948 married Michael G. Sweet born May 10, 1944; they have two children; Tesa born June 9, 1970 and Todd born Oct. 30. 1975.

2) Brenda Lee born Mar. 5, 1951 married Theron (Butch) A. White born Apr. 26, 1943; they have two children; Tisha Lee born Dec. 29, 1970 and Aaron Lee born June 17, 1973 (born on Father's Day). 3) Almon Gary born Aug. 12, 1953, not married and 4) Crystal Lynn born Apr. 3, 1968, not married.

Wait information obtained from Almon and Jennie Wait, St. Regis Falls.

THE WHITE FAMILY

Walter F. White born June 27, 1889 in Potsdam, N.Y. and died 1955. He was the son of Frank and Angeline White. Walter's father died when he was 7 years old, and his mother died when he was between 12 and 14 years old. Walter had a brother, Vernon J. 1892–1954, Vern was a World War I veteran, married, but had no children. A sister, Mabel, married John Johnson; they had two children—Richard and Madeline. Mabel died and John married Maude Brown.

Walter came to St. Regis Falls and married Charlotte M. Tripeny, who was born Aug. 25, 1891 in St. Regis Falls and died 1978. She was the daughter of Raphael and Anna (Strand) Tripeny, Sr. Raphael was from Tripenyville (near the vicinity of Norfolk, N.Y.—see *Tripeny family*).

The children of Walter and Charlotte White were; 1) Gerald born Sept. 10, 1914, married Gladys Brown. There were no children by this marriage; however, Gladys had children by a previous marriage. 2) Willard born July 2, 1916 married Doris Niche and had two children Susan and Carol. Both Gerald and Willard were team members of the "Wonder Five" basketball team. 3) Harriet born Sept. 16, 1917 married Nillie D. Noyes (from Harrisville) and had two sons; Brandon and Nillie Walter. 4) Helen Marie was born Sept. 8, 1920 and died 1940. 5) Carlton Strand was born, Apr. 19, 1924 in New Hampshire; he married Rita Palmer (see *Palmer family*). Their children—baby (stillborn) 1947, Dona Rae born 1948, Gary Carlton born 1950, Douglas James born 1951, Helen Marie born 1954, Carl Michael born 1962, John Patrick born 1965, Pamela Lynn and Tamara Lee (twins) born 1967.

Walter White worked at the Brooklyn Cooperage Co. mill and in 1940 he went to Tonawanda, N.Y. to work, while the family stayed in St. Regis Falls.

White information obtained from Carlton White, Hamburg, N.Y.

WINTERS—LA CLAIR FAMILIES

Lan Winters (1865-1915) married Mattie _____ (1868-1934). They were the parents of Forest E. Winters (1886-1959). Forest married Glencie L. Prentice (1891-1971). Forest and Glencie Winters' children were; 1) Lan (died at birth), 2) Walter Lan born Aug. 28, 1913, married Regina LaClair , he died Apr. 28, 1972, they had no children.

3) Wallace Henry born Oct. 12, 1916, married Kathryn LaClair, they had three children; Gerald married Betty LaPage, Linda married Peter Soteman, and Sharon married Gary Patraw. 4) Helen S. born 1923 and died 1943 at age 19 years. 5) Wilta W. born and died 1918.

John LaClair/LaClaire born 1846 and died Jan. 4, 1937; he was from Canada. John married Zoa Jandrews. They had eight children—Celinda, Jane, Anna, Frank, William, John, Jeffery, and George.

Frank was born June 22, 1881 and died Sept. 23, 1963. He married Oct. 12, 1909 to Charlotte (Lottie) Seymour born Oct. 10, 1887 and died Dec. 26, 1976. They had seven children—1) Lloyd born July 28, 1910 and died Nov. 27, 1951, 2) Regina Kathryn born July 4, 1912 married Walter Winters, 3) Irene born Jan. 22, 1914 and died Jan. 28, 1937, 4) Kathryn Agnes and Margery (twins) born Aug. 25, 1915—Margery died Dec. 12, 1915, Kathryn married Wallace Winters, 5) Gerald born July 12, 1918 and 6) Walter born Apr. 26, 1921.

Winters and LaClair information obtained from Mrs. Kathryn LaClair Winters, St. Regis Falls.

THE YOUNG FAMILY

Robert Young, father to James Henry Young, was born in England about 1778 and came to this country as a young man. He died in May 1844, at the age of 66 years at Gilboy, Schoharie County, N.Y. Robert married Phebe Buckhout, born at New Paltz, Ulster County, N.Y., the daughter of John Buckhout, of the Knickerbocker ancestry.

The children of Robert and Phebe Young were, 1) James, 2) Henry, 3) Jacob, 4) Theodore, 5) John, 6) George, 7) Alexander, 8) William, 9) Margaret, 10) George, 11) Willis and 12) William. (Note: two Williams and two Georges, many times if a baby died the next child born of the same sex would be given the same name as the dead child.)

James Henry Young born Nov. 17, 1820, a native of Poughkeepsie, N.Y.; married Caroline Egbertson, born in Jewett, Green County, N.Y. in 1832 and died in 1900. James Young was the superintendent of the tannery in St. Regis Falls around the mid 1860s. The children of James and Caroline were, 1) Ophelia, 2) Charles H., 3) Arthur and 4) Frank Stanley.

Ophelia Young born at Pottersville, Warren County, N.Y.; July 26, 1853 and died 1932. She married William T. O'Neil, Nov. 19, 1872 (see *O'Neil lineage*).

Charles H. Young born Nov. 26, 1857 at Bleeker, Fulton County, N.Y.; located at St. Regis Falls with his parents in 1866 and continued to make it his home until 1896. Mr. Young worked at merchandising and lumbering and was a surveyor. He served as town supervisor for several years, and was active in the Republican party. He moved to Texas in 1896 to represent two land and timber companies of New York City in developing and marketing their Texas properties. Then he made his home in Malone after 1912. He died Sept. 15, 1940.

Charles' wife, Orpha Berry, was born Jan. 11, 1860 in Trout River. They were married Nov. 23, 1885 and she died Feb. 11, 1938. A daughter, Janet, died Aug. 30, 1896 at the age of 8 weeks, and a son, Jamie, died May 5, 1895 at the age of 6 weeks.

Frank Stanley Young was born Jan. 29, 1869 and died Aug. 31, 1945. He married in Aug. 1920 to Jane C. Donaghy, the daughter of Hawley and Christina Kopanski Donaghy. Jane was born July 13, 1899 in West Virginia. Frank and Jane had two children—Nelda born July 14, 1924 and died Sept. 1, 1969 and Stanley.

Chapter 15
ST. REGIS FALLS CEMETERIES

Forest Cemetery
St. Ann's Cemetery
Cataloged July, 1980

The oldest marked grave in the Forest Cemetery: David Conger, died Jan. 24, 1850, aged 31 yrs. 2 mos.

The oldest marked grave in the St. Ann's Cemetery: Mary (Parent) Deno died May 18, 1879, aged 36 yrs, wife of Ambrose Deno.

FOREST CEMETERY

AIKEN

1. Deforest M.   1899-1938
   Pearl M.   1902-
   Matilda Bailey Landry   1890-1975
2. Robert E.   Mar. 24, 1920-July 9, 1945   N.Y. Cpl., 402 Bomb Sq., AAF WW II; PH

ALDRICH

1. Alvin S.   died Sept. 23, 1887   age 58 yrs, 7 mos., 14 days
2. C. Y.   1861-1951
   Flora D., his wife   1866-1900
3. Frederick W.   1864-1931
   Mary C., his wife   1866-1916

ALLEN

1. Bert   1880-1945   father
   Gertrude   1920-1920   dau.
   Nora Cook   1892-1945   mother
2. Clara   1887-1969   (see Richard Lyons)
3. Dorothy   1918-   (see Harold N. Kelley)

4. Eunice	1893-	(see B. A. Biggers) husband
5. George	1886-1954	wife
Lucy	1893-1974	
Margarite	1912-1922	dau.
6. Lemuel B.	1846-1917	father
7. Leonard	1913-	
Ernest B.	Oct. 1, 1901-June 1, 1979	MABT, U.S. Army, WWII
8. Sarah Bero Allen	1876-1967	
9. W. Dunham Allen	1856-1932	
Lillian	1862-1927	

ATWOOD

1. May A.	1883-1968	(see Ezra M. Barkley)

AUSTIN

1. Albert H.	1884-1959	
Jessie M.	1884-1958	
2. Charles W.	1850-1919	
Hannah M., his wife	1857-1914	
3. Dora S.	1888-1964	(see Ernest O. Brabon)
4. John W.	died 1925	
Vera M.	1906-1928	
Henry A.	1908-1968	

5. Wesley C.   Aug. 30, 1894-Sept. 2, 1977 Pvt. U.S. Army, WWI
6. Wesley C.   1894-1977
   Ethel Brabon, his wife   1901-

BADGER

1. Floyd E.   1894-1958
   Nettie   1867-1894   dau.   (see Benjamin F)

BAILEY

1. A. F.   died Mar. 23, 1892   age 33 yrs.
   Leo   died Aug. 22, 1885   age 1 mo.   son of A. F. & L. Bailey
   Georgie   died July, 1900   age 9 yrs, 10 mo.
        son of A. F. & L. Bailey

2. George F.   1870-1953
   Sarah his wife   1871-1956
   George A., son   1888-1910
3. Lawrence L.   1906-
   Mildred E., his wife   1900-1971
4. Wilbur H.   1900-1975
   Dorothy Williams, his wife   1904-

BAIRD
  1. Anna   1868-1964   (see Gordon Hannay)

BALDIN
  1. Alton O.   1875-1961
     Mary J. Gardner   1875-   his wife

BALDWIN
  1. Frederick R.   1945-1946
     Jackie K.   1943   age 2 mos.

BANDY, BANDY-CAMP
  1. Loretta Alice Bandy   1909-
     Raymond Harry Camp   1906-1943
     Edmund Raymond Camp   1932-1932
  2. Edmund E.   1883-1941
     F. Frank Day   1886-1951   his wife
  3. Ruth Day Bandy   1916-1952   his wife
  4. Sarah   1858-1901   (see Hugh Raymo)

BARKLEY
  1. Arnold E.   1912-1974

ST. REGIS FALLS CEMETERIES • 207

Ruth E.	1914-	son of Arnold & Ruth Barkley
Roger Irving May	19(20), 1955	(see George I. Fadden)
2. Daisy	1909-	
3. Ezra M.	1874-1950	
May A. Atwood	1883-1968	
4. Inez Barkley Heywood	1904-1970	(see Inez Heywood)

BARNES

1. Charles	1859-1919	
Mary his wife	1857-1910	
2. Lowessa	died Jan. 1919	age 93 yrs. (see Joseph P. Smith)
3. Lucy	died Oct. 17, 1920	age 72 yrs. (see Joseph P. Smith)

BELMORE

1. Lewis D.	1896-1918	Co. B 504 Eng's Bat.
Lucinda	1862-1948	mother

BERDROW

1. Barbara	1928-	(see James E. Sochia)

BERO

1. Sarah Bero Allen	1876-1967	

BESA

1. Alex   Co. F, 193 N.Y. Inf.

BESAW

1. Amelia   1894-   (see Frank Jones)
2. Alexander   Sept. 23, 1888-Dec. 25, 1913
3. Gilbert   1887-1969
    Ella C.   1895-1974
4. Margaret   1853-1939

BICKFORD

1. Tracy A.   1892-
    Ruth Cheney, his wife   1894-1968
2. Edward   1890-1967
    Martha   1885-1958
3. Edward   Nov. 7, 1890-Apr. 1, 1967   N.Y. Sgt. Co. C 346 Inf., WW I

BIGGERS

1. B. A.   1887-   husband
    Eunice Allen   1893-   wife
    Eunice Meyers   1910-1959   dau.
2. Beverly A.   May 9, 1887-Nov. 7, 1974   Pvt., U.S. Army

BLADE

1. Bert E. — 1869-1941
   Elizabeth Olmstead — 1870-1957 — his wife
2. Leo J. — 1893-1960
   Edna G. — 1902-1975

BOARDROW

1. Henry H. — 1865-1964
   Phoebe E. — 1875-1959
2. Joseph — 1850-1922

BOICE

1. Eva — 1896-1968
2. Walter H. — 1863-1936 — (see Wm. Y. Grant)
   Etta — 1876-1972

BOMBARD

1. Earl L. — 1902-1955
   Leila E. — 1909-
2. Laura — 1862-1954 — wife of Charles Camp (see Bert Camp)

BRABON

1. Ernest O.	1884-1967	
Dora S. Austin	1888-1964	his wife
2. Ethel	1901-	(see Wesley C. Austin)
3. Eugene W.	1908-	father
Arietta C.	1911-	mother
their sons		
Austin	1932	
Hayden	1942	
4. Frank	1883-1944	
	1893-	
5. George E.	1897-1975	
Emma Martin	1921-1932	his wife
6. Harold H.	1907-	
7. Carroll	1916-1926	
Wesley	63-65	sons of E. & D. Brabon
8. 16th N.Y. Cav. Co. F	1869-1918	
footstones--William	1846-1929	
Oliver F.	1851-1935	
Katherine	1891-1948	his wife
Harry		

BRAY

1. Floyd E.	1909-1980	

ST. REGIS FALLS CEMETERIES • 211

    Evelyn J.   1914-
2. Frank   1901-1924
3. John F.   1874-1957
    Dora E.   1877-1959

BRAYMON

1. Harry   1905-1914   son of T. & A. Braymon

BRIGGS

1. Allen D.   died Dec. 10, 1902   age 64 yrs., 8 mos., 23 days.
    Henrietta   died Jan. 1, 1903   age 53 yrs., 4 mos., 20 days.

BROWN

1. Alexander   Feb. 28, 1835-July 3, 1923   N.Y. Pvt. Co. F, Civil War
2. Alexander   1836-1923
    Jane, his wife   1847-1921
    Claud   1897-1920
    Peter   1870
    Fayette   1872
3. Benjamin   1839-1904
    Huldah L. Clary, his wife 1845-1936
    Nettie Badger   1867-1894   their dau.

footstone—Frank O. Brown		
4. Clarence F.	1871-1934	
5. Claude	1871-1925	
	May 5, 1895-May 29, 1921	N.Y. Pvt. Btry., F 13 Reg., Fard WW I
6. Fred	1866-1930	
7. Maud E.	1879-1964	(see David F. DeShaw)
8. Vern	1889-	father
Emma	1896-	mother

BRUCE

1. Henry Walton	died Jan. 19, 1913	age 60 yrs.
2. Jonah C.	died Mar. 17, 1908	age 62 yrs. Co. D, 142 Reg. N.Y.V.
3. Mina A.	died June 14, 1887	age 5 mos. 14 days
		dau. of E. D. & E. M. Bruce
4. Phoebe	died June 2, 1966	age 79 yrs., wife of Jonah C. Bruce
5. Timothy	died Oct. 21, 1894	age 67 yrs.
Melisa V.	died June 28, 1903	age 70 yrs. his wife

BRUNELL

1. Effie W.	1874-	(footstone near Hiram Walker)

BUCK

1. Mary	1870-	(see Moses E. Ludrick)

BUGBEE

  1. Gertrude E.   1842-1893   wife of L. A. Raymond
  2. W. B.   1845-1913
      Annie T. O'Neil, his wife   1847-1901

BUMP

  1. Will   1876-1962
      Delia   1876-1929
      Mina A.   1902-1940

BURDICK

  1. Clarissa M.   Apr. 27, 1809-Nov. 14, 1887

BURNETTE

  1. Effie M.   1880-1969   (see Milo M. Gale)

BURTON

  1. Harriette J.   1918-1962   wife of Chester R. Burton, dau. of Vern Brown

BUTLER

1. Myrton W.	1881-1932	
Orril C. Turner	1877-1946	his wife
Ruth E.	1920-1921	dau. of M. W. & O. C. Butler
Mabel	1894-1922	
Adelin	1914-1932	
2. Ralph T.	1916-	
Vera Westurn	1919-	his wife

BYAM

1. John M.	1815-1945	
Mae C.	1890-1964	
Freda M.	1913-1915	dau., buried at Salisbury Center

CAMP

1. Daisy C., his wife	1881-1958	
Bert	1883-1954	
Nora Rivera	1887-1938	his wife
Charles	1861-1948	
Laura Bombard	1862-1954	his wife
2. Charles	died Dec. 19, 1898	age 66 yrs.
3. Elizabeth	1896-1946	(see Fred W. Lang)

4. Elizabeth, his wife 1903-
   Lymond R. 1908-

CAMPE

1. Bert   died Jan. 9, 1903   age 32 yrs.

CAMPBELL

1. Antoine   1851-1914
   Inez, his wife   1864-1942
   Leila   1877-1891
   Somner   1889-1910
   Randolph   1906-1913

CARPENTER

1. Martha M.   wife of O. S. Southworth (see O. S. Southworth)

CARR

1. Ezekel   1808-1878
   Polly, his wife   1820-1901
   Charley   1865-1886
   Bial J.   1850

    Hattie A.   1848
    2. Noel O.   died Mar. 21, 1882   (stone in very poor condition)

CATURA
    1. Hattie M.   1869-1954

CATURIA
    1. Jennie   1876-1938   mother

CHENEY
    1. Ruth   1894-1968   (see Tracy A. Bickford)
    2. Wayne R.   1942-1947   their son
        Glen H.   1901-1966
        Joyce Ploof   1923-   his wife
    3. Watson L.   1899-1929
        Harriet   1922-1923
    4. Willard G.   1898-
        Beulah Hicks   1906-   his wife

CHRISTIAN
    1. Richard E.   Jan 20, 1926-May 31, 1972   N.Y. Cpl. 413 ORD HV MAINT
                                                                    CC. Korea

CHYLER

1. Clista — died Dec. 19, 1895 — age 28 yrs. (see John B. Ford)

CLAFLIN

1. Walter E. — Sept. 16, 1882-Nov. 28, 1922
   footstone—father
   Albert E. — Sept. 11, 18__-Aug. 11, 1925

CLARK

1. Clara P. — died Feb. 11, 1890 — age 1 yr, 11 mos., 27 da. dau. of H. & H. Clark

2. Hiram — 1854-1922
   Hattie — 1861- — his wife
3. Milon C. — 1906-1964
   Nellie Hart — 1916-
4. Nellie — 1875-1917 — wife of Peter DeLair

CLARY

1. Huldah L. — 1845-1936 — (see Benjamin Brown)

CLOOKY

1. William B. — died Oct. 20, 1917 — age 74 yrs. Pvt. Co. G, 142 Reg.

		N.Y.S. Vol.
COMBS		
1. Elizabeth J.	1848-1907	
CONGER		
1. A. P.	died Mar. 24, 1895	age 74 yrs.
Clara B.		his wife (on other side of stone)
Tryphena, his wife	died Dec. 3, 1856	age 24 yrs.
Mary Jane	died Sept. 26, 1853	age 29 yrs.
Nettie	died June 1, 1862	age 5 mos., dau. of A. P. & C. Conger
2. David	died Jan. 24, 1850	age 31 yrs, 2 mos.
3. Mary Miller Conger	1884-1919	wife of M. A. Conger
CONLEY		
1. William A.	1859-1954	
Ada Belle	1862-1916	his wife
COOK		
1. Carrie Sochia Cook	1872-1958	mother
2. Effie M.	died Apr. 11, 1884	age 10 mos., dau. of H. & E. Cook
3. Ella A.	1893-	(see Bert A. Hart)

4. Hial   died May 28, 1907   age 54 yrs., 10 mos., 29 da.
5. Hiram   died Sept. 30, 1894   age 73 yrs.
   Hitty   died May 3, 1900   age 67 yrs.   his wife
6. LaRoy   1890-1910
7. Lucinda   1821-1899   (see David Parks)
8. Luther H.   1880-1945
9. Nora   1892-1945   (see Bert Allen)
10. Orin H.   1869-1952   father
    Carrie Sochia   1872-1959   his wife   mother

COTTER
1. Margaret M.   1863-1939

COWLEY
1. Jane B.   1837-1890   (see Daniel W. Flack)

CRANDALL
1. Samuel W.   1870-1905
   Nona E.   1874-1942 (43)

CRONK
1. Delmar A.   1890-1918

2. Jesse W.   1882-1969
   Laura B. Winters   1880-1956   his wife
   Anna L.   1908-   their dau.
3. Wilbur W.   1850-1936
   Mary L.   1850-1880
   Anna L.   1856-1903

CUMMINGS

1. Charles A.   1870-1951   father
   Mary E.   1879-1936   mother
2. Efard S.   1909-1973
   Lillian Merrill   1917-   his wife
   footstone—
   Allan S. Cummings Sept. 7, 1940-Feb. 17, 1980 Sp. 4, U.S. Army
3. J. Wesley   1910-1925
   John   1883-1954   father
   Christena   1891-1970   mother
   Shirley E.   1918-   dau.
4. James   1848-1932
   Jane LaValley   1850-1932   his wife
5. Kenneth   1915-
   Evelyn Jones   1917-

CURRIER

1. Alfred M.   1864-
   - Marcia   1864-
   - Eleanor   2 mos. 14 days.
   - Leon   14 days
   - Ruth   11 weeks
   - Isreal C.   1834-1876
   - Adaline   1843-1898   his wife

DAVIDSON

1. Mary H.   1876-1915   wife of Bert T. Parks
2. Sarah   1844-1921
3. Thomas   1841-1917

DAY

1. F. Frank   1886-1951
2. John S.   died May 11, 1894   (see Edmund E. Bandy)
   - Fidelia   1843-1918   age 58 yrs. his wife
3. Ruth Day Bandy   1916-1952

DELAIR

1. Nellie Clark   1875-1917   wife of Peter Delair

DESHAW

1. Albert C.　　　　Sept. 5, 1870-July 18, 1911　N.Y. Pvt. TRPE 3 Reg. Calvary
   Adelaide　　　　1833-1917
   Gilbert　　　　　1829-1913
   Albert　　　　　 1869-1911
   Nell　　　　　　 1861-1897
   Lydia　　　　　　1864-1892
   Minor　　　　　　1863-1907
   Edna C.　　　　　1888-1907
   George H.　　　　1852-1914
   Mary　　　　　　 1854-1946
2. David F.　　　　 1879-1969
   Maud E. Brown　　1879-1964　　　　　　　　　his wife

DILLION

1. Annabell　　　　Apr. 30, 1903-Aug. 16, 1974
   Victor　　　　　 1905-1952

DIMICK

1. Alice　　　　　　1923-　　　　　　　　　　(see Elmer R. Wagner)
2. John M.　　　　　1869-1958　　　　　　　　 father

Mildred B.	1902-1980	dau.
3. Linus J.	1901-1962	
Esther A.	1899-	

DORA-DREW

1. John	1881-	
Lena Drew	1880-1955	his wife
Frank	1878-1924	
Delbert	1897-1948	son
2. Myrtle Wade Dora	1886-1956	

DOUGALL

1. Fred	1864-1933	
Theo	1871-1941	
2. Leo L.	May 5, 1889	age 5 mos 3 days (son of unreadable) (near Nellie L. Dougall stone)
3. Nellie L.	died Nov. 7, 1893	age 1 yr, 11 mos., 15 da. dau. of Mr. & Mrs. Fred Dougall

DOUGLAS

1. Isabelle Douglas McKennon 1860-1945 (see Fraser-McKennon)
2. Ruth   died Oct. 8, 1895   dau. of H. B. & G. Douglas

DOUGLASS

1. Gertrude J.   1871-1906   wife of H. B. Douglass
2. Henry B.   1867-1934
   Helen A.   1877-1938   his wife
3. Lawrence R.   1910-1914

FARR

1. Isaac   1836-1908
   Lura   1836-1916   his wife
2. Willis Prentice   Oct. 29, 1904-Apr. 5, 1906   (on left side of Isaac Farr Stone)
   Ethel L. Parks   Aug. 20, 1902-Feb. 14, 1903

FETTERLEY

1. Elmer   1877-1949
   Maude Amy   1893-1939

FILES

1. Adnor P.   1897-1952

ST. REGIS FALLS CEMETERIES • 225

2. Charles	Feb. 8, 1869-Aug. 16, 1928	father
Clara E. Johnson	Apr. 13, 1874-Nov. 4, 1957	mother
Mattie H.	1902-1926	footstone
George E.	Jan. 20, 1899-July 14, 1945	N.Y. Cpl. 30 Inf. 3 Div.

FLACK

1. Daniel W.	1831-1904	
Jane B. Cowley	1837-1890	his wife

FLEMING

1. Elizabeth	1879-1960	(see Fred S. Ramsdell)
2. John	1847-1914	
Harriet	1857-1922	his wife
Milton M.	1881-1939	footstone
		age 5 yrs., 7 mos.
		son of M. E. & N. R. Fleming
3. Patrick	died Mar. 26, 1903	

FLYLES

1. Arthur E.	1891-1955	
2. William H.	1867-1933	
Rhoda A. Thomas	1870-1958	his wife

FLYNN

1. Hobart L.	died Jan. 22, 1886	age 3 mos. son of E. W. & M. J. Flynn
2. Martha J.	Apr. 30, 1867-May 4, 1928	

FORD

1. Frank H.	1900-1933	
2. Harold F.	1923-	
Helen I.	1925-1978	
3. John B.	died Sept. 27, 1897	age 56 yrs.
Clista Chyler	died Dec. 19, 1895	age 28 yrs.
4. John F.	1873-1926	
Dora E. Emlaw	1882-1945	his wife
Manfred A.	1912-1929	

FORTIES

1. Jennie M.	1898-1957	dau.
footstone—Alvin (nearby)		

FRASER-MC KENNON

1. Isabelle Douglas McKennon	1860-1945	
James M. McKennon	1859-1934	

Emma McKennon Fraser	1887-1967	
Emma McKennon Fraser	1887-1962	(Emma had two different stones)
2. John A.	1853-1930	
3. John W.	1887-1943	
4. Louise Little Fraser	1853-1931	

FRENCH

1. Susie A.	died Oct. 5, 1886	age 10 mos. 5 da.
		dau. of E. W. & E. B. French

FREY

1. Herman	1884-1943
Rose	1885-1946

FULLER

1. Rose	1856-1925	(see George W. McNeil)

FYE

1. Harry H.	1876-1935	
Luna	1883-1910	his wife
Martha Hase	1875-1957	his wife
2. Harry H.	1908-1979	

Alvena Gokey	1914-	his wife
GAGE		
1. Bessie R.	1888-1915	(see Rolly R. Wait)
GALE		
1. Mila M.	1878-1942	
Effie M. Burnette	1880-1969	his wife
GALUP		
1. Eva	1889-1894	dau. of F. & F. Galup
GARDNER		
1. Mary J.	1875-	(see Alton O. Baldin)
GEDDES		
1. Best	1883-1929	
Gertrude W.	1865-1948	his wife
2. Roydon B.	1888-1961	
Georgianna	1892-1964	his wife

GENAWAY

1. Mildred — 1914- — his wife

GHRIST

1. Lester L. — 1893-1968
   Rosella Radloff — 1895-1980 — his wife

GIBBS

1. Carrie — 1877-1957
   (see Fred H. Hunkins)
2. Amelia — 1850-1920
   James — 1848-1916
   Bert — 1870-1931
3. John C. — born Dec. 12, 1837
   Mary J. Race, his wife — Jan. 29, 1830-June 17, 1910 — age 80 yrs., 4 mos., 19 days.
4. Henry H. — 1868-1958
   Shirley Palmer — 1884-1951 — his wife
5. Lois — 1882-1960
   (see Vernon H. Palmer)
6. Norma — 1915-1916
7. Samuel E. — 1866-1898

GIFFIN

1. Martin E. 1836-1898
   Mary E. 1851-1931
   Abbie M. 1878-1885
   2. Rollin G. 1875-1947
   Frank M. 1870-1946
   Mary M. 1878-1965

GILMAN

1. Hattie   died June 29, 1899   age 43 yrs.
   Ida   died Oct. 10, 1892   age 18 yrs.

GOKEY

1. Alvena   1914-   (see Henry H. Fye)

GOODRICH

1. Dorothy P. 1914-1937

GORDON

1. Marcia   1873-1961   (see William Rockhill)

GRANT

1. Francis C.   Dec. 4, 1897-Apr. 18, 1959
2. William Y.   1903-1971   brother
   Eva Boice   1896-1968

GRAVELLE

1. Rose M.   1883-1951   (see Fay H. Trim)

GREENE

1. Horace A.   1849-1912
   Mary Ellen   1856-1911
2. Nellie J.   died Oct. 9, 1893   age 7 yrs. 18 days
   dau. of W. H. & A. J. Greene

GRENE

1. Willaim H.   1861-1902
   Alpha J.   1867-   his wife

GRIFFIN

1. Charles   1867-1923
   Emma   1867-1914   his wife   (back of stone) SINDO
   Fred   1881-1946

GRIFFIS

1. Jennie E.   died Oct. 15, 1889   age 37 yrs.   (see William E. King)

HALEY

1. Amanda   1834-1906
2. Clark   died Feb. 7, 1901   age 70 yrs.   Co. 142 Reg., N.Y.V.
3. George W.   1868-1937
    Mina P.   1872-1954   his wife
    Ben F.   1858-1927

HANLEY

1. Edward G.   1884-1956
    M. May   1883-1949
2. Frank   1860-1939
    Amy L.   1859-1931   his wife
    Watson E.   1887-1913   their son
3. George   1827-1905
    Carrie Hill   1839-1904   his wife

Grace   1885-1919
2. Herbert N.   1865-1946   his wife

HANNAY

1. Gordon 1865-1942 father
   Anna Baird 1868-1964 mother
   Agnes Maloney 1907-1942 wife of Gordon Hannay
   Gordon 1901-1971
   Margaret Reynolds 1906- wife of Gordon Hannay Jr.
2. Mary A. 1899-1968 (see Vernon D. Parks)

HANSON

1. Hattie R. 1872-1950 (see Joseph C. Johnson)

HART

1. Bert A. 1882-1957
   Ella A. Cook 1893- his wife
2. Herman 1868-1944
   Belle 1882-1948
3. Norman
   Loretta
   Hiram J. 1829-1916 father
4. Nellie 1916-
   (see Milon C. Clark)

HARTLEY
1. Mary A.   1862-1932
   (see Charles Weller)

HARTNETT
1. Dora Hartnett   Mar. 1, 1891-
                     Jan. 18, 1977

HARVEY
1. Edson   1868-1926
2. Eugene   1870-1931   father
   Floyd E.   1907-1968

3. Girtta M. died Apr. 23, 1882 age 3 yrs. 10 mos.
   dau. of W. C. & B. M. Harvey
4. Glen Roy died Sept. 28, 1891 age 2 mos. 11 days son of E. L. &
   H. D. Harvey
5. Sarah J. 1857
   (see Millard F. Sabin)
6. William H. 1840-1921 Priv. LD F 16 Brig. N.Y. Vol.
   Laura 1855-1925 his wife

HASE

1. Martha 1875-1957
   (see Harry H. Fye)

HASKINS

1. Fanny E. 1870-1946
   (see John Kidney)

HASKINS

1. Clarence 1892-1930
   (see Forest E. Winters)

HAZEN
   1. Harriet   1895-1903
      Mary   1865-1916
      Fred   1863-1951

HEWITT
   1. Ada M. Maxam Hewitt   died Dec. 25, 1892   age 25 yrs.   wife of F. M. Hewitt
   2. Flora D.   1871-1925
      Bert H.   1868-1923
      Russell   1904
      Baby   1905
   3. William J.   1885-1972
      Bessie   1888-1914
      Effie   1887-1960

HEYWOOD
   1. Inez Barkley Heywood   1904-1970

HICKS
   1. Beulah   1906-
      (see Willard G. Cheney)
   2. Luella   1904-1940

HILL

1. Carrie 1839-1904
   (see George Hanley)
2. James S. died Aug. 14, 1890 age 50 yrs. 10 mos. Co. F 193 Reg., N.Y.V.

HOLLISTER

1. Harry D. 1904-1967
   Agatha Wood 1918- his wife
2. Madge Hollister McNeil 1906-1952
   (see Madge McNeil)
3. William B. 1876-1946
   Elizabeth D. 1879-1953

HOWE

1. Dorothy 1912-
   (see Deforest C. Patraw)
2. Evely M. died Nov. 10, 1913 age 1 mo.
3. George V. 1876-1945
   Jessie M. Story 1886-
4. Monroe C. 1856-1908
   Mina S. 1863-1965 his wife
5. Catherine Ryan "Bitty" 1926-

  Norbert G. "Mickey"   1918-
 6. Ralph R.   1914-1973

HOY

1. Ann J.   1848-1928
 (see MILLER-CONGER)

HUCKINS

1. Marie Odette   Sept. 24, 1937-Dec. 2, 1979

HUGHES

1. Elaine S.   1919-
 (see SMITH-HUGHES-SLATTERY)
2. William J.   1866-1944
 Ruth   1875-1940   his wife
 Victoria Ada   1898-1908

HULL

1. Douglas Palmer Hull   1921-1943
 Elva Palmer   1893-1967   his wife
 Jesse A. 1895-1947

HUNKINS

1. Fred H. — 1878-1954
   Carrie Gibbs — 1877-1957 — his wife
2. W. Hunkins — 1855-1935
   Eltha — 1857-1926 — his wife
   Ralph — 1876-1893
   Bessie — 1880-1915
   Dora — 1896-1898

IRELAND

1. Andrew — died July 27, 1883 — age 82 yrs. — Native of England

JEROME

1. William F. — 1890-1967
   Charlena Lalone — 1896- — his wife

JESMER

1. Sada — died June 6, 1897 — age 9 mos. — dau. of J. & M. Jesmer

JOHNSON

1. Adnor — 1842-1933 — Co. F 142 Reg.
   Marion — 1842-1927 — his wife

Matie	1881-1885	
2. Allie W.	1903-1904	
3. Clara E.	Apr. 13, 1874-Nov. 4, 1957	
(see Charles Files)		
4. Effie R.	1874-1909	
(see Justin W. McNeil)		
5. Fred A.	1877-1963	
Jennie Orton	1881-1969	his wife
Kenneth F.	1905	
6. Joseph C.	1872-1924	
Hattie R. Hanson	1872-1950	
7. Kenneth S.	1902-1979	married July 9, 1928
Doratha B. Locke	1905-	
8. Samuel C.	Oct. 17, 1854-Apr. 30, 1890	

JOHNSTON

1. Edna	1906-1976
(see Floyd C. Rockhill)	
2. John Sr.	1863-1922
Ruth M.	1862-1938
3. John W.	1891-1971
Maude L.	1891-1971

JONES

1. Evelyn   1917
   (see Kenneth Cummings)
2. Frank   1882-1945
   Amelia Besaw   1894-   his wife
3. James J.   1889-1951
   Jennie E.   1883-1956
   Ruth M.   1913-1929
4. Ronald H.   June 10, 1920-Sept. 22, 1947   N.Y. Sgt., 180 Inf., 45 Inf. Div. WW II Pvt. U.S. Army WW II
5. Vranous A.   1914-1976

KELLEY

1. Clyde A.   1901-
   Millicent M.   1902-
2. Darwin A.   1922-
   Della Mashtare   1931-
   our baby   1950
3. George   1824-1916
   Abigail   died Feb. 4, 1902   age 73 yrs.
4. Georgiana   1862-1923
   (see John J. Lang)
5. Harold N.   1903-1977

Dorothy Allen	1918-		his wife
6. Hiram	1866-1934		
Clara	1888-1903		his dau.
7. infant dau. of M. & D. Kelley died May 22, 1895			
8. Kattie	died Apr. 13, 1895	age 7 yrs. 14 days	dau. of Silenous & Mary Kelley
9. Pearl	1907-1925		
10. Scott Michael	Dec. 29, 1955-Feb. 27, 1956		son of C. B. & C. H. Kelley
11. Silenous	1859-1915		
Mary J. Minnis	1870-		his wife

KETCHAM

1. J. Avery	1859-1938
Frances	1858-1932	his wife
Caroline A.	1891-1909	dau.
Leslie O.	1883-1939	son
Jessie M.	1887-1958	his wife

KIDNEY

1. Caroline M.	1893-1968
2. Hiram C.	1891-1954
3. John	1860-1900

Fanny E. Haskins	1870-1946		his wife
John Jr.	1889-1889		
baby	1898-1898		
footstone—Johnie died	Nov. 4, 1888,		age 7 wks., 4 days son of John & Fannie Kidney
4. John Sr.	1822-1909		
William	1872-1944		

KING

1. Theodore	died May 30, 1910	age 83 yrs.	Priv. Co. C, 5 Reg. N.Y. Vol.
2. William E.	died Feb. 20, 1896	age 46 yrs. 11 mos. 20 days	
Jennie E. Griffis	died Oct. 15, 1889	age 37 yrs.	his wife

LA BONTE

1. Gideon   1903-1980

LA BOUNTY

1. C. H.	1875-1959	
(see Richard Sawyer)		
2. Edmund D.	1870-1950	
Alice M.	1877-1956	
3. Elwin P.	Nov. 21, 1925-Dec. 12, 1977	QMS U.S. Navy WW II

4. Ernest 1879-1957
   (see John McNeil)
5. Harold E. 1908-1975 married Nov. 28, 1933
   Evelyn Ploof 1917-
   footstone—Harold E. LaBounty Nov. 2, 1908-Apr. 12, 1975 PFC U.S. Army WWII
6. Hatty 1878-1934
   (see Ratty LaBounty Palmer)
7. Louisa 1847-1935
8. Simeon 1845-1920 Pri. Co. K, 118 N.Y.V., Inf. UFF

LACROIX

1. Jacob died Feb. 7, 1889 age 53 yrs. a member of Co. D 98 N.Y.S.V.
2. John E. 1868-1939
   Electa M. White 1871-1951 his wife

LANDRY

1. Matilda Bailey Landry 1890-1975
   (see Deforest M. Aiken)

LADUE

  1. Mary J.   1856-1927   wife of Joseph LaDue

LAFRANCE

  1. Joseph   Mar. 27, 1892-Aug. 19, 1969   N.Y. Pvt. Co. A 1 Prov. Div Brig. WW I

LAHAIR

  1. Clarence   1893-1978
     Ethel E.   1898-

LALONE

  1. Charlena   1896-
    (see William F. Jerome)

LAMB

  1. Calvert D.   died Feb. 20, 1899   age 40 yre.
     Cornelia   1858-1929   his wife

LAMBERT

  1. Aliza   1845-

(see-Richard McGovern)

LANG

1. Fred W.		July 2, 1891-Dec. 14, 1975	Pvt. U.S. Army WW I
Elizabeth Camp		1896-1946	his wife
2. John J.		1818-1885	
Mariah J.		1834-1915	his wife
3. John J.		died June 13, 1917	age 65 yrs.
Georgiana Kelley		1862-1923	his wife
footstone at right—Wesley J.		1898-1924	
4. John J.		died June 23, 1885	age 66 yrs. 9 mos.
5. Martha J.		Apr. 11, 1887-	
(see-Oscar O. McNeil)			

LA POINT

1. Earl J.		Mar. 25, 1890-Mar. 4, 1971	N.Y. WAGR Co. B
			304 Ammo Train WW I
2. Earl J.		1890-1971	
Marion D.		1896-	his wife
James W.		1926	our son
3. John		1837-1900	
Henry		1866-1897	
Halcyon L.		1892-1951	wife of J. H. Rusterholtz

Roy W.   1888-
Guy A.   1884-1886
Mattie B.   1865-1945
Jerry   1862-1920

LAQUE
1. Lucille M.   1923-1974

LAROW
1. Ambrose   1847-1939
2. S. Ambrose   1885-
   Arvilla   1860-1929   his wife

LARRABEE
1. Asaltel P.   1853-1934
   Sarah A.   1855—1936   his wife
   Percival W.   1894-1912
   Glenn R.   1888-1972

LAVALLEY
1. Jane   1850-1932
   (see-James Cummings)

LA VOY

1. Arthur — died July 7, 1886 — age 4 yrs. — son of C. Z. & Emily LaVoy
2. Charles Z. — died Sept. 7, 1892 — age 63 yrs. 7 mos.
   Mary — died Jan. 7, 1891 — age 97 yrs.
3. Emma — May 24, 1873-Nov. 18, 1915
4. Freddie B. — died May 24, 1875 — age 4 yrs. 8 mos. — son of C. Z. & Emily LaVoy

LAWRENCE

1. Olive — 1877-1962 — mother

LEFFLER

1. Iva — 1871-1927
   (see Percy Snyder)
2. William Frank — died Nov. 9, 1906 — age 36 yrs. 2 mos.

LENNON

1. Grace B. — 1877-1948
   (see Percival L. Rowell)

LEAVENWORTH

1. Chloe 1894-
   (see Henry G. Trudeau)
2. Henry 1851-1923
   Christie 1854-1927 his wife
   Letty 1888-1914
   Rufus 1891-1892

LEONARD
1. Harriet (baby) died May 19, 1893 age 1 no. 17 da. dau. of F. W. & H. W. Leonard

LERCH
1. George 1875-1957
   Dinah 1879-1959

LOCKE
1. Doratha B. 1905-
   (see Kenneth S. Johnson)

LUDRICK
1. Moses E. 1868-1917
   Mary Buck 1870- his wife

LYONS
1. Richard — 1885-1970
   Clara Allen — 1887-1969

MAC DONALD
1. Edith C. O'Neil — 1874-1934 — wife of A. MacDonald
   (see O'Neil-MacDonald)

MALONEY
1. Agnes — 1907-1942
   (see Gordon Hannay)

MARKHAM
1. Arthur — 1887-1901
2. Bertha — 1866-1927
3. Clara Bertha — Feb. 6, 1892-Mar. 18, 1960
4. Clark L. — 1829-1911
5. Fred Leslie — June 27, 1895-Feb. 26, 1955
6. Leslie C. — 1865-1931

MARTIN
1. Emma — 1897-1975
   (see George E. Brabon)

MASHTARE

1. Christopher E.   Oct. 29, 1966-Mar. 28, 1967   son of Marshall & Roberta Mashtare

2. Earl L.   1914-1964
    Fannie M.   1915-
3. Mary   1887-1945
    (see James J. Meacham)

MAXAM

1. Ada M.   died Dec. 25, 1892   age 25 yrs.   wife of F. M. Hewitt
    (see-Ada M. Hewitt)
2. Marshall   1832-
    Amarilla Parks   1843--1904   his wife
3. Myrtle   1876-1904
    (see Howard McNeil)

MC CALLUM

1. John   1877-1906

MC GARVEY

1. Kenneth G.   Mar. 13, 1924-Oct. 7, 1969   N.Y. Tec 5 920 TECH SVC Unit WW II

MC GOVERN
1. Richard   1835-1890
   Aliza Lambert   1845-   his wife

MC KENNON
1. Isabelle Douglas McKennon 1860-1945
   James M. McKennon   1859-1934
   (see Fraser-McKennon)

MC LANE
1. Robert R.   1858-1933
   Alice C.   1869-1919

MC NEIL
1. Sr.   1826-
   Nancy R.   1832-1901   his wife
2. Anna   1884-19
   (see-Archie A. Niles)
3. Eva   1884-1927
   (see Newton Parks)

4. Eva	1884-1927	wife of Newton Parks
5. Frederick D.	1858–	
Elizabeth	1864-1918	his wife
Alane	1890-1897	
Guy H.	1880-1918	
6. George W.	1857-1940	father
Rose Fuller	1856-1925	his wife
		mother
7. Howard	1875-1955	
Myrtle Maxam	1876-1904	his wife
8. Laura C.	died Oct. 21, 1907	age 52 yrs.
John W.	died May 9, 1929	age 77 yrs.
Ernest LaBounty	1879-1957	
Carol McNeil	1878-1943	his wife
Elwin	1904-	
Esther Pulling	1903-1980	his wife
9. Effie R. Johnson	1874-1909	wife of W. F. McNeil
Justin W.	1903-1918	
Walter F.	1875-1954	
footstones—mother-Justin-father		
10. Madge Hollister McNeil	1906-1952	
11. Martha	1881-1909	dau. of Ira &
12. Oscar	Mar. 7, 1883-June 14, 1955	

Martha J. Lang	Oct. 11, 1887-	his wife
13. William D.	1878-1945	
Katherine A.	1876-1955	
Howard C.	1899-1904	

MEACHAM

1. Henry	died Sept. 12, 1893	age 13 yrs. 3 mos. son of J. & C. Meacham
2. James J.	1886-1944	
Mary Mashtare	1887-1945	his wife
3. John	Oct. 8, 1853-Oct. 12, 1906	age 48 yrs.
4. Lena M.	1917-1975	
(see-Bernard W. Rivers)		

MENZIES
1. William A.   born in Scotland Nov. 6, 1862
drowned in St. Regis Falls River—Apr. 30, 1885

MERDICK
1. Gordon E.   1886-1972   (two other blank stones)

MERRILL
1. Lillian 1917
(see-Efard S. Cummings)

MILLER
1. Mary   1884-1919   wife of M. A. Conger
James M.   1841-1928   father
Ann J. Hoy   1848-1928   his wife   mother
Emma   1871-1906   wife of J. H. Thompson
Hubert H.   1902-1907
Wilbert Jr.   1930-
Hubbard   1866-1935   father
Jennie his wife   1869-1959   mother
Clara Palmer   1895-1975   his wife   mother
Wilbert Conger   1895-1977   father
2. Fred Miller   May 5, 1900-Sept. 6, 1963   (metal plaque)

MILLIS
1. Hattie J.   1876-1929   wife of Otis V. Millis
2. Mary J. 1870
   (see Silenous Kelley)
3. William 1849-1912
   Malinda   1848-   his wife

MOSIER
1. Catherine   1889-1966
2. Hershel J.   1884-1945
3. Luella   1899-1966
4. Margaret O.   1851-1936
5. Timothy   1895-1974

MOTT
1. Mary   1864-1953
   (see George A. Weller)

MULHOLLAND
1. Frank   1887-1962
   Gladys M.   1895-   his wife
   Mary   1923-1923   dau.
2. Lominda   1861-1929   (metal plaque)

MURRY
  1. George 1860-1927

MUSHTARE
  1. Delia   1931
     (see Darwin A. Kelley)
  2. Ruth Winkle Mushtare   9-20-1909/4-17-1980   mother

MYERS
  1. Eunice   1910-1959   dau.
     (see B. A. Biggers)

NELSON
  1. Harry B.   1882-1952
     Pearl Sabins   1895-   his wife
     Kathryn N.   1922-1957   dau.

NILES
  1. Archie A.   1880-1950
     Anna McNeil   1884-19   his wife

NORTON
  1. Daniel   died Aug. 24, 1903   age 78 yrs.

Anna   died Mar. 27, 1896   age 74 yrs.   wife of Daniel
Ambrose J.   Oct. 19, 1851-May 19, 1920

O'DONNELL
1. Sadie B. Parka O'Donnell   1895-1949

OLMSTEAD
1. Elizabeth   1870-1957
   (see Bert E. Blade)

O'NEIL
1. Annie T.   1847-1901
   (see W. B. Bugbee)
2. Edith C.   1874-1934   wife of A. MacDonald
   Henry Coward 1876-1909   his wife
   footstone--Ophelia Young   1853-1932

ORTON
1. Ida   died Apr. 27, 1894   age 42 yrs.   wife of G.G. Orton
2. Jennie 1881-1969
   (see Fred A. Johnson)

ST. REGIS FALLS CEMETERIES • 259

PAGE
1. Dan — 1900-1944
2. Frederick A. — Jan. 18, 1894-Dec. 20, 1964 — N.Y. Pvt. Co. C 328 Inf. Reg. WW I PH

PALMER
1. Azro I.J. — 1870-1943
   Hattie — 1873-1960 — his wife
   Homer — 1897-1935
2. Clara — 1895-1975 — wife of Wilbert Conger
   (see MILLER-CONGER)
3. Douglas — 1899-1973
   Lillian — 1907-1983
4. Elijiah A. — died Nov. 9, 1901 — age 77 yrs.
   Harriet A. — died May 28, 1900 — age 71 yrs. 6 mo. 22 da. wife of Elijiah A. Palmer

   Agusta A. — 1856-1911 — wife of Alfred Palmer
5. Ellen A. — died Sept. 18, 1921 — age 69 yrs.
   (see John A. Ramsdell)
6. Elva — 1893-1967
   (see Jesse A. Hull)
7. Fred — 1860-1935
   Sadie — 1873-1920
8. Hatty LaBounty Palmer — 1878-1934

Ovett Palmer	1898-1939	Corp. Co. A 14th N.Y.H. Art.
9. Henry S.	1833-1905	his wife
Nancy M.	1842-	married Feb. 12, 1918
10. Hoyt A.	1896-1976	
Clara Weller	1894-	dau. of Casper & Beatrice Palmer
11. Linda Eva	1943-1943	age 61 yrs.
12. Mary A.	died Apr. 25, 1917	
(see Danny G. Parks)		
13. Milton H.	1875-1933	
14. Shirley	1884-1951	(see-Henry H. Gibbs)
15. Vernon H.	1882-1974	
Lois Gibbs	1882-1960	his wife

PARIS

1. Alpha	died June 19, 1880	age 1 yr. 9 mos.
		dau. of Ira & Elizabeth Parks
2. Amarilla	1843-1904	
(see-Marshall Maxam)		
3. Claude F.	1886-1970	
Eva Wood	1894-1971	his wife
4. Daniel	1905-1964	
George D.	1863-1924	father

Annice	1868-1941	his wife	mother
5. Danny G.	died June 1, 1897	age 17 yrs. 3 mos.	
footstone—DANA			
Mary A. Palmer	died Apr. 25, 1917	age 61 yrs.	his wife
William	died Jan. 3, 1895	age 38 yrs.	
6. David	1816-1899	father	
Lucinda Cook	1821-1899	mother	
7. Ethel L.	Aug. 20, 1902-Feb. 14, 1903		
(see-Isaac Farr)			
8. Eva McNeil	1884-1927	wife of Newton Parks	
9. Eva McNeil Parks			
(see-Eva McNeil)			
10. Frank	1859-1919		
Irene his wife	1864-1937		
11. Howard D.	1879-1949		
footstones—			
MOTHER	1850-1931		
FATHER	1844-1920		
12. Ira	1844-1918		
Elizabeth M.	1858-1934	his wife	
13. Laurence	died June 9, 1905	age 2 yrs. 8 mos.	
		son of N.C. & E.R. Parks	
14. Lenna	1897-1972		

	(see-Frank L. Taylor)		
15. Leo S.		Aug. 17, 1890-Sept. 14, 1968	N.Y. Cpl. 548 Co. MTC WW I
16. Marjory H.		1888-1933	
17. Martha		1881-1909	dau. of Ira & Elizabeth Parks
	(see-Martha McNeil)		
18. Mary H. Davidson		1876-1915	wife of Bert T. Parks
19. Rev. R.		Apr. 10, 1818-Dec. 8, 1901	
Amanda Dow		Dec. 16, 1812-Mar. 28, 1896	his wife
20. Sadie B.		1895-1949	
	(see-Sadie O'Donnell)		
21. Vernon D.		May 10, 1893-Oct. 6, 1959	N.Y. PFC Quarter Master Corps.
22. Vernon D.		1893-1959	
Mary A. Hannay		1899-1968	his wife
23. children of Vernon & Mary Parks			
Irene M.		1921-1934	
V. Leo		1923-1927	
Harry K.		1925-1927	

PATRAW

1. Deforest C.		1906-	
Dorothy Howe		1912-	his wife

2. Randy W.   Feb. 22, 1965   our baby

PECK
1. Franklin O.   1893-1932   father
   Ada Peck Whitcomb   1894-1966   mother
2. Norman H.   1870-1956
   Loretta his wife   1870-1954
   Wilbur E.   1899-1911   their son
3. Otis W.   died Feb. 2, 1909   age 66 yrs.   Co. F 92 Reg. N.Y.VOL.
   Warren   1874-1954
   Herbert   1899-1912
   Elvira   1843-1924

PERIA
1. Charles G.   1888-1961

PHILLIPS
1. Alta May   May 3, 1883-Aug. 10, 1889   dau. of M. M. & A. B. Phillips
2. George M.   1877-1926
   Pearl E.   1877-1905
   Lena W.   1888-1967
   Charles M.   1874-1959
   Eliza L.   1876-1945

Rosaltha A.	1847-1932		
James M.	1839-1899		
3. Merton E.	1890-		
Beatrice M.	1893(4)-1939		
4. Myron M.	1851-1925	father	
Annabel	1861-1940	mother	

PHIPPS

1. John	died Jan. 26, 1908	age 75 yrs.	Priv. Co. 10 Reg. N.Y. Ca.
2. John	1832-1908		
Jane E.	1833-1915		

PIERCE

1. Henry M.	died June 8, 1902	age 57 yrs. 10 mos. 5 da.	Co. D 11 Reg. N.Y. Cal. Vol.
		(footstone & "Green" metal marker)	
Annis M.	1854-1939		
Fannie W.	1887-1915		

PLOOF

1. Adam	1882-1942
Lottie	1887-1962
2. Evelyn	1917-

(see Harold E. LaBounty)
3. Joyce 1923-
(see Wayne R. Cheney)

POTTER
1. Henry T. 1868-1938
   Bernice A. 1878-1942 his wife
   William H. 1907-1909 their son

PROSPER-TALBOT
1. Mary Talbot 1877-1951
   Madge H. 1900-1933
   Irving M. 1869-1941 father

PULLING
1. Esther 1903-1980 wife of Elwin laBounty
   (see John McNeil)

PRENTICE
1. George F. 1878-1956
   Minnie B. 1887-1929
2. Henry and Susan
   Harley and Mildred

3. Willis
   (see Isaac Farr)

QUICK
1. William   Oct. 29, 1904-Apr. 5, 1906

RACE
1. Mary J.   died Oct. 13, 1920   age 39 yrs.
   (see John C. Gibbs)

RADLOFF
1. Charles   1865-1939
   Elizabeth   1873-1957
2. Charles E.   1865-1939
3. Rosella   1895-1980
   (see Lester L. Ghrist)

RAFTER
1. George Alex   Apr. 15, 1895-Sept. 8, 1958   N.Y. PFC Co. G 59 Pioneer Inf. WW I
2. Mary Rafter St.Dennis   1871-1924
   Allen   died 1917   (funeral metal marker)

Jan. 29, 1830-June 17, 1910   age 80 yrs. 4 mos. 19 days

RAMSDELL

1. Fred S. — 1867-1947
   Elizabeth Fleming — 1879-1960 — his wife
   infant son — July 1908
   Melvin
   Francis
2. John A. — died May 12, 1914 — age 63 yrs.
   Ellen A. Palmer — died Sept. 18, 1921 — age 69 yrs.
   Millie E. — died May 21, 1893 — age 20 yrs.
   dau. of J. A. & E. A. Ramsdell
3. Elizabeth Shaw — 1870-1952 — his wife
   Melvin Blanchard — 1869-1949
4. Rev. Nelson — May 19, 1833-Dec. 18, 1917
   Eliza C. Smith — May 6, 1829-Aug. 31, 1916 — his wife

RAYMO

1. Hugh — 1859-
   Sarah Bandy — 1858-1901 — his wife
   their children—
   Alice age — 8 mos.
   Luella — age 2 wks.

RAYMOND
  1. Gertrude E. Bugbee Raymond   1842-1893   wife of L. A. Raymond
     (see-Gertrude E. Bugbee)
  2. Nelson F.   1871-1965
     Gertrude S.   1873-1966
     Velma L.   1905-1906

REYNOLDS
  1. Margaret   1906-   wife of Gordon Hannay Jr.
     (see Gordon Hannay)

RHOADS
  1. Margaret   died Dec. 12, 1890   age 48 yrs.
     wife of Charles H. Rhoads

RHODES
  1. Fred R.   1885-1959
     Coral   1887-   his wife
     Charles   1905-1921   their son

RICHARDS
  1. Elmer
     Mildred

RIVERS

1. Bernard W.	1914-	
Lena M. Meacham	1917-1975	married Oct. 21, 1939
2. Melanie S.	Mar. 24, 1971-Mar. 25, 1971	dau. of Lawrence & Jeane Rivers
3. David	1845-1922	
Amelia his wife	1862-1921	
footstones—		
Theodore	died Mar. 18, 1887	age 3 yrs. 11 mos.
son of D. & A. Rivers		
4. Nora	1877-1938	
(see Bert Camp)		
5. William	1889-1965	father
Delia	1875-1954	mother
Ethel	1910-	dau.

ROCKHILL

1. Floyd C.	1903-1976	
Edna Johnston	1906-1976	
2. William	1868-1938	
Marcia Gordon	1873-1961	his wife

ROGGENBAMP
1. see Smith-Roggenkamp-Wacker

ROLLINS
1. Rhoda A.   1879-1964
(see George D. Smith)

ROSS
1. John G.   died Feb. 16, 1901   age 76 yrs. Co. F 142 Reg. N.Y.V.

2. W. W.   1850-
Emma   1854-   his wife
Anna M.   1882-1910

ROWELL
1. Percival L.   Mar. 19, 1892-Jan. 30, 1969   N.Y. QM Sgt. U.S. Army WW I
Lynn Avon   1889-1927
Jennie L.   1864-1944
Mark A.   1864-1923
Grace B. Lennon   1877-1948

RUSTERHOLTZ
1. Halcyon L.   1892-1951   wife of J. H. Rusterholtz
   (see John LaPoint)

RYAN
1. Catherine "Kitty"   1926-
   (see Norbert G. Howe)

SABIN
1. Millard F.   1852-1913
   Sarah J. Harvey   1857-   his wife
   Verona   1887-1924

SABINS
1. Ella M.   1864-1938
2. Pearl   1895-
   (see Harry B. Nelson)

SAMPSON
1. Mother-Monroe-Willie-Jerrie

SAWYER
- 1. Charlotte — 1875-1959 (funeral home marker)
- 2. Leon J. — 1887-1942 (funeral home marker)
-    Milo F. — 1898-1962 (funeral home marker)
- 3. Richard — 1872-1918
- 4. Richard — 1872-1918
-    C.H. LaBounty — 1875-1959
- 5. Stanley J. — 1907-1959

SCHARF
- 1. Vern A. — Aug. 10, 1905-Sept. 25, 1975   son   Pvt. U.S. Army WW I
-    Effie L. — 1876-1955   mother

SCHENK
- 1. William — 1893-1957
-    Anna E. — 1898-

SHAMPINE
- 1. Charles — died Dec. 13, 1913   age 67 yrs.   Co. C 6 Reg. N.Y.V.

SHAMPO
- 1. Ruby E. dau. — 1923-

Bernice C.	1906-1967	mother
John S.	1901-	father

SHARPE
1. Lottie M. 1878-19
   (see Clayton C. Southworth)

SHAW
1. Elizabeth 1870-1952
   (see Melvin Blanchard Ramsdell)

SHONYO
1. Harold M. 1915-1974

SINDO
1. Fred 1881-1946
   Grace 1885-1919   his wife
   (see Charles Griffin)

SLATTERY
1. Rosemond F. 1904-
   (see Smith-Hughes-Slattery)

SMITH-HUGHES-SLATTERY

1. John Thompson   1861-1888
   Nellie D. Smith   1897-1966
   Elaine S. Hughes   1919-
   Rosemond F. Slattery 1904-

SMITH-ROGGENKAMP-WACKER

1. John Wacker   1873-1949
   Katherine   1868-1946   his wife
   Lena C.   1894-1934
   Johnny   1916-1929
   (SMITH side)
   Willaim J.

SMITH

1. Charles P.   1874-
   Grace M.   1880-1910   his wife
   Eva A.   1886-   his wife
2. Eliza C.   May 6, 1829-Aug. 31, 1916
   (see Rev. Nelson Ramsdell)
3. Frank A.   1876-
   Harriet M.   1872-1915   his wife
   baby dau. of F. A. & H. M. Smith   1904-1904
   Lucy H.   1908-1913   dau. of F. A. & H. M. Smith

```
 4. Fred N.                1880-
    Emma L.                1883-1946
 5. George D.               1869-1965
    Rhoda A. Rollins        1879-1964
 6. Joseph P.               died Dec. 2, 1930    age 85 yrs.
    Lucy Barnes             died Oct. 17, 1920   age 72 yrs.   his wife
    footstones—grandmother-mother-father
 7. Nellie D.               1897-1966
    (see Smith-Hughes-Slattery)
 8. Thomas B.               1890-1961
    Gertrude                1880-1957                          his wife
 9. Wendell L.              Jan. 14, 1920-                     husband
    Nelda Young             July 14, 1924-Sept. 1, 1969        wife
10. William J.              1897-1931                          US Navy
```

SNELL

```
 1. Anna Snell Dubuque      Sept. 15, 1913-Nov. 11, 1972
    (see Charles N. Dubuque)
```

SNYDER

```
 1. Perry                   1865-1942
    Iva Leffler             1871-1927                          his wife
    William J.              1900-1921
```

SOCHIA

1. Carrie   1872-1942   wife of Frank Sochia
   (see Orin H. Cook)
2. Harold M.   1914-1918
   Almeda L.   1881-1928
3. infant dau. of B. & J. Sochia
4. James E.   1923-1972   his wife
   Barbara Berdrow   1928-

SOETEMON

1. Peter W. Sr.   June 15, 1867-Oct. 20, 1950   N.Y. 1st Sgt. Co. B
   203 N.Y. Inf.
   Spanish-American War

SOMERS

1. Benjamin C.   1841-1920
   Lylias J.   1845-1928   his wife
   footstones—Mary—baby
2. G. Arba   1845-1917   Co. F 142 Reg. N.Y.V.
   Addle J.   died Oct. 14, 1928   mother
   Ora A.   dau.
   Eugene   1874-1894

SOUTHWORTH

1. Clayton C.   1868-1941
   Lottie M. Sharpe   1878-19_   his wife
2. Lena M.   died Oct. 24, 1885   age 7 mos. 4 days
   dau. of O. S. & M. M. C. Southworth
3. O. S.   1839-1910
   Martha M. Carpenter   his wife

ST. DENNIS

1. Mary Rafter   1871-1924
   (see Mary Rafter)

STEWART

1. Noble   1880-1950   (metal marker)

STINEBOUR

1. Annie   1880-
   (see Malcolm Tweed)

STONE

1. infant son of E. L. & F. E. Stone   died July 15, 1893
2. Joseph   died July 25, 1899   age 78 yrs.   Co. K 17 Reg. Vt. Vol.
3. Mary   died Dec. 14, 1887   age 25 yrs.   wife of ____ Stone

4. Willie   died Dec. 21, 1900   age 4 yrs. 10 mos
   son of J. & A. Stone

STORY
1. Jessie M.   1886-
   (see- George V. Howe)

SUMMERS
1. Cecil H.   1899-
   Eliza B.   1904-   his wife

TALBOT
1. Mary   1877-1951
   (see Prosper-Talbot)

TAYLOR
1. Deforest G.   1874-1910
   Alma M.   1875-1945
2. Frank L.   Mar. 29, 1897-Nov. 20, 1959   his wife   N.Y. PFC 320 Bakery Co.
                                                                                             QMC WW I
3. Frank L.   1897-1959
   Lenna Parks his wife   1897-1972

THOMAS
1. Addle   died Dec. 9, 1887   age 34 yrs. 10 mos.
   wife of Wilbur Thomas
2. Matthias E.   died May 4, 1907   age 67 yrs.   Co. D 7 Reg. N.Y.H. Artl.
3. Rhoda A.   1870-1958
   (see William H. Flyles)

THOMPSON
1. Emma Miller Thompson   1871-1906   wife of J.H. Thompson
   (see Miller-Conger)
2. John   1861-1888
   (see Smith-Hughes-Slattery)

TOWER
1. Ambrose   1825-1890
   Elizabeth   1832-1925   his wife
   Carrie   1863-1917
   Sarah E.   1865-1949
   Horace J.   1869-1904

TRIM
1. Fay H.   1876-1945
   Rose M. Gravelle   1883-1951   his wife

(also buried here—3 infant daus. of Gerald and Marie Trim)
2. Frank   1855-1931
   Carrie A.   1858-1936   his wife
3. William R.   1881-1962
   Lulia L.   1886-   his wife
   Donald L.   1909-1909

TROTTER
1. Ira   1900-
   Mildred M.   1913-1963

TRUDEAU
1. Henry F.   1893-1952
   Chloe Leavenworth   1894-   his wife

TURNER
1. Orril C.   1877-1946
   (see Myrton W. Butler)

TWEED
1. Malcolm   1868-1954
   Annie Stinebour   1880-

VANSCHAICK
1. Charles L.   1870-1943

WACKER
1. John   1873-1949
   (see Smith-Roggenkamp-Wacker)

WADE
1. Myrtle Wade Dora   1886-1956
   (see Myrtle Dora)

WAGNER
1. Elmer R. "Ed"   1910-
   Alice Dimick   1923-   his wife
2. Robert E.   1875-1958

WAIT
1. Myron A.   1900-1971
   Archie   1902-1926
   Mary E.   1861-1932
   Almon A.   1863-1934
2. Rolly R.   1867-
   Nina M.   1869-   his wife

Hattie	1890-1891	
Bessie R. Gage	1888-1915	

WALKER
1. Florence L.	1914-1936	dau. of Rev. & Mrs. A. D. Walker
2. Hiram	died Mar. 30, 1906	age 63 yrs.
Evaline	died Sept. 21, 1904	his wife age 56 yrs.

WARDNER
1. L. M. Wardner M.D.	died Jan. 12, 1896	age 54 yrs. Co. C 1 Vt. Cav. Vol.
footstones—		
mother	1853-1899	
father	1842-1896	
infant	1906-	
Laurens, A.	1878-1937	
Joseph E.	1878-1948	wife of J. E. Wardner

WARDS
1. William E.	died Jan. 29, 1898	age 79 yrs. Co. A 142 Reg. N.Y.V.

WEBB
1. J. W.		
Viola M.	1858-1895	his wife

footstones—
Marcurite
Viola M.

WELLER
1. Arthur A. 1882-1947
2. Charles 1849-1926
   Mary A. Hartley 1862-1932 his wife
3. Clara 1894-
   (see Hoyt A. Palmer)
4. George A. 1854-1923
   Mary Mott 1864-1953 his wife
   Earl N. 1890-1949
   Erma E. 1888-1930
   Elmer E. 1921
5. Lonnie 1885-1893 (near Charles Weller)

WESTURN
1. Vera 1919-
   (see Ralph T. Butler)

WHITCOMB
1. Ida Peck 1894-1966

(see Frank O. Peck)
2. Roy J.   1883-1941   (metal plaque)

WHITE
1. Elects, M.   1871-1951
   (see John E. LaCroix)
2. Frank L.   1889-1963
   Gladys W.   1892-

WILBUR
1. Glen H.   died Feb. 23, 1884   age 5 mos 25 days
   son of C. H. & C. M. Wilbur

WILKINS
1. Roy L.   Apr. 10, 1894-Oct. 18, 1944   N.Y. Pvt. 105 Inf. 27 Div.
   Dorothy   1908-1928
   wife of R. L. Wilkins

WILLIAMS
1. Dorothy   1904-
   (see Wilbur H. Bailey)

ST. REGIS FALLS CEMETERIES • 285

WILSON
1. Orin L.   1856-1925
   Lucina   1863-1932   his wife

WINKLE
1. Ruth   9-20-1909/4-17-1980
   (see Ruth Mushtare)

WINTERS
1. Clyde & Carmine
2. Flossie Winters Dubuque   Dec. 10, 1892-Feb. 10, 1935
   (see Charles N. Dubuque)
3. Forest E.   1886-1959   children of Carl & Effie Winters
   Glencie L.   1891-1971
   Helen S.   1923-1943
   Wilta W.   1918-
   Sandra J.   1942
   Clarence Hawkins   1892-1930   husband
4. Beulah   1866-1957   wife of John Durr
   Eliza A.   1860-1943   mother
   Henry G.   1884-1964   father
   Carl O.
   Caroline   1920-

5. Lan	1865-1915	
Mattie	1868-1934	his wife
6. Laura B.	1880-1956	
(see Jesse W. Cronk)		
7. Walter L.	Aug. 28, 1913-Apr. 28, 1972	N.Y. Cpl. Hq. & SVC Co. 85 Inf. WW II BSM

WOOD

1. Agatha	1918-	
(see Harry D. Hollister)		
2. Eva	1894-1971	
(see Claude F. Parks)		

WOODBURY-WILSON

1. Edgar A.	1845-1925	footstone
Ethan A.	1860-1911	footstone
Eva	1889-1894	dau. of F. F. Galan
(footstone near above stones)		

YOUNG

1. Arthur Y.	died Feb. 15, 1968	age 9 mos. 20 days
2. Bernice B.	Sept. 24, 1887-Jan. 24, 1971	dau.
3. Charles H.	Nov. 26, 1857-Sept. 15, 1940	father
4. Frank S.	Jan. 29, 1869-Aug. 31, 1945	husband

Jane C.	July 13, 1899- Nov. 1983		wife
5. James H.	1820-1910		
Caroline E.	1832-1909		his wife
footstones—			
Ophelia	1853-1932		his wife
(next to William T. O'Neil stone)			
6. Janet	died Aug. 30, 1896		8 wks.
Jamie	died May 5, 1895		age 6 wks.
children of C. H. & O. C. Young			
7. Morris	1867-1925		
8. Nelda Young Smith	July 14, 1924-Sept. 1, 1969		wife
Wendell L. Smith	Jan. 14, 1920-		husband
9. Ophelia	1853-1932		
(see O'Neil-MacDonald)			
10. Orpha L.	Jan. 11, 1860-Feb. 11, 1938		mother

ST. ANN'S CEMETERY, ST. REGIS FALLS

indexed August 1980

ALDRICH
1. Allene M.   died Sept. 16, 1899   age 10 mos. 20 days
 dau. of E. S. & J. M. Aldrich

ANTONIO
1. Daniel   1881-1954
 Jennie   1879-1926   his wife
 Edward   Oct. 10, 1908 (side of stone)   their son
 May Woods Cucinotta   1883-1966
 Gussippe Cucinotta   1898-1950   (other side of stone)

ARCADI
1. Shirley Garro Arcadi   1944-1973   dau.

ARNO
1. George A.   1882-1966
 Myrtle E.   1891-
2. Stanley L.   1930-
 Mary Simpson   1937-1973   his wife

ARQUETT
1. Mary J. — 1892-1910 — wife of Arthur Arquett

BAGNATO
1. James Andro — May 23, 1933-Dec. 27, 1937

BAILEY
1. Fred J. — 1890-
   Nora E. Crowley — 1883-1945 — his wife

BAKER
1. Archie — died Feb. 6, 1899 — age 9 yrs.
   George — died Feb. 25, 1899 — age 3 yrs.
   children of A. &. M. Baker
2. Donald C. — 1915-
   Marie Doherty — 1911-1972
3. Henry J. — 1892-1975
   Fannie R. Smith — 1896-1948 — his wife
4. Henry J. — Dec. 27, 1892-Feb. 27, 1975 — PVT. U.S. Army WW I

BARCOMB
1. Virginia — 1889-1975 — mother
   (footstone to Julius A. Susice)

BARNES
1. Wayne D.   1894-1968
    Edna Gokey   1904-1968
    footstones
    Frank   1866-1921
    Laura H.   1873-1949
2. Wayne D. Apr. 5, 1894-July 18, 1968

BARRETT
1. (no name)   Sept. 17, 1932-June 24, 1974   CPL U.S. Army

BAITER
1. Frances D.   Oct. 19, 1906-Aug. 19, 1979   mother of William D. Baxter
2. William A.   Dec. 30, 1897-Oct. 25, 1970

BEAN
1. Harvey F.   June 23, 1894-Dec. 28, 1970   N.Y. PVT Co. H 59 Pioneer Inf. WW I

2. Peter   1858-1930
    Margaret   1861-1941

3. Rosanna   1901-

(see George P. Caskinette)
4. Rosella 1896-
(see Richard H. Caskinette)

BEGOR
1. Frank 1849-1896
   Exeriene LaBombard 1860-1910

BENNETT
1. Laura 1882-1968
   (footstone to the left of above stone)
   Louis A. 1884-1949 brother

BESAW
1. Jane 1874-1905
   (see Benjamin Guyett)

BESSET
1. Julia 1819-1909

BEYETTE
1. Mayne D. 1890-1974
   (see Fred W. LeMieux)

BISHOP
1. Charles   May 24, 1907-
   Ida Susice   Dec. 20, 1907   his wife

BLADE
1. Earldean   1918-
   (see Albert J. Farmer)

BOUCHARD
1. Louis   1848-
   Sophie   1850-1906   his wife
2. Louis W.   July 17, 1874-Nov. 20, 1916   (on side of stone)
   Louis W.   1874-1916
   Anna   1878-1964   his wife
   Francis N.   1914-1980

BOUCHER
1. Joseph S.   1839-1922   father
   Mary S.   1869-1931   sister
   Odena E.   4-24-1877—11-7-1899
   William Joseph   8-30-1878—3-26-1898
2. Stella M.   1904-1977

BOURDAGE
1. Frank X. 1905-1972
   Doris M. Susice 1916- his wife

BOYCE
1. Ernest J. Sr. Aug. 9, 1943-Sept. 12, 1971

BRAATZ
1. Florence Ploof Braatz 1906-1973

BRISBOIS
1. Rose 1888- wife of Joseph W. Bushey
   (see Bushey—Wilcox)

BROOKS
1. Rose 1870-1948
   (see Jerry Debien)

BROWN
1. DeEtta 1906-
   (see Joseph F. Clookey)
2. Freddie 1895 age 1 mo.
   Ralph 1899 age 6 mos.

3. John	1827-1901		
Julie	1844-1910	his wife	

BURDO

1. Harold A.			
Anne Mayville		husband	
2. Harold Albert	Feb. 23, 1925-Nov. 21, 1970	wife	N.Y. PFC Co. C 155 Engr. CBT BN WW II

BURNETT

1. Ethel	1906-1933		dau.
(see Joseph G. Dora)			
2. Joseph F.	1880-1967		
Hattie LaCombe	1881-1947	his wife	

BUSHEY

1. Addie	1872-1963		
(see Eugene Goodrow)			
2. David	died Nay 1, 1907		age 60 yrs.
3. Jennie	1879-1967		
(see Amos Forkey)			
4. John	1870-		
Ellie	1872-1918	his wife	

5. Wallace A.　　　　　　　　Aug. 19, 1845-Mar. 7, 1907

BUSHEY-WILCOX
1. Joseph W. Bushey　　　1887-1976　　father
   Rose Brisbois　　　　　1888-　　　　mother
   Louise B.　　　　　　　1928-　　　　dau.
   Grant J. Wilcox　　　　1930-　　　　husband　　married Nov. 18, 1912

BUTIN
1. Philanda　　　　　　　　1848-1911
   (see Moses Richards)

BUTLER
1. Catherine J. Daly　　　1854-1908　　his wife
   George H.　　　　　　　1854-1933

CARDINAL
1. Amelia　　　　　　　　died Aug. 2, 1892　age 15 mos.
2. Laura　　　　　　　　　1838-1918　　wife

CARON
1. Ernest L.　　　　　　　Nov. 5, 1914-Nov. 11, 1974 Cpl. U.S. Army

CASCANETTE
1. Dorothy E.   1903-1964   married-June 6, 1946
   Floyd J.   1912-
2. Irene   1915-1942   wife of Raymond Holmes
3. Joseph G.   1884-1949

CASKINETTE
1. Daniel   died June 11, 1906   age 21 yrs.
2. Edward H.   1899-
   Mary Deon   1908-   his wife
3. Eva M.   June 19, 1929-June 11, 1935
4. George P.   1899-1970
   Rosanna Bean   1901-   his wife
5. Gilbert   1851-1945
   Mary   1865-1957
6. Joseph H.   1893-1961   father
   E. Frances   1910-   mother
   Eva M.   1929-1935   dau.
7. Maureen   1933-1967
   (see Bernard M. Richards)
8. Richard H.   1890-1945   married 1913
   Rosella Bean   1896

CASKINETT
1. Richard died   Apr. 21, 1909   age 62 yrs.   Priv. N.Y.S.

CATURA
1. Archie C.   1894-1949
    Mabel LaVoy   1896-1974   his wife
    Glenford A.   1918-1976
    Millie Richard   1914-   his wife
2. Fred   1856-1934
3. Gloria   1935-1959
    (see Carroll Hayle)
4. Lewis   1845-1899
    Ellan Richards   1845-19–   his wife
    Milent   1889-1906   son
    footstones—
    Bernice   1911-
    Edna   1904-1959

CENTER
1. Louisa   1846-1931
    Julia   1814-1909
    (see Thomas Dubuque)

298 • WATER OVER THE FALLS

CHENEZ ??? (French)
1. Desire — 1892 — dye de 7 seinaines (almost impossible to read)
2. Helene — decede la 20 Mai 1891 — agie de 3 ans 10 mois
   Joseph A. B. — decade la 23 Mars 1892 — age de 4 mois 4 jours
   enfants de Desire Chenez ??

CHAGNON
1. Joseph — 1869-1957
   Adaline — 1874-1908 — wife of J. C. Chagnon

CHESBROUGH
1. Flora G. Farmer — 1909-1943 — wife of Roy Chesbrough
   Richard Farmer — 1930-1936 — their son

CHRISTIAN
1. Fred — 1881-
   Alzina — 1884-1957
2. Fabian E. — 1886-1956
   Sadie A. — 1893-1956
3. Loyd L. — died Sept. 16, 1922 — age 1 yr. 6 mos.
   son of F. E. & S.A. Christian
4. William — 1892-1970

ST. REGIS FALLS CEMETERIES • 299

Eva	1895-1976	his wife	
5. William R.	Apr. 21, 1892-Jan. 28, 1970		N.Y. PVT 75 Inf. Reg. WW I

CLEMENT
1. Lewis   1 yr. 10 mos. (no dates)
    Charley   2 mos.
    sons of A. & A. Clement
2. Rose   1888-1963   (metal plaque)

CLEMENTS
1. Joseph   1861-1924   father
    Mary   1865-1941   mother

CLOOKEY
1. Joseph F.   1902-1954
    DeEtta Brown   1906-   his wife
2. Margaret   1924-1980
    (see Raymond Holmes)

COLLETTE
1. Edward J. Jr.   1940-1960
    Nola M.   1920-
    Edward   1915-

CONKLIN-FOURNIER
1. Roy Leonard Fournier 1913-1956 N.Y. MM3 USNR WW II
   (dates on separate footstone)
   Mary A. 1891-1943
   Bernice M. Fournier
   Bessie A. Fournier

COURCEILE
1. Eugenie 1876-1976 mother
   (see PROULX-ROKAHR)

COURTNEY
1. John T. Oct. 28, 1904-May 29, 1967 N.Y. M. Sgt. Scv. Co.
   318 infantry WW II

COX
1. Wendell F. 1918-
   Winifred Story 1918- his wife

CRAMER
1. Jennie 1906-
   (see Bert Susice)

CROSS
1. Florence T.   died Jan. 16, 1899   age 6 yrs. 10 mos. 11 days

CROWLEY
1. Nora E.   1883-1945
   (see Fred J. Bailey)

CUCINOTTA
1. May Woods Cucinotta   1883-1966
   Gussippe   1898-1950
   (see Daniel Antonio)

CUTURIA
1. Joseph   1842-1899   Co. E 8 Reg. Vt. Vet. Vol.
   Mary Ploof   1846-1927   his wife
   Seymore   1866-1886   son

DAEHLER
1. Elsie   1896-1973   wife of Harry J. Paradise

DALAIRE
1. David J.   1878-1938
   Violet Perry   1878-1929   wife of David Dalaire

Valina Raymo	1882-1914	wife of David Dalaire
2. Peter J.	1876—1931	brother
George J.	1874-'938	brother
David	1849-1931	father
Florestine	1854-1902	mother

DALLAIRE
1. Eilenne 1827-1890
2. Marie 1818-1888

DALY
1. Catherine J. 1854-1908
(see George H. Butler)

DANCOUSE
1. Frank X. 1868-
Maggie 1867- his wife
Mable 1893-1900

DASHNAW
1. Emma 1891-1942 sister
(see Joseph G. Dora)

DAVIGNON
  1. Amedee   died Aug. 29, 1910   age 49 yrs.
     Mary   died June 1, 1928   age 66 yrs.   his wife

DAWSON
  1. Robert   May 2, 1926-July 24, 1926

DEBIEN
  1. Francis   died May 18, 1896   age 60 yrs. Co. I 118 Reg. N.Y.I. Vol.

  2. Jerry   1862-1933
     Rose Brooks   1870-1948   his wife
     Frederick   1890-1953
  3. Lydia   1889-1962   wife of Frank LaVoy
     (footstone to LaVoy)

DEBUQUE
  1. Joseph T.   1897-1959
     Rose M.   1903-
     Evelyn   1934(24)-1950
     Thomas J.   1877-1955
     Flenda R. 1876-
     (all footstones)   IN LOVING MEMORY

DECARR
1. Eli — died Nov. 30, 1894 — age 53 yrs.
2. Sgt. Seymour DeCarr, died in France 1920-1945 In memory of fought with 14th Armored Div. 3rd Army

DEION
1. Alfreda — 1902-1968 — wife of Joseph E. Votra
   (see Harold J. Votra)

DELAIRE
1. Helen R. Sullivan — Mar. 16, 1976 — wife of Bernard T. DeLaire
   (see Helen R. Sullivan)
2. Fred G. — 1897-1957
   Elizabeth L. — 1900- — his wife
   their sons
   Leon W. — 1920-
   John F. — 1924-1966
   Larry — 1928-
3. Fred G. — May 1, 1896-Feb. 27, 1957 — N.Y. Pvt. Co. E 306 Inf. WW I
4. James — 1861-19__
   Virginia — 1859-1916 — his wife
5. Paul T. — 1880-1951 — father
   Clara G. — 1882-1971 — mother

DELANIA
1. John D.   died June 24, 1900   age 59 yrs.   Co. Reg. N.H. Vol.

DELON
1. Josephine   1882-1946
    (see Frank Gokey)

DE LOSH
1. William H.   1889-1948   father
    Alice   1886-1979   mother
    Robert J.   1915-   son

DENO
1. Alfred E.   1903-1967
    Lila E.   1903-
2. Ambrose   died June 29, 1911   age 69 yrs. 9 mos.
    Mary Parent   died May 18, 1879   age 36 yrs.   His wife
3. Dorothy   1927-
    (see Merrell G. LeBar)
4. Edward   1836-1913
    Lucy   1850-1936   his wife
    John   1880-1895   their son
5. Frederick A.   Apr. 20, 1901-

Margaret LaGray Feb. 13, 1904- married July 25, 1921
6. George F. 1875-1962
7. William E. 1862-1915 father

DENNO
1. John 1878-1950
   Mary Gaff 1888-1956

DENUE
1. Clara 1884-1924
   (see Laporte Dresye)
2. Frank A. 1875-1935
   Moses died Oct. 24, 1924

DEON
1. Mary 1908-
   (see Edward H. Caskinette)
2. Philip R. 1864-1931
   Elizabeth LaComb 1877-1922

DERON
1. Stella 1876-1912
   (see Elias Richards)

DESHAW
  1. Burt   1897-1918
  2. Cora B.   died Mch. 23, 1902   age 24 yrs.   wife of John DeShaw

DILLON
  1. Ronald O.   1922-1952
  2. infant dau. Kathy Jean   1952-

DION
  1. Paul   1838-1913
     Emele Pepin   1837-1907   his wife
     their children—
     Emma   1874-1886
     Arthur   1879-1898

DORA
  1. Joseph G.   1877-1963
     Emma Dashnaw   1891-1942
     Eva W.   1892-1971   sister
     Ethel Burnett   1906-1933   dau.

DOW
  1. Edward M.   1904-19 63

	Lena M.	1909-	

DRESYE

1. Laporte	1882-1929		
Clara Denue	1884-1924	his wife	

DUBOIS

1. Lydia M.	1889-1949

DUBUQUE

1. Thomas	1838-1928	Co. I 60 Reg. N.Y. Vol.
Louisa Center	1846-1931	his wife
Julia Center	1814-1909	
(info. on other side of stone)		
Ferdinand Hewitt	1861-1950	
Julia Dubuque	1869-1948	his wife
(info. on other side of stone)		

DUFFY

1. Bridget	1844-1903	wife of W. H. Harvey
(see Bridget Harvey)		

DUFRANE
1. Joseph   1864-1925
   Elizabeth 1872-1949   his wife

DUGALL
1. Joseph   1843-1909   Pvt. Co. 22 Reg. N.Y. Vol.
   (stone broken in 3 large pieces)

DUHAME
1. Louise   1840-1916

DOHERTY
1. Marie   1911-1972
   (see Donald C. Baker)

DONOVAN
1. Daniel J.   1934-
2. Daniel H.   1895-1961
   Ruth V.   1903-1945
3. Daniel   1861-1939
   Phoebe   1877-1964

DUNN
1. Julia
   (see John White)
2. Mary M. — died June 11, 1889 — age 6 mos.
   Alexander P. — died Mar. 5, 1892 — age 8 yrs. 5 mos.
   children of Charles and Katie Dunn

DOUGALL
1. Nellie — 1917-1921
   Harold — 1919-1920
   children of L. F. & O. M. Dougall (back of stone)
   Harold M. Dougall — died Sept. 30, 1920 — age 1 yr. 8 mos. 16 days.

DUVAL
1. Garriel — died Oct. 9, 1898 — age 76 yrs.
   Caroline Miville — died Mar. 5, 1916 — age 84 yrs. — his wife

EMLOW
1. Edward L. — died June 27, 1896 — age 3 mos. — son of J. & C. Emlow

ESELTINE
1. Lloyd E. — 1900-1973
   Odella M. 1905-

Bella Madeleine   Feb. 14, 1931-June 12, 1931

FAGERSTROM
1. August B.   1866-1948
    Bridget M.   1867-1950   his wife
2. Mary C.   1898-
   (see Raphael Tripeny Jr.)

FALVEY
1. William   1871-1950
    Jennie Perry   1885-1968   his wife
2. FALVEY   Jan. 19, 1907-July 30, 1957   N.Y. SKI U.S. Navy WW II

FARMER
1. Albert J.   1911-1973
    Earldean Blade   1918-   his wife
    Judith P.   1942-1964   dau.
2. Arthur J.   1877-1965   father
    Libby C.   1886-1961   mother
    Carlton A.   Nov. 26, 1922-Oct. 8, 1967   N.Y. S1 U.S. Navy WW 11
3. Commodore A.   1867-
    Sophia M.   1870-1901   his wife

4. Doris S.
5. Elizabeth Mar. 17, 1892-Jan. 9, 1944
   (see Percy K. Ploof) 1922-
6. Flora G. 1909-1943 wife of Roy Chesbrough
   Richard Framer 1930-1936 their son
   (see Flora G. Chesbrough)
7. George F. 1887-1953
   Nora M. 1887-1974
8. Mary Ingland died Mar. 26, 1896 age 81 yrs. wife of John Farmer
   (see Mary Ingland)
9. Warren J. 1893- father
   Spencer 1917-1935
   Mary Louise Ploof 1897- mother

FAUCHER
1. Doris M. 1898-1973
2. Enile A. 1904-1975

FERRIS
1. Delia 1894-1960 mother

FILLION
1. Louis 1911-1913

FLANAGAN
1. Charles   1857-1937
   Phoebe   1858-1931
   Mary E. Gremore 1879-1956

FOLEY
1. Alice   1898-19__
   (see Edward W. Martin)

FOOS
1. Althea M.   1933-   wife of Orville D. Perry
                                 married Apr. 22, 1924
2. Raymond M.   1897-1979
   Lillian Watson 1900-

FORD
1. Esther King   1926-
   (see Esther King)
2. Floyd G.   1925-   his wife

FORKEY
1. Amos   1876-1951
   Jennie Bushey 1879-1967
2. Antoinette   1901-1982

(see Sibley J. Palmer)
3. Lenore　　　　　　　1911-1965
　　(see Edward H. Ploof)

FOURNIER
1. Joseph G.　　　　　　1869-1921
　 Eva　　　　　　　　　1871-1959　　his wife
　 Maude G. Snyder　　　1894-1918　　footstones—Father—Mother
　 Harry J. 1897-1940
　 Myrle V. 1907-1945
　 Maude C.

FRASER
1. Haven Jerry Fraser Jr.　Sept. 26, 1977-Sept. 27, 1977

GADOUA
1. Ernest J.　　　　　　 1912-1971
　 Velma Griffin　　　　 1913-　　　　his wife
　 Thomas E.　　　　　　 -1949-　　　 son

GAFF
1. Mary　　　　　　　　 1888-1956
　 (see John Denno)

GAGE
1. Elizabeth   Apr. 11, 1823-May 19, 1892   wife of John Moot
                                              age 64 yrs.
                                              Co. K 1 Reg. Vt. A

GARDNER
1. Joseph   died Nov. 5, 1890

2. Nettie   1896-1928
(see Augus A. Martin)

GARRO
1. Shirley   1944-1973
(see Shirley Garro Arcadi)

GARULSKE
1. infant dau. of V. G. & A. G. Garulske died Aug. 16, 1899

GAUTHIER
1. Joseph M.   1870-1966
   Melvina Supernant 1874-1962   his wife

GILBERT
1. Archie E.   1892-1960
   Exzildia Sochia 1893-1944   his wife

GIRARD
Lena M. 1903-1924

GOKEY
1. Ambrose 1854-
   Martha 1875-1913 his wife
2. Dennis 1868-1943
   Eliza S. 1872-1966 his wife
3. Edna 1904-1968
   (see Wayne D. Barnes)
4. Frank 1880-1979
   Josephine Delon 1882-1946 his wife
5. Fred 1854-1930
   Mary Norman 1850-1917 his wife
   footstones—Melford J. 1879-1948
6. Joseph Gokey 1830- 1909
   Elizabeth 1833-1935 his wife
7. George 1862-1950
   Neoma St. Hilaire 1878-1911 his wife
   George F. 1896
   Napoleon 1907
8. Henry G. 1881-1951
   Odena Stacy 1883-1951 his wife

9. infant son of Lionel H. Gokey Jr. 1948
10. Josephine 1875-1947 wife of Mederic laChance
    (see Fred G. LaChance)
11. Pauline Oct. 7, 1916-
    (see Burlan J. Holmes)
12. Rose B. died Aug. 28, 1916 age 68 yrs. wife of S. Gokey
13. Virginia M. 1873-1966
    (see Joseph L. LaChance)
14. Virginia 1899-
    (see Wallace D. Story)
15. William F. July 3, 1890-May 28, 1956
    Mabel M. Aug. 16, 1893-Oct. 28, 1961

GOODROW
1. Ernest H. Mar. 4, 1900-Oct. 5, 1957 N.Y. Pvt. Army Air Forces WW II
2. Eugene 1865-1959
   Addie Bushey 1872-1963 his wife
3. Floyd H. 1919-1924
4. Joseph 1884-1957
   Emma M. 1889-1970
5. Napoleon age 6 yrs.
   Eva age 5 mos.

6. Oscar 1891-1951
Barbara Haynes May 14, 1891-Jan. 25, 1972 his wife
7. Thomas A. 1907-1955

GORYIER
1. Lewis M. 1819-1907
Mary Louise 1812-1892

GREMORE
1. Helen A. 1878-1904
F. Gremore M. 1881-1935
(all footstones)
Flanagan 1889-1921
2. Mary E. 1879-1956
(see Charles Flanagan)

GRIFFIN
1. Velma 1913-
(see Ernest J. Gadoua)

GULLO
1. James J. 1903-
   Beatrice A. 1898-
   (all footstones)
   Donna D. Olig 1927-

GUYETTE
1. Sophia C. 1884-1942

GUYETT
1. Benjamin 1869-1944
   Jane Besaw 1874-1905
   Odena 1889-1902

HARRIG
1. Olive M. 1901-1936 dau. of V. & Wm. Harrig

HARVEY
1. Bridget Duffy 1844-1903 wife of W. H. Harvey

HAYLE
1. Carroll 1922-
   Gloria Catura 1935-1959

HAYNES
1. Barbara   May 14, 1891-Jan. 25, 1972
   (see Oscar Goodrow)
2. Howard   1885-1957
   Eva Paradise   1900-1944   his wife
   (footstones right in back of this stone)
   Nettie   1903-19   mother

HEWITT
1. Ferdinand Hweitt   1861-1950
   (see Thomas Dubuque)
2. Lewis   1849-1923
   Eliza   1856-1936   his wife
   Maranda   1877-1892
3. Nelson   1883-1956
   Bertha   1911-1973
4. S. J.
   (see D. H. Raymond)

HOLMES
1. Burlan J.   Feb. 7, 1907-Feb. 21, 1978
   Pauline Gokey   Oct. 7, 1916-   his wife

2. Irene   1915-1942   wife of Raymond Holmes
   (see Irene Cascanette)
3. Laura Votra Cascanette 1892-1977

HOLMES-CASCANETTE
4. Raymond O.   1916-1966
   Margaret Clookey   1924-1980   his wife

HOOLE
1. Victor   1891-1947
   Rose   1893-19__   his wife
   (also a metal plaque)
   Thomas
   Aida   his wife

HUNKINS
1. Harrison   1839-19__   12 N.Y. Cal. Vol.
   Mary Sucese   1841-1917   his wife
2. John   1863-
   Ellen   1886-1906   his wife   ROCK OF AGES

HURLME
1. Gracy died   June 23, 1886   age 9 mos. 18 days
   dau. of J. H. & E. H. Hurlme

INGLAND
1. Mary   died Mar. 26, 1896   age 81 yrs.   wife of John Farmer

JANDREW
1. Napoleon   1885-1959
   Elmer   1911-
   Nellie   1889-
   Isabell   1926-

JESMER
1. Wallace   1877-1968
   Mattie   1877-1917   his wife

JESMUR
1. Daniel   1869-1953
   Mary   1866-1953

KELLEY
1. Mary Delia   1877-1950   (metal plaque)

KENNEDY
1. Alice Gegelia   died Sept. 19, 1892   age 1 yr. 7 mos.
    dau. of P. & Alice Kennedy

KING
1. Ellen   1880-1899   wife of John White
2. Esther   1926-   wife of Floyd G. Ford
3. Jennett   1850-1943   his wife
    (between Wallace & David Bushey stones)

KIRCHNER
1. Falcones   (ROCK OF AGES)

KOHL
1. Frederick A.   Jan. 27, 1898-Dec. 15, 1969
    Beulah Paradise   July 17, 1906-

LA BAR
1. Merrell G.   1924-   married July 25, 1946
    Dorothy Deno   1927-

LA BOMBARD
1. Exeriene   1860-1910
   (see Frank Bedor)

LA BOUNTY
1. Louesa M.   1868-1947
   (see Oscar Rivers)

LA CHANCE
1. Alexander   July 28, 1874-Jan. 7, 1942 (FROM A FRIEND)
2. Fred G.   1894-1972
   Ruby Wells   1901-   his wife
   Mederic   1872-1956
   Josephine Gokey 1875-1947   his wife
3. Fred G.   June 27, 1894-Nov. 1, 1972 N.Y. PVT U.S. Army WW I
4. Joseph L.   1869-1951
   Virginia M. Gokey 1873-1966   wife
   Benny   1899-1921   son
5. Paul O.   1901-1971
   Lillian M.   1904-1951

LA CLAIR
1. Cathleen M.   born Aug 1, 1899   age 17 days.
   dau. of Mr. & Mrs. Daniel J. LaClair
2. Frank   1881-1963
   Lottie   1887-1976
3. Irene   1914-1937   dau.
4. Kathryn   1915-
   (see Kathryn LaClair Winters)
5. Regina   1912-
   (see Regina LaClair Winters)

LA COMB
1. Elizabeth   1877-1922
   (see Philip R. Deon)
2. Joseph   1839-1912   age 73 yrs.
   Elizabeth   1841-19   his wife

LA COMBE
1. Hattie   1881-1947
   (see Joseph F. Burnett)

LA FAVE
1. Eli   1862-1915

Clara 1863-1928
2. Mary LaRose LaFave   died Apr. 30, 1913   age 17 yrs.
   wife of Ernest LaFave
   (see Mary LaRose)
3. Napoleon   died May 26, 1913   son of E. & M. LaFave

LAFLEUR
1. Jusph (only letters that could be seen)   died Feb. 16, 1902   son of H. & A. LaFleur

LA GRAY
1. Albert   1881-1941   father
   Cecelia   1886-1948   mother
2. Barbara E.   1914-
3. Eleanor M.   wife of Irving D. Perry
   (see Edward J. Musthare)
4. H. LaGray
   R. Sausville
5. Margaret   Feb. 13, 1904-
   (see Frederick A. Deno)
6. Ralph G.   Mar. 5, 1909-Sept. 25, 1968

LA HARE
1. Melia   1889-1912
   (see YOUNG-LA HARE)

LAMOTT
1. Adeline   1822-1898   wife of Antoine LaMott
   (see John St. Onge)

LANCTO
1. Philomena   1886-1927   wife of Herman LaVoy
   Gladys E. LaVoy   1903-1928   wife of David F. Nisoff

LANTEIGNE
1. Edward E.   1888-1957

LAROCQUE
1. Joseph   1845-1919
   Harriet D.   1843-1914   his wife

LARONE
1. Helen   age 33 yrs. 4 mos.
   wife of Ambrose Larone
   Libbey   age 11 yrs. 3 mos.

LA ROSE
1. Charles W.   Oct. 1, 1909-July 29, 1974   U.S. Army WW II
2. Mary   died Apr. 30, 1913   age 17 yrs.   wife of Ernest LaFave
3. Richard 1880-1913
   Ida LaFave   1870-1939   his wife
   Charles W.   1909-1974
   Mary O. Pero   1918-

LA ROUSE
1. Prosper   1854-
   Martha   1859-1908   his wife

LA VAIR
1. Charles   1889-1955
   Agnes   1899-1960   his wife

LA VA RE
1. Berthat   1911-1957
   (see Augus A. Martin)
2. Ida   1870-1939
   (see Richard LaRose)

ST. REGIS FALLS CEMETERIES • 329

3. Sarah M.	1895-	mother
Dorothy M.	1911-1968	dau.
Lester F.	1905-	brother

LA VOY

1. Elmer L.	1890-1975	
Dora M. Cook	1894-1952	his wife
2. Frank F.	1885-1962	
3. Lewis	1860-1937	father
Margaret Masthare	1862-1929	mother
4. Mabel	1896-1974	his wife
(see Archie C. Catura)		
5. Philomena	1886-1927	wife of Herman LaVoy
(see Philomena Lancto)		
Gladys E. LaVoy	1903-1928	wife of David Nisoff
6. Walter J.	1905-1951	

LE BOEUF

1. Mamie F.	1892-1962	

LE MIEUX

1. Fred W.	1890-1958	WW I
Mayme D. Beyette	1890-1974	his wife

2. Fred W.   1890-Mar. 28, 1958   N.Y. Pvt. Co. K3 Casual Reg. WW I
3. Joseph A.   1897-1960   son
   Paul   1863-1958   father
   Josephine Morin   1865-1939   his wife   mother
   Laura I.   1902-   dau.
   Lionel O.   1910-   son
   Margaret McLaughlin   1908-   his wife
   (all footstones)
4. William W.   1900-1952   father

LINCOLN
1. Doris   1915-1964
   (see Bernard H. White)

LODER
1. Louise James Loder   1890-1936   (footstone)

LONGTIN
1. Eva

LOSEY
1. Esther   1914-
   (see Raymond E. Rouselle)

2. Thelma 1914-1962
   Stephen L. 1907-1969
   infant baby 1950-

MAC DONALD
1.

MALLETTE
1. Francis L. 1899-1912

MALLETTE
1. Francis L. 1933-1953
   Betty M. 1930-1935

MARSHEY
1. Julia 1858-1926
   (see Eli M. Russell)

MARTIN
1. Augus A. 1894-1974
   Nettie Gardner 1896-1928
   Bertha LaVare 1911-1957
2. Benjamin 1903-
   Barbara 1911-
   Fred G. 1869-1943   his wife
   Phoebe 1871-   his wife

footstone—Frederick
3. Donald P. — 1932-1956 — son
4. Edward W. — 1892-1958
   Alice Foley — 1898-19__ — his wife
5. Jerry — 1865-1954
   Elizabeth — 1876-1961
   Walter C. — -1917- — son

MASHTARE
1. Herbert — 1903-1919
2. Maggie — 1862-1929
   (see Lewis LaVoy)

MASHTAR
1. John — died Mar. 10, 1904 — age 67 yrs. — Co. A 95 Reg. N.Y.V.

MAYVILLE
1. Anne — wife
   (see Harold A. Burdo)
2. Francis J. — 1899-1969
   Helen M. — 1889-1954 — his wife

MC GARVEY
1. Edward P.   1875-1958
   Martha   1883-1956   his wife

MC LAUGHLIN
1. Margaret   1908-   wife of Lionel O. LeMieux
   (see Paul LeMieux)

MC NULTY
1. Mary E.   1855-1921
2. Thomas E.   1855-1903

MEACHAM
1. Viola   1915-1959

MEPE
1. Omear   July 1, 1897-Mar. 18, 1903   son of P. F. & L. G. Mepe

MIVILLE
1. Caroline   died Mar. 5, 1916   age 84 yrs.
   (see Garriel Duval)

MOOT
1. Elizabeth Gage — wife of John Moot

MORE
1. Mary A. Richards 1878-1909 wife of Walter I. More
footstone nearby—Frank J. L.

MORIN
1. Josephine 1865-1939
(see Paul LeMieux)

MORGAN
1. Henry 1884-1956
Bessie M. 1896-1980

MUSHTAR
1. David 1867-1943
Nellie Story 1875-1955 his wife
2. Edward J. 1907-
Eleanor M. LaGray 1914-

MUSHTARE
1. Henry Feb. 27, 1898-Nov. 3, 1961 N.Y. Pvt. HQ Btry. 8 Coast Arty. WW II

2. Joseph 1865-1942
Margaret 1872-1957
Mother—Father

MYNER
1. Mayme Story Myner 1877-1965
   (see Gilbert Story)

NEWTOWN
1. Loisa 1876-1908 mother
2. Melvin 1879-1959
   Nettie 1880-1952 his wife
   their children—Eva 1900-1901
   Garfield 1902-1904
   Gladdys 1908-1910
   baby 1898

NISOFF
1. Gladys E. LaVoy 1903-1928 wife of David F. Nisoff
   (see Philomena Lancto)

NOONAN
1. William 1879-1959

Jerry 1886-1955

NORMAN
1. Mary 1850-1917
   (see Fred Gokey)

O'BRIEN
1. Minna   died July 19, 1906   age 20 yrs. 5 mos.   wife of J. E. White

O'KEEFE
1. Leonard   died Nov. 12, 1907   age 74 yrs.

O'NEIL
1. Bernard P.   Mar. 17, 1904-Sept. 23, 1979   Pvt. U.S. Army WWII

O'SULLIVAN
1. John   1909-1909   children of J. & S. O'Sullivan
   Adora   1910-1911

PAGE
1. Delena   1860-1912

PALMER

1. Sibley J. 1894-1981
   Antoinette Forkey 1901-1982 his wife

PARADISE
1. Beulah July 17, 1906-
   (see Frederick A. Kohl)
2. Eva 1900-1944
   (see Howard Haynes)
3. Gerald E. Nov. 1, 1915-Apr. 24, 1961 N.Y. Sgt. 9 Air Force WW II
4. Gerald E. 1915-1961
5. Harry J. 1904-1973 footstone
6. Henry 1872-1943
   Emma A. 1881-1975 his wife
   Harry J.
   Elsie R. his wife

PARENT
1. Mary died May 18, 1879 age 36 yrs.
   (see Ambrose Deno)

PARTLOW
1. Alice J. 1890-1973
2. Angus A. 1887-1971

   3. Kenneth   1909-1913   OUR DARLING   son of A. & A. Partlow

PATRAW
   1. Bruce J.   Nov. 20, 1959   OUR BABY

PEPIN
   1. Emele   1837-1907
      (see Paul Dion)

PERO
   1. Mary C.   1918-
      (see Richard LaRose)

PERRY
   1. Althea   1933-   wife of Orville D. Perry
      (see Althea M. Foos)
   2. Barbara   1907-   wife of Irving D. Perry
      (see Barbara E. LaGray)
   3. Dorothy   wife of Leon I. Perry
      (see Dorothy M. Richards)
   4. Irving D.   1908-1976
      Barbara LaGray   1907-   his wife
      Ronald J.   1940-   their son

their sons—Orville D. & Leon I.
5. Irving D.
6. Jennie   In memory of Irving D. Perry by his Sunbeam Lodge Friends
     1885-1968
(see William Falvey)
7. Leon I.   1934-   their son
8. Martin   died July 5, 1906   age 80 yrs.   Co. A 98 Reg. N.Y.S. Inf.
9. Orville D.   1933-   their son
10. Ronald John   their son
11. Violet   1878-1929
(see David J. DaLaire)

PLANTY
1. Nicholas   1820-1908
    Arilla   1831-1916   his wife

PLOOF
1. Andrew   1856-1935
    Lucy   1860-1948   his wife
2. Arthur   1895-1979
3. Donald L.   Sept. 13, 1922-Feb. 1, 1966 N.Y. PFC U.S. Army WW II
4. Edward H.   1911-
    Lenore Forkey   1911-1965   his wife
5. Elaine   1923-1961

(see Harold J. Votra)
6. Florence 1906-1973
(see Florence Ploof Braatz)
7. Francis 1857-
Miranda 1862-1926 his wife
children—
Alice 1899-1899
Howard 1901-1906
8. Frank A. 1884-1936
9. Gerald L. March 8, 1916-Aug. 13, 1957 N.Y. Pvt. Medical Dept. WW II
10. Hattie died Feb. 21, 1909 age 21 yrs. wife of Joseph Ploof
11. Helen L. 1927-
Lois F. 1932-
(see WHITMAN-PLOOF)
12. Howard died Sept. 8, 1906 age 5 yrs. 3 mos.
son of F. & M. Ploof
13. Laura 1889-1914
(see Theodore Wood)
14. Leona E. 1910-1977 (see Walter A. Scott)
15. Leonard 1890-1959
Emma L. 1899-
Earl G. 1906-1947
Regina B. 1910- (footstone—Leonard)

16. Mary 1846-1927
    (see Joseph Cuturia)
17. Mary A. 1884-1959 mother
18. Mary Louise 1897-
    (see Warren J. Farmer)
19. Percy K. 1913-
    Elizabeth Farmer 1922-
    Brain R. -1961- his wife
    Mary J. -1952- son
                     dau.
20. Peter 1849-1943
    (see Felix Premo)
21. Royal F. May 27, 1908-
22. Russell B. 1918-1937
23. Seymore L. died Aug. 19, 1897 son
    son of L. & E. Ploof age 4 yrs. 6 mo. 19 da.

PREMO

1. Felix 1880-19
   Ida 1878-19
   Peter Ploof 1849-1943
   Everest Gay 1869-1905
   Sophia 1856-1938
   Ida Premo 1879-1966 (metal plaque)

PRIORE
1. Angela M.   *morte 31 Marzo 1889 anno 24*
2. Lenard 1845-1899
   Mary   1853-1911
   Cora M. Prior   1887-1961   footstone

PRESPARE
1. Joseph J.   1856-1925
   Flavia   1852-1937   his wife
   Jenny   1882-1977
2. Joseph   1837-1912
   Mary   1837-1923   his wife

PRESPER
1. Roy   Jan. 6, 1894-   son of George S. & Fanney Presper

PROULX-ROKAHR
1. Theodore Rokahr   1896-1977
   Geraldine Proulx   1901-   his wife
   John B. Proulx   1879-1941   father
   Eugenie Courcelle   1876-1976   mother

RAFTER
1. Frank J. 1890-
   Rose M. 1893- his wife

RAYMO
1. Alexander 1855-1936
   Jennie 1860-1938
2. Hugh 1857-1931
   Sarah 1852-1925 his wife
   Frederick J. 1882-1971
   Anna E. 1886-1963 his wife
3. Thomas 1869-1930
   Martha 1878-1969 his wife
   children—
   Joseph 1915
   Jennie 1920
   footstones—Thomas J. 1913-1929 father
   Jennie mother
4. Valina 1882-1914
   (see David J. DaLaire)

RAYMOND
1. Agatha   1908-
   (see Gay E. Sweet)
2. D. H. Raymond
   S. J. Hewitt
   Melvina   1901-1938
   Stephen   1890-1967
   Eva   1894-1918
3. Etta E.   June 2, 1894-Feb. 24, 1954
4. Fred L.   1909-1979
   Blanche D.   1916-
   Marjorie M.   1921-1975
5. Frederick L.   Oct. 12, 1909-May 28, 1979   CPL U.S. Army WW II

REGIS
1. Joseph P.   1870-1952   father
   Mary Sochia   1875-1952   mother

RICHARD
1. Millie   1914-   wife of Glenford A. Catura
   (see Archie C. Catura)

RICHARDS

1. Adelia	died May 25, 1889	age 9 yrs. 9 mos. dau. of M. & P. Richards
2. Elias	1864-194	
Stella Deron	76-1912	
Elizabeth	1901-1904	
3. Bernard M.	1931-	
Maureen Caskinette	1933-1967	his wife
4. Catherine A.	11-30-1956—12-2-1957	dau. of Andrew & Martha
5. Dorothy M.	1935-	wife of Leon I. Perry
6. Ellan	1845-19	
(see Lewis Catura)		
7. Francis R.	1837-1916	Piv. Co. H. 106th Reg. N.Y. Inf.
8. Fred	1876-1947	
Elizabeth	1839-1912	
9. Joseph	died June 15, 1899	age 4 yrs. 8 mos.
son of M. & P. Richards		
10. Ma A.	1878-1909	wife of Walter I. More
(see Mary A. More)		
11. Maurice G.	1906-	
Mayfred P.	1910-1974	
12. Moses	1841-	
Philanda Butin	1849-1911	his wife

RIVERS

1. Oscar — 1868-1948
   Louesa M. LaBounty — 1868-1947
   Ray J. — 1907-1964
2. Ray John — July 23, 1907-Dec. 17, 1964
   N.Y. TEC 4 HQ & HQ Btry. 49 Ca. Brg. WW II
3. Rosie — (no dates)
   Maude — (no dates)
   Mildred — (no dates)
   Earl Simeon — (no dates)
4. Simeon — died Jan. 8, 1889   age 1 yr.   son of O. & L. Rivers

ROKAHR

1. Theodore Rokahr — 1896-1977
   (see PROULX-ROKAHR)

ROUSELLE

1. Raymond E. — 1908-1975
   Esther Losey — 1914-   his wife

ROY
1. Roger A. 1939- father
   Joan A. 1940- mother
   Rolland R. 1962-1969 son

RUSSELL
1. Bert A. 1871-1963
   Emma R. 1870-1956 his wife
   M. Mabel 1900-1974 dau.
2. Eli M. 1857-1961
   Julia Marshey 1858-1926 his wife
3. Joseph 1855-1904
   Agnes 1860-1895 his wife
   Iven 1890-1895 their son

RUGAR
1. Georgia Hoole Rugar 1925-1972

SABRAY
1. Joseph O. 1910-1918
   Raymond L. 1912-1913
   Mary R. 1915-1915
   Oliver O. 1873-

Delia	1875-	
Burt J.	1906-1909	married Jan. 12, 1963

SATHER
1. Kenneth F.	1935-	
Wilda A. Story	1943-1976	
2. Oscar E.	1888-1977	
Anna V. Surprise	1896-	
Frank Surprise	1864-1949	
May Marie	1920-1946	

SAUSVILLE
1. Edward E.	1896-1918	
2. R. Sausville		
H. LaGray		
3. Rhoda	1874-1965	(metal plaque)

SAVOY
1. Lawrence W.	1894-	
Lillian Tuper	1900-	his wife

SAWYER
1. Alex	1870-	

   Ellen 1874-1911 his wife
2. Peter

SCOTT
1. Walter A. 1909-1960 husband
   Leona E. Ploof 1910-1977 his wife

SERVANT
1. John S. 1882-1951
   Blanche M. 1893-1924 his wife

SHAMPINE
1. John F. died Apr. 13, 1894 age 19 yrs.

SIMPSON
1. Mary 1937-1973
   (see Stanley L. Arno)

SMITH
1. Otto H. 1882-1936
   Margaret M. 1881-1955 his wife

SNYDER

1. Angline — 1882-1940
   (see Arthur B. Wood)
2. Maude G. — 1894-1918
   (see Joseph G. Fournier)

SOCHIA

1. Beatrice C. — 1901-1969
2. Edison E. — 1888-1956
3. Hattie Caskinette — 1892-1876 — his wife
4. Elizabeth — died Sept. 26, 1903 — age 27 yrs. — wife of R. A. Sochia
5. Exzildia — 1893-1944
   (see Archie E. Gilbert)
6. Frank J. — 1878-1954
7. Gilbert E. — 1912-1932 — father
8. Elsie M. — 1930-
9. Joseph — died Jan. 26, 1906 — age 77 yrs.
10. Julian — died May 11, 1902 — age 73 yrs. — wife of Joseph Sochia
11. Leo W. — 1913-1949
12. Leon E. — 1850-1911
    Chloe M. Young — his wife
13. Mary — 1852-1913
14. William — 1875-1952

(Note: items renumbered as originally: 1. Beatrice C., 2. Edison E., 3. Elizabeth (Hattie Caskinette his wife), 4. Exzildia, 5. Frank J., 6. Gilbert E. (Elsie M.), 7. Joseph, 8. Julian, 9. Leo W., 10. Leon E. (Chloe M. Young his wife), 11. Mary, 12. William)

STACY
1. Amos F. — 1866-1933
   Helen E. — 1898-1968
2. John E. — died Apr. 21, 1889 — dau. age 29 yrs.
3. Joseph N. — 1888-1956
   Sarah J. — 1885-1962
4. Odena — 1883-1951
   (see Henry G. Gokey)

STACY (or) **STAGY**
1. D. twin babies

ST. DENNIS
1. Mary — died Mar. 4, 1904 — age 33 yrs. wife of John St. Dennis
   (see Mary White)

ST. HILAIRE
1. Edmund — 1872-1937 — father
   Sophia — 1868-1918 — mother
   Florence — 1903-1915 — sister
2. Neoma — 1878-1911
   (see George Gokey)

ST. ONGE
1. John — 1844-1922 — his wife
   Sophia — 1843-1926
   Adaline — 1822-1898 — wife of Antoine LaMott

STOREY
1. Lewis — 1882-1959 — his wife
   Estells Sullivan — 1885-1961

STORY
1. Gilbert — died Oct. 3, 1903 — age 63 yrs. — his wife
   Mary — died Sept. 20, 1936 — age 84 yrs.
   Mary Story Myner — 1877-1965 — footstone
2. Wallace D. — 1892-
   Virginia Gokey — 1899- — married July 12, 1917
3. Wilda A. — 1943-1976
   (see Kenneth Sather)
4. Winifred — 1918-
   (see Wendell F. Cox)

SUCESE
1. Mary — 1841-1917
   (see Harrison Hunkins)

SULIA
1. Angeline   1889-1974
   (see Thomas J. Susice)

SULLIVAN
1. Estella   1885-1961
   (see Lewis Storey)
2. Helen R.   Mar. 16, 1976   wife of Bernard T. DeLaire

SURPERNANT
1. Maude M.   1884-1945
   Modest L.   1886-1936
2. Melvina   1874-1962
   (see Joseph M. Gauthier)

SURPRISE
1. Anna V.   1896-
   Frank   1864-1949
   (see Oscar E. Sather)
2. Frank   1856-   B. of Rt. 183 of O.N.Y.
   Mary   1864-   wife
   Edward   1889-1914   son
3. Louise   1890-1926

4. William E.	1900-1950	
5. William E.		1 yr. 3 mos. 15 days.

SUSICE

1. Bert	1902-1976	
Jennie Cramer	1906-	married July 5, 1923
2. Doris M.	1916-	
(see Frank X. Bourdage)		
3. Frederick J.	June 22, 1945-Oct. 28, 1969	N.Y. SFM3 U.S. Navy Vietnam
4. Ida	Dec. 20, 1907-	
(see Charles Bishop)		
5. James	1949-1953	(footstone to Bert Susice stone)
6. John J.	1871-1956	
7. Julius A.	1886-1957	footstone
8. Julius A.	1886-1957	
Virginia M.	1889-1975	his wife
Matilda	1924-1939	
Richard A.	1926-1945	killed at Okinawa
Norman G.	1928-1950	killed in Korea
9. Norman G.	Mar. 13, 1928-Aug. 18, 1950	
		N.Y. Cpl. 34 Inf. 24 Inf. Div. Korea Ph
10. Richard A.	Feb. 28, 1926-May 18, 1945	
		N.Y. Pvt. 7 Marines 1 marine Div. WWII

11. Richard E. 1945-1946
    Frederick J. 1945-1969
    Katie L. 1968-1971
12. Thomas J. Mar. 14, 1879-Feb. 17, 1942
    Angeline Susice 1889-1974 his wife

SWEET
1. Gay E. 1905-1970 father
   Agatha Raymond 1908- mother

TAYLOR
1. Edward L. 1919-
   Frances M. 1915-1978

TEBO
1. Ernest A. 1881-1960
   Margaret A. 1883-1972
   Lawrence E. -1904-
2. son of E. A. & M. A. Tebo died July 25, 1904 age 3 mos. OUR DARLING

THOMPSON
1. Henry H. May 29, 1891-May 10, 1964 N.Y. 20 Lieutenant Infantry WW I

2. Henry H. 1891-1964
   Harriet T. 1900-

TREVETT
1. Marcell   Dec. 6, 1820-Apr. 9, 1903   wife of J. H. Trevett

TRIPENY
1. Ernest C.   1893-1950
   Geraldine Ward   1900-19   his wife
   infant son   1928   son of Ernest & G. Tripeny
3. Raphael W. sr.   1866-1942
   Anna S.   1864-1943
4. Raphael Jr.   1897-1974
   Mary C.   1898-
   Bernard   1919-1932
   Raphael W. 3rd.   1921-1930
   Evelyn A.   1895-1918
   Raphael W. J.   1897–1974   "Budd"
   Mary C. Fagerstrom   1898   "Mamie"
5. William   1856-1897
   Angelica   1859-1934   his wife   (buried in Casper, Wyoming)

TRUDO
1. Freddie   died Apr. 20, 1888   age 11 days   son of W. & E. Trudo

TUPER
1. Lillian   1900-
   (see Lawrence W. Savoy)

VILLNAVE
1. Daniel A.   1889-1962
   Angie   1891-1957   his wife
   Ralph   1909-1910   their son

VOTRA
1. Harold J.   1924-1979
   Elaine Ploof   1923-1961   his wife
   Joseph E.   1897-1970
   Alfreda Delon   1902-1968   his wife
2. John L.   Feb. 28, 1895-May 6, 1960   N.Y. Pvt. U.S. Army
3. Laura   1892-1977
   (see Holmes-Cascanette)
4. Linda Lou   1959-1963   OUR BABY
5. mother   1902-1969
   father   1897-

WARD
1. Geraldine   1900-19_
   (see Ernest Tripeny)

WATSON
1. Lillian   1900-
   (see Raymond M. Foos)

WELBURN
1. Darley   1891-1952
   Yvonne   1893-1961

WELLS
1. Ruby   1901-
   (see Fred G. LaChance)

WITCHER
1. Joseph Milon   died Mar. 9, 1900   age 19 yrs.   son of J. & S. Witcher

WHITE
1. Bernard H.   1906-1966
   Doris Lincoln   1915-1964   his wife
2. Doris L.   1911-1916

3. Ellen	1880-1899		wife of John White
(see Ellen King)			
4. George	1888-19		
Nora	1896-1969		
Alexander	1842-1914		
Mary	1851-1923		
5. Helen M.	1920-1940		
6. infant son of R. & C. White	-1947-		
7. John	1875-1946		
Adeline	1843-1924		
Joseph	1839-1914		
8. John	1878-1951		
Julia Dunn			his wife
9. Mary	died Mar. 4, 1904	age 33 yrs.	wife of John St. Dennis
10. Minna	died July 19, 1906	age 20 yrs. mos.	wife of J. E. White
(see Mary O'Brien)			
11. Silas	1886-1963		
12. Steven	1852-		
Phebe	1851-		his wife
13. Vernon J.	1892-1954		Vet. WW I
14. Walter F.	1888-1955		
Charlotte	1891-1978		

WHITMAN-PLOOF
1. Carl N. — 1924-
   Helen L. Ploof — 1927- — his wife
   Lois F. Ploof — 1932- — her sister

WILCOX
1. Grant J. — 1930-
   Louise B. Bushey — 1928-
   (see Bushey-Wilcox)

WINTERS
1. Kathryn LaClair Winters — 1915- — dau.
2. Regina LaClair Winters — 1912- — dau.

WOOD
1. Arthur B. — 1880-1941 — father
   Angeline Snyder — 1882-1940 — mother
2. Gertrude A. — 1898-1972
3. Herbert J. — Aug. 30, 1930-Feb. 1, 1977
4. John E. — Apr. 11, 1916-Dec. 2, 1967
   N.Y. Pvt. Co. B 23 BN 6 Regt. 1 RTC WW II
5. Lyle Joseph — Aug. 31, 1922-Jan. 19, 1945
   N.Y. TEC 5 Co. C 19 armo inf. BN WW II BSM-P

6. Theodore   1890-
   Laura M. Ploof   1889-1914   his wife

WOODS
1. Antione   1856-1921   his wife
   Malvina   1864-1935
2. Rosa   Oct. 8, 1910   age 4 yrs. 2 mos.   dau. of A. & M. Woods

YEDDO
1. Richard   1890-1890
   Frank   1891-1891
   Marcell   1906-1907
   Olive   1892-1908   (footstone—Olive)

YELL
1. Joseph   died Mar. 20, 1888   age 62 yrs.
2. Leona E. 1903-1970   (metal plaque)
3. Louis   born Aug. 6, 1824
   Cecelia   born-Oct. 18, 1830-Died-Nov. 25, 1909   IN MEMORY OF
   Hattie   died Oct. 8, 1885   age 18 yrs. 5 mos.
   dau. of Louis & Cecelia Yell   (footstone)

YOUNG
1. Antione 1846-
   Louise 1847-1912 his wife
2. Chloe M. 1852-1913
   (see Leon E. Sochia)
3. Gilbert died July 20, 1889 age 5 mos. son of J. & R. Young
4. John 1850-1910
   Rosy 1858-1929
   Gilbert 1889-1889

YOUNG-LAHARE
1. Melia LaHare. 1889-1912
   Amelia Young 1867-1926
   Theodore Young 1862-1953

SELECTED BIBLIOGRAPHY

Publications

The Adirondack News. St. Regis Falls, NY: Mark A. Rowell and Grace Lennon. 1887–1933.

Allen, Gove, Maloney, and Palmer. *Rails in the North Woods*. 1973.

Amigo, Eleanor and Mark Neuffer. *Beyond the Adirondacks: The Story of St. Regis Paper Company.*

Bethke, Robert D. *Adirondack Voices Woodsmen and Woods Lore*. 1945.

Diocese of Ogdensburg Centennial. 1872–1972.

Fox, William F. *History of the Lumber Industry*. 1976.

Franklin County Atlas.

World War I Records. Compiled by Edward C. Rider, County Historical. Malone, NY: Franklin County. 1931.

Franklin Historical Review. Malone, NY: Franklin County Historical and Museum Society.

Sanfords, Carl E. *History of the Town of Hopkinton*. 1903.

Seaver, Frederick J. *Historical Sketches of Franklin County and its Several Towns with Many Short Biographies*. Albany, NY: J. B. Lyon Company, 1918.

Smith, H. P. *History of Essex County*. 1885.

Taylor, Sister Mary Christine, S.S.J., Ph.D. *History of Catholicism in the North Country*. 1972.

St. Regis Falls Newsletter. St. Regis Falls, NY. 1968–1973.

St. Regis Falls Central School Yearbook. 1957.

Informants

Ralph Farmer. Town of Waverly Historian.

Rev. Msgr. Robert J. Giroux.

Troop "B" NYS Police, Ray Brook, NY.

INDEX

A

A. J. Norton & Co. 117
Achcroft
  Donald 143
  Michelle 143
  Thomas 143
Adirondack Mission 108
Adirondack News 30, 96, 117, 119, 190
Adirondacks 43
Adirondack Sanatorium 97
Agnew, D. M. 118
Aiken
  Beulah Smith 193
  Deforest M. 203
  Matilda Bailey Landry 203
  Pearl M. 203
  Robert E. 88, 203
Albany 123
Albany Business College 127
Albany Law School 126
Albany Medical College 123, 127
Alburg, NY 151
Aldrich
  Alvin S. 203
  C. Y. 203
  Cherol 70
  Edwin S. 119
  Flora D. 203
  F. W. 61
  Frederick W. 203
  Mary C. 203
Alfred, W. J. 21
Alfred Lumber Company 7
Allegheny College 121
Allen
  Beatrice 140
  Bert 140, 203
  Clara 203
  Dorothy 140, 203
  Ernest B. 88, 204
  Eunice 204
  George 204
  Gertrude 140, 203
  Lawrence 140
  Lemuel B. 204
  Leonard 204
  Lillian 204
  Lucy 204
  Margarite 204
  Neva 109
  Nora Cook 203
  Sarah Bero 204
  Vergie 140
  W. Dunham 204
Altamont 6, 116
American Legion 146, 147, 163
American Legion Hall 96
American Sugar Refining Co. 14
Amyot, Philomena 37
Anderson, David M. 106
Andre, Maj. 159
Antonio
  Daniel 172
  Daniel and Jennie Mashtare 173
  Edward 173
  May 173
Arcadi
  Peter 132, 168
  Darlene 142
  Harry 141
Arey, Maddock & Locke 10
Arnold
  Benedict 195

Atwater
  A. W. 97, 119
  H. H., M.D. 97
Atwood
  May A. 204
Ausable Forks 127
Austin
  Albert H. 204
  Charles W. 70, 204
  David 137
  Dora S. 134, 204
  Ethel Brabon 205
  Hannah M. 204
  Heath 137
  Henry A. 204
  Jessie M. 204
  John W. 204
  Mathew 137
  Raymond 88
  Sands H. 36
  Vera M. 204
  Wesley 194
  Wesley C. 70, 86, 133, 205

B

Babcock
  Benjamin 4
  Mr. 96
Badger
  Floyd E. 205
  Nettie 205
Bailey
  A. F. 205
  Albert 165
  Barbara 132
  Bernard 33, 132
  Bruce 132
  Cynthia 132
  Donna 132
  Dorothy Williams 205
  Elsie 132
  George A. 205
  George F. 205
  Georgie 205
  Lawrence L. 205
  Lynn 132
  Leo 205
  Michael 132
  Mildred E. 205
  Rose 132
  Sarah 205
  Sharon 132
  Sheila 132
  Susan 132
  Wilbur 132
  Wilbur H. 205
Baird
  Anna 159, 206
  Mattie 162
  William and Anna Sharp 159, 160
Baker
  Ann 187
  Daniel 88
  Fannie 70
  Henry J. 86
  Henry Joseph 70
  Joseph 85
Baldin
  Alton O. 206
  Mary J. Gardner 206
Baldwin
  Frederick R. 206
  Jackie K. 206
Bandy, Ed and Fanny 106
Bandy's Bakery 106
Bangor 26, 116
Barber
  Caroline Adelia 195
  William and Sally Owens 195
barber shop 119
Barkley, Ezra M. 204
Barlow, Doe 141
Barnes
  Charles A. 70
  Lucy 192
  Wayne D. 70

Bassette, Dr. Peter 36
Bastin, Allan 68
Battle of Shiloh 187
Baxter
 William A. 143
 William P. 143
Bean
 Amelia 194
 Harriet 180
Bean
 Harvey F. 70, 86
 James D. 103
 Mr. and Mrs. Peter 70
Beaudry, Anna 147
Beauhanois, Canada 133
Bellmont 19
Bellmore
 David 88
 Lewis D. 86
Benham, Curtis 47
Bennett
 David 144
 Jay 144
 John 144
 Joyce 144
 K. 51
 Kenneth 144
Berdrow, George 119
Bernadot, Leon C. 98
Bernard, Cascanette 136
Besa, Alex 67
Besaw 51
Best, Helen 182
Betterley, Audrey 88
Beyette
 Mayme 171
 Rev. P. V. 33
Bickford
 Edward 86, 194
 Henry 21
 Minnie 136
 Ruth 136
 Tracy 136

 Tracy, Jr. 136
Bigelow
 William 185
Bigelow, Blake, M.D. 97
Big Five, The 47
Biggers
 B. A. 204
 Beverly A. 86
Big Pond 110
Binan
 Captain 44
 D. 51
 Doug 44
 Douglas 47, 50
Bingo Town 112
Bishop
 Aaron 132
 Arlene 132
 Charles 132
 Charles Andrew 132
 Charles Eugene 132
 Darien 132
 Debbie 132
 Delores Genevieve 132
 Elsie 132
 George 21
 Gloria 132
 Ida Susice 132
 Joan 132
 John Paul 132
 Linda Ida 132
 Rose Marie 132
 Shawn 132
 Susan 132
 Tammy 132
 Violet 132, 162
 William Eugene 132
 Yvonne Marie 132
Bishop's Hotel 61
Bishop Foss 121
Bishop Merrill 121
Black Bridge 154
Black Horse Troop 62

blacksmith shop 119
Blade
  Fay E. E. 71
  Leo J. 71
  Mr. and Mrs. B. E. 71
blockhouse 105
Blood
  J. L. 35, 63
  John L. 36, 120
Blouf 187
Blue (Azure) Mt. 98
Blue Mountain Lodge #874, F.&A.M. 63
Blue Mountain Road 107, 108, 109, 111
Blue Mt. Lodge 163
Bombay 42, 43, 50, 106
Boston Celtics 43
Bouchard
  Edna 197
Boucher, Stella Susice 131
Boulds
  Phyllis 163
Bowes, Bruce, Mrs. 148
box factory 117
Boy's Camp 108
Boyce
  Ann Susice 132
  Betsey 158, 191
Boyer, Pauline 110
Braatz
  _____ 188
Brabon 133
Brabon
  Alton 134
  Austin 134
  Barclay 134
  Bernard 133, 194
  Carroll 134
  Daniel 134
  Eldred 133
  Ernest 133
  Ernest O. 134, 204
  Ethel 133, 194
  Eugene 133, 134
  Eugene W. 134
  Frank 133
  George E. 133
  Harley 134
  Harry 133, 134, 146
  Hayden 134
  James 134
  John 134
  Judy 134
  Keith 133
  Laura 134
  Lyndon 133
  Marshall 88, 134
  Mickey 134
  Oliver 31
  Oliver F. 67
  Pearl 134
  Reginald 134
  Reginald, Mrs. 146
  Robert 88, 134
  Susan 134
  Wesley 134
  William 133
Brabon House 37
Brabont, Oliver F. 133
Bradford, Sam 132
  _____ 194
Brandon 6, 32, 111, 116, 117, 125
Bray
  Harold 88
  Lillian 182
Bredrow, Ellen 85
Breyer, Margaret 63
Brighton 108, 178
Brisbois, Rose 134
Bristol
  G. Edward 192
British troops 105
Broadfield, Capt. Charles J. 62
Brooklyn-Cooperage Lumber Company 131

Brooklyn Cooperage Co. 14, 102, 111, 146, 153, 154, 161, 199
broom handle factory 117
Brown
  Alexander 67
  Alice 147
  Claude 86
  Edward 88
  Elwood 88
  Gladys 199
  Judson 71
  Laurice 88
  Maude 199
  Robert 88
  Ronald 89
  William 89
Brown Tract Sawmill 109
Brown Tract School 109
Bruce
  Abner 157
  Charles 154
  Floy 109
  Henry 135
  Jonah C. 67
  Mary 157
Brunette, Regina 187
Brushton 31, 127
Buckhout
  John 200
  Phebe 200
Buckley, Irene 185
Buelah, Hicks 136
Bump, Goldie 89
Burdo, Harold Albert 89
Burke 120
Burns, R. N. 26
Bury, Dr. 143
Bushey
  Addie 134
  Annie 134
  Beatrice 135
  David 134, 152
  Ellie 134
  George 134
  Helen 135
  Irene 135
  Jennie 134, 152
  Joe 135
  John 134
  Joseph 32, 134
  Joseph W. 134
  Leo 134
  Louise B. 135
  Lucy 134
  Mary 134, 135
  Maude 134
  Rose 135
  Vivian 135
Bushy, Mary 162
Butler, Ralph 89
Buttermilk Hill 14

C

"Calendar Club" 145
"Camp Cheerio" 170
Cahill, Gerald 169
Callaghan, Rev. P. 33
Camp
  Charles and Nancy Farmer 182
  Eugene 89
  Hattie 180, 182
  James, Mrs. 161
  Jim 18
  Liz 18
  Lyman (Jim) 89
  Lymond R. 160
  Maurice 89
Campbell
  Benjamin L. 71
  Inez 71
Canaserago High School 121
Canton 42
Carlin
  Charles H. 71
  Mr and Mrs. Charles 71
Caron, Ernest L. 89

Carpenter
  Clara 135
  Martha M. 195
Cascade Chair Co. 11, 178
Cascade Wood Products Co. 11, 19, 124
Cascanette
  Bernard 89
  Floyd 89
  Harold 89
Caskinett
  Alfred 72
  Emma 72
  George 72
  Mose 72
  Mr. and Mrs. Hays 72
  Richard 67
Caskinette
  Floyd 153
  Harry J. 153
  Hattie 194
  Leslie 89
Cassidy, _____ 173
Caswell, Hannah 189
Cat Hill 109
Cat Mountain 8
Cayea, Katherine Cayea 131
Center
  Julia 141
  Louise 141
Center Camp Logging 174
Central University 120
Chaffee, William 192
Chagnon, _____ 134
Chamberlain, Wilt 42
Chandler, F. L. 118
Chapman
  Ethel 137
  Gerald 150
  Lillian 135
Chase, Bert 180
Chateaugay 50, 122
Cheektowaga 46

Cheney
  Ann 135
  Arlene 135
  Bertha 135
  Debbie 188
  Deborah 136
  Eileen 136, 188
  Ellen 135
  Eva 193
  Eva A. 192
  Eva Ann 135
  Evelyn 136
  Fred 135
  George 135
  Gilbert 135
  Giles 107, 135
  Glen H.
  Glenn 136
  Glenn H. 136
  Harold W. 72
  Harriet 135, 136
  Helen 136
  Ivan 136
  Josephine 135
  Laurence 136
  Laurenzo 135
  Lawrence 188
  Leon 136
  Lillian 135
  Lois 136, 188
  Loren 135, 136
  Lucena Moffett 135
  Merchant 136
  Mr. and Mrs. Fred 72
  Nancy 136, 188
  Nora 136
  Norma 136
  Ruth 136
  Silas 135
  Velma 136
  Watson L. 136
  Wayne R. 136
  Wayne 188

INDEX • 371

Willard 136
Willard G. 136
Wyotte 135
Chesbrough
  Clara 136
  Cynthia Ann 137
  Ethel P. 137
  Eula 152
  Eula Autumn 136, 137
  Fred 136
  Gary Thurston 137
  George and Lowessa Finlayson 152
  George F. 152
  George Fred 136
  Haven 152
  Haven Grant 136, 137
  Herbert L. 136
  Jessie R. 136
  John B. 136
  Julie 137
  Julie Ann 169
  Kathleen 137
  Kathleen Mary 169
  Leila 137
  Lesley 137
  Louise 136
  Lowessa 136
  McCrae 136
  Richard 151
  Roy 151
  Roy J. 136
  Sandra 137
  Starr 137
  Thurston 89, 136, 152, 175
  Thurston McCrae 137
  Verlie 136, 137, 152
  Walter E. 136
  Wayne 137, 169
  Wayne and Glenda 169
  Wayne Morris 137
Christian
  Eva 72

  William P. 72
  William R. 86
Churchill, Jessie M. 123
Cimbric, Michael 150
Civil War 63, 67, 68, 126, 133, 141, 161, 164, 172, 180, 187, 192, 195
Cladin, A. A. 119
Clarence Creek, Ontario 134
Clark
  C. G., Mrs. 84\
  Edward 89
  Lester 89
  Mary 175
Clarlen, Dr. 97
Clary, Florence 134
Clinton County 123
Clookey
  Walter 188
  William B. 67
clothespin factory 14
Clothier, Marshall 73
Cobb, Eunice 189
Coffin, _____ 187
Collins, Libby 150
Compo
  _____ 142
  Annabel 142
  Darin 142
  Donald 142
  Edward 142
  George 142
  Leli 142
  Louise 142
Comstock
  Lucy 178
  Samuel and Annie Weller 178
Conger
  David 202
  Donald 186
  Edith 186
  Ernest 73
  Hubert 89

Ralph 136, 186
Wilbert 186
Conger Mountain 8
Conklin
　Isaac 109
　Jennie 109
　Mary 109
Conley, E. Vaughn 35
Connally, Newton 36
Conroy, Bishop J. H. 33
Contu, Prof. H. 37
Cook
　Bessie 139, 141
　Carrie 140
　Dora Mae 139, 140, 169
　Ella M. 139, 140
　Emma 139, 141
　Ethel 139
　Florence 139, 141
　Fulton 141
　George, M. D. 98
　Gertrude M. 139, 140
　Hiram 4, 139
　Hiram, Jr. 140
　Jesmer and Hettie 139
　Lawrence 141
　Luther H. 193
　Margaret 141
　Nora 139, 140
　Oliver 139
　Orin 139, 140
　Orin and Carrie (Sochia) 169
　Orin H. 139
　Theodore 139, 140
　Warren 119, 139
Cooney, Mary A. 36
Courtney, John T. 89
Covell
　Bruce 157
　Jack 157
　Jeff 157
　Tim 157
　Wendell O. 157

Crandall, Samuel W. 157
Cronk, William 89
Cross, John 173
Crown Point 4
Cummings
　Arietta 134
　Arthur 89
　Earl 89
　Kenneth 89
　Martin B. 73
　May 152
　Mr. and Mrs. James 73
　Sheldon 89
Cunningham, Patricia 143
Cunnion, R. F. 97
Curran
　Candace 162
　Theresa Haynes 161
　Thomas 162
Cutting family 174
Cutting Lumber Company 173
Cutting Tract 174
Cuturia, Joseph 67

D

Dabiew
　George C. 73
　Mr. and Mrs. Frank 73
Daggett
　Anna Kenny 135
　Darius 135
　George 135
　Harriet 135
　Lucien 135
　Ruth Parks 135
　Willard 135
　William 135
Dandorand, S., Ph.D. 97
Daney, _____ 151
Danforth
　G. 51
　Gene 48, 49, 50
　Larry 50

INDEX • 373

Daniels 98
  Carl 47
  Carl O. 36
Darling
  John 120
  Mary 120
  Norman Addison, Rev. 120
Darrah, Ralph 151
Dauray, _____ 134
Davidson, Bessie 127
Davies
  Elmer 163
  Halcyon 195
  Halcyon LaPoint 145, 163
  Halcyon Lapoint, Mrs. 161
Day
  Darwin 170
  Edward 68
  Lovell 85
Days Mills Road 47
Debien, Francis 67
Debiew
  Lydia 167
  Margaret 172
DeBoice, George 61
DeBuque 141
  David 141
  Donnie 141
  Dorothy Fay 141
  Evelyn 141
  Flenda R. 141
  Floyd 89, 141
  Glenford 90, 141
  Greg 141
  Howard 90, 141
  Jeanne 141
  Jimmy 141
  Joseph T. 141
  Kenny 141
  Larna 141
  Loren 141
  Ralph 141
  Ronnie 141

  Stacie Jo 141
  Steve 141
  Tammy 141
  Thomas 141
  Windy 141
DeCarr
  Louise 73
  Prescott 90
  Samuel 73
  Seymour 90
Deer River 7
Defore, Clara 77
DeLair 142
  Dave 104
DeLaire
  Alfreda 143
  Alice J. 144
  Ann Marie 144
  Bernard 90, 143, 144
  Bernice 143
  Carol 143
  David 74, 142
  David J., Jr. 143
  Dennis 143
  Dewey 90, 143
  Doris 143
  Dorothy 144
  Ellen 143
  Etienne and Marie 142
  Frances 143
  Fred G. 86
  Fred G. 74
  George 142
  George Morton 90, 143
  James 74
  Kenneth 144
  Laura 144
  Linda 143
  Louis 144
  Mark 144
  Mary 144
  Paul 143, 144
  Paul, Jr. 143

Peter 144
Peter J. 143
Roger 143
Thomas 144
Thomas H. 74
DeLania, John D. 67
DeLlaire 142
Delosh
  Donald 90
  Harold 90
  Robert 90
Delude
  Blanche Levesque 131
  Ida Levesque 131
Demar
  Gertrude 182
  Phil 165
Democratic County Committee 127
Denning, Myra 35
Deno
  Alfred E. 167
  Ambrose 202
  Floyd 167
  Frederick 167
  Fredrick A. 167
  John J. 194
  Mary Parent 202
  Phebe 173
Densmore
  Albert 141
  Percy 141
  Ruth 141
  Wilfred 141
Desaw
  Andrew 136
  Betty 136
  Fred 136
  Fred, Jr. 136
DeShaw, Albert C. 69
Dewey
  Clara 143
  Sidney 188
  Susan 188

Terrence 188
Timothy 188
Dexter 108
Dexter, Mr. 110
Dexter, Orrando P. 108
Dexter Lake 108
Dexter Lake Road 109
Dickinson 7, 11, 21, 36, 97, 111, 115, 116, 123, 124, 125, 126
Dickinson Center 18, 29, 37, 103, 122, 126, 127
Disotelle, Kenneth 134
Dodge, George E. 106
Donaghy
  Hawley and Christina Kopanski 201
  Jane C. 201
Donovan
  Daniel H. 74
  Phoebe 74
Douglas, Henry 145
Douglas, Robert 111
Douglass
  Bertha 145
  Claire 145
  Donald 145
  George 144
  Harold 145
  Henry 145, 163, 195
  Henry and Gertrude 145
  Henry Bancroft 144
  John 144
  John and Harriet Bancroft 144
  Lawrence R. 145
  Marion Dorothy 145, 163
  Ruth 145
  Thera 145
  William 144, 145
Douglass & Southworth 145, 195
Dow
  Elaine 187
  Floyd 74
  Frank B. 74

Dr. Trudeau prize 171
Dresye, Gerald 90
Drew
  Alvira 195
  Donald D. 90
  Michael and Nancy Reynolds 195
Drew Theological Seminary 121
Duane 111
Duane Road 110, 196
Duane Street 30
DuBuque
  Bonnie 142
  Charles 142
  Flossie 142
  Gary 142
  Gladis 142
  Julia 142
  Loren 142
  Mary 142
  Muriel 142
  Racheal 142
  Thomas 67, 141
Dufore, Amos 132
Dufrene, Anna 168
Dugall, Joseph 67
Dupee, Dupee 119
Dupre, Bayard T. 75
Dupree
  "Bert" 158
  Burton 27
  Eileen 90
Duprey, Henry, 75
Durkee Post, G.A.R. #504 63
Dwyer, Addle 83

E

Eaton
  Francis 189
  Rachel 189
Eddie Road 110, 196
Edwin Aldrich 70
Egbertson, Caroline 201
Eleven Miles Woods Road 4

Elizabethtown 4, 50
Ellis, Fanny B. 180
Elmer, LaVoy 140
Emmons, Ebenezer 105
Erbach, Eunice Farrington 169
Essex County 4
Everett
  Percy 160
  Percy, Mrs. 161
Everton 7, 32, 110, 111, 125
Everton Lumber Company 7, 111
Everton Railroad 7
Everton Road 155

F

F. L. Tryon block 170
Fadden
  Arthur 146
  Arthur H. 75
  Barkley 147
  Basil E. 147
  Beatrice 146
  Bernard 90, 146
  Betty 146
  Carol 146
  Claude 147
  Doris 146
  Evelyn 146
  George I. 147
  Graceann 134
  Graceanne 146
  Ida 146
  James A. 145
  Joy 147
  Leroy 147, 174
  Lyman 90
  Lymon W. 147
  Mr. and Mrs. James 75
  Nelson 147
  Oral Marie 148
  Orie Peter 148
  Pansey 148
  Pearl 148

Ray 146
Swamp 147
Theda 146
Fairchilds, Eleanor 134
Fairfield Seminary 121
Fairmont Creamery 14
Fairview Cemetery 136
Falusha, Anna D. 63
Falvey
  Bernard 171
  (no name) 90
  Bernard 90
Fargerstrom, Mary C. 197
Farmer
  Albert Alexander 151
  Alice 150
  Arthur J. 150
  Beatrice Eva 151
  Belva Jean 151
  Betsey 150
  Blade 151
  Catherine 175
  Carlton A. 90, 150
  Clarence 75
  Commodore A. 150
  Daniel 90
  Daniel Oliver 151
  Elizabeth 150, 188
  Elizabeth Philena 151
  Ethel 150
  Evelyn 150
  Flora Gertrude 151
  Floyd 75
  Francis 150
  Fred 150, 194
  Gertrude 152
  James 150
  James Lindon 151
  John 75, 150, 180
  John and Mary England 150
  Judith P. 151
  Kathryn 194
  Lester 194
  Lindon James 151
  Lindsay 150
  Lucy 150
  Lyndon and Nettie LaPage 188
  Margaret Violet 151
  Maude 150
  May 150
  Nelma 150
  Nelson, Jr. 136
  Ralph 88, 90, 150, 151
  Robert 150
  Royal 90, 150
  Sophia M. 150
  Thelma Louise 151
  Walter Leo 151
  William 90
  William Harold 151
  William Wallace 150
Farr
  Allan 68
  Columbus 68
  Isaac 68
Farr District 37
Farrington, Sarah 189
Federal Government 101
Federman, Jay S., M.D. 98
Ferris, Stanley 41, 46
Festival of St. Regis 1
Files, George E. 86
Finlayson
  Arliegh Lynn 152
  Arnold 140
  Audrey 152
  Bessie Denise 152
  Carmen Fern 152
  Darrell 152
  Donald 140
  Donald McRae 152
  Fern 140
  Isabel 140
  Isabel Mae 151
  Janis Mae 152
  Jennie B. 152

John 151, 192
John and Clarabelle Surprise 152
John Clayton 152
Katie Jennifer 152
Leroy 152
Lowessa M. 136
Lowessa Myrtle 152
Lulu Lenora 151
Lulu, 196
Patsy 152
Stanley 152
Finnell, Mary 152
fireproof windows 13
First Free Baptist Church 30
First Free Will Baptist Church 107
First Methodist Episcopal Church 29
Fisk
  C. A. 118
  G. 51
  George 43, 46, 47, 48
  Marry Brabon 133
Fitts (Peitz), Lois 189
Fitzgerald
  Loren Richard 141
  Terrance 141
Flack
  Daniel W. 29
  William H. 63
  Wm. H., Congressman 123
Flanagan
  Benjamin 171
  Evelyn 171
Fleming
  Elizabeth M. 190
  Mary Jane 127
Fleming Store 96
Flenning, M. E. 97
Flynn
  Charles 196
Flynn Crossing 110
Foley, Kenneth 90
Fontcouverte 3

Ford
  Allie 90
  Floyd 91
  Harold 91
  John 84
Forest Cemetery 140, 164, 167, 202
Forest Home Road 187
Forkey
  Adolphus 152
  Amos 134, 152, 153
  Antoinette 153, 182
  Charles 153
  Cora 153
  Diane 153
  Dorothy 153
  Earl 135, 153
  Ellen 153
  Forkey 153
  Frank 153
  Frederick 153
  Gail 153
  Irene 153
  Jennie 153
  Jerry 153
  Lenore 153, 187
  Libby 153
  Lillian 153
  Nancy 153
  Sherry 153
  Terisa 153
  William 153
Fortier
  Henry 171
  Joseph A. 75
  Mr. and Mrs. E. J. 75
Fosdick, Harry Emerson 109
Foster
  Henry 118, 128
  Lucina 128
Fournier, Roy Leonard 91
Franklin Academy 44, 51, 124, 126
Franklin County 2, 114, 115, 122, 125, 127

Franklin County Board of Supervisors 128
Franklin County Republican Committee 123
Fraser
  "Old Jack" 154
  Bessie 154
  Hal (Jeff) 155
  Harold 154, 155
  Harold (Jack) 155
  Haven (Jerry) 155
  Helen 154, 155
  Howard (Jim) 155
  Hugh (John) 155
  J. A. 153
  Jean 155
  Jennifer 155
  Joanne 155
  John 19, 154
  John W. 154, 174
  Louise 154
  Rita 154
Frazza Construction Company 101
Free Will Baptist Society 126
Frey, Melvin J. 91
Frontier House 21, 118
Fronzack
  Edward 197
  Evelyn A. 197
  Harriet 197
Fulks, Joe 43
Fullerton
  Muriel 75
  Willis 75

G

"Goose Pond" 131
Gadoua
  Ernest 137
  Grace 137
  James 137
  Kimberly 137
  Lynn 137
  Mary Ann 137
  Michael 137
  Thomas 137
  Velma Griffin 137
Gadway, James 134
Gage, Rollin 91
Gale, Clifford 152
Galyen, Lonnie G. 76
Gardner, Joseph 67
Garrity, Jack 150
Garrow
  Bert 91, 141
  Billy 141
  Eleanor "Tootie" 141
  Larry 141
  Shirley 141
Gasper, Dr. 98
Gertrude, Cook 152
Geyer, Robert 144
Gibbs
  James 68
  John 68
Giffin
  Bertha 158
  Calvin and Rhoda Hewett 157
  Frank 158
  Frank M. 157
  Helen 157
  Helen Abbie May 157
  Jeanne Terese 158
  Martin 68, 157
  Martin and Mary 157
  Martin E. 157
  Mary 157
  Mary Maher 157
  Nona 157
  R. G., Mrs. 35
  Rollin 102
  Rollin, Jr. 18
  Rollin and Mary 157
  Rollin George 157, 158
  Rollin Glenville 18, 157
Giffin family 157

Giffins 158
Gilbeault, Caroline Levesque 131
Gilber, Archie E. 194
Gile 109
  Rich 109
  S. R. 63
  Steve 109
Giles, Azro 117
Gillett, Samuel W. 96
Gleason, Lyle 19
Glenda M. LaVoy 137
Glover, Pearl E. 173
Godreau, Robert 134
Gokey
  Fred Jr. 91
  Lawrence 91
Goldstone, H. A. 117
Goodrich, L. C. 7, 21, 118
Goodrow
  Clarence 91
  Clifford 91
  Dwight 91
  Ernest H. 91
  Eugene 134
  Harold 91
  Howard 91
  Karen 163
  Lawrence 91
  Thomas 91
Goose Pond 109
Gordon, Anthony 1
Gorman, _____ 135
Gott
  Jonathan 163
Gould
  Baird 162
  Chester 162
  Earl 162
  Earl Jerry 162
  Guy 162
  John 162
Graffin, Grace 35
Grand Seminary of Montreal 125

Gravel
  Michael and Melvina Campbell 196
  Rose M. 196
Graves, Calvin 118
Green
  Anabel 48
  Anabel Hewitt 35
  Bessie 159
  E. E. 159
  Frank, Dr. 62
  Frank M. 122
  Frank M., Dentist 97
  Frank Morton 91
  I. Clayton 159
  I. L. 118
  Ira 159
  Ira C. 2, 158, 159, 192
  Nettie 159
  Rosa 159
  Silas 159
  Thomas 159
  Willard 159
Greene, Nancy 134
Greenville 2, 159
Gremore, Fred Flanagan 97
Griffin, Myrtle 35
Grimes, Orrin and Harriet Knowlton 179
grist mill 195
Guide Board 108, 109
Guide Board School 37
Guth, Cindy 198
Guthrie, E. Julian 76
Guyton, Coriea, Mrs. 148

H

Hadlock, Waren 91
Haggerty, Minnie 177
Hail, Cook 139
Haley, Clark 67
Hall
  Dona L. 151

Donald 91
Jack 146
Maurice 91
Vila 91
Ham, Robert 162
Hamilton College 121
Hammond 96
  Charles 159
  Charles F. 159
  Daniel 159
  John 159
  Charles 2, 4, 159
  Charles F. 159
  Daniel 159
  John 2, 4, 159
  Thomas 159
  Thomas, Hon. 159
Hammond Falls 2
Hammond Mill 4
Hammonds 10
Hammonds Mill 139
Hanley
  Carmen 152
  Edward 167
  Helen 152
  Kathleen 152
  Kay 152
  Peggy 152
  Robert 152
  Rodney 152
  Rodney and Jennie Finlayson 152
  Ronald 152
Hannay
  Anna 160
  Elizabeth 160
  Gordon 159, 161
  Gordon, Jr. 160
  Gordon and Anna Baird 160
  Jessie 160
  Mary A. 160
harness shop 118
Harrietstown. 116
Harris, Elinor 143
Hart
  Bert A. 140
  Elmer 91
Hartman, Tim, Mrs. 146
Harvey
  Amos 4, 139
  William H. 67
Harwood Corners 151
Haskell
  Jan 198
Hathaway
  Albert 169
  Albert and Carla 169
  Andrew Palmer 169
  Barbara Ann 169
  Elizabeth Mary 169
  Nathaniel Joseph 169
Hawkins
  Clarence F. 76
  Mr. and Mrs. Henry 76
  Mrs. Henry 76
  Warren H. 76
Hawleyton 121
Haynes
  Alton 162
  Claire 162
  David 162
  Debbie 162
  Eva 162
  Gisele 162
  Harry 162
  Harry, Jr. 162
  Helen 162
  Howard 162
  Howard C. 161, 162
  Howard L. 162
  John Henry 161
  Levi 161
  Marietta 162
  Robbie 162
  Susan 162
  Theresa 162
  Walter 162

INDEX • 381

William 162
Haynes
  Adams 68
  Alton 91, 132
  Alton Charles 132
  Gisele Marie 132
  Howard 91
  Jacqueline 132
  Stanley Harris 132
  Violet 132
  William 132
Haynes Road 111
Haynes Road School 37
Haywood, Jefferson, Mrs. 146
Hazen
  Fred 76
  Kyle 76
  Lauriston 148
  Pansey Fadden 149
  Richard, Mrs. 147
health officer 128
Heath
  Frederic M. 110
  James A. 30
Herkimer County 120
Herne, Edith 195
Heuvelton 120
Heuvelton Union Free School 120
Hewitt
  Dewey 168
  Dollie 142
  Ezeckel 68
  Ferdinand 142
  Forest 92
  Herbert 168
  John 77
  Madge 168
  Marshall 168
  Sadie 142
  Steve 142
  Violet 142
  Whiter 92
  William 142

  William J. 168
Hewlett, Mollie Jane Galyen 76
Hill
  Gertrude 193
  Greg 194
  James S. 67
Hill-crest 8
Hillcrest Inn 22
Hitchcock, W. G. 36
hockey sticks 19
Hogansburg 97
Hoit, Myra C. 30
Hollifield
  Virginia 184
Holister
  Agatha Wood 133
  Guy 68
Hollister House 14
Holmes
  Linda 133
  Melissa Mary 133
  Reginald 132, 133
  Reginald, Jr. 133
Holy Name Society 171
Hopkinton 4
Howe
  Bert 165
  Violet 165
Howe Road 161
Hubbard & Lowell 19
Hudson, Brooks 180
Hughes, Mary 110
Hull, Jesse 182
Hunkins, Harrison 67
Hurd, Hotchkiss and Mac Farland 5
Hurd, John 4, 5, 6
Huse, Nancy 180

I

Iby
  Henry and Phoebe Sweet 145
  Ida 145
Indians 113

International Paper Company 154
Irish, Sydney 68
Ives Seminary 121

J

"John Hurd's Road" 8
J. & J. Rogers Co. 127
jackworks 154
Jandrew, Eileen 169
Jandrews, Zoa 200
Jarecki, Rev. M. 33
Jeanette, Ezra 187
Jennings Road 104
Jesuit College of Seziers 3
Joanette
  Ezra 68
  Hubert 169
John Hurd Lumber Co. 4
John Hurd Railroad 170
Johnson
  Adnor 67
  Alexander 21
  199
  Joseph C. 35
  Katherine Pickham 133
  Kenneth 22
  Madeline 199
  Orton 19, 92
  Richard 199
Johnson Saw Mill 19
Johnston
  Alexander H. 77
  Frederick W. 77
  John 12
Jones
  James J. 192
  Michael 135
  Paul 135
  Phillippe 135
  Ronald H. 92
  Stephen 135
  Theresa 135
  Vranous A. 92

Judware, Alfreda Susice 132

K

"Kill or Cure" Sanitarium 63
Keese's Mills 108
Kelley
  Harold N. 203
  Claire 27
  Darwin 26, 92
  Orvil 92
Kelly
  Darwin 173
Ketcham, J. A. 29
Kidney, William 62, 101
Kidney Ave. 106
Kilbourne, Barry, M.D. 98
Kimball
  Deanna 198
  Donald (Jack) 198
  Donald, Jr. 198
  Kevin 198
King
  Janet 152
  Theodore 67
  W. E. 117
  William E. 29
Kingsley
  A. 117
  Ella 192
Kinnear
  K. W. 118
  Kenneth W. 21
Kirby
  Johanna 157
  Josephus 4
Kirkey, Clarence 187
Klein, Dr. 98
Knapp, S. D. 30
Knickerbocker 200
Knights of Columbus 171
Knoxboro Union School 121
Koch, Sarah 110
Kujawsky, Alton 184

L

L'Verte 131
LaBarr, Buddy (Peck) 92
LaBarr, Merrill 92
LaBounty
  Charles 137
  Dawn 137
  Elwin P. 92
  Floyd 92
  Harold E. 92, 188
  Jack 18
  Jackson 188
  Linda 188
  Lorraine 137
  Marsha 188
  Martin 188
  Paula 137
  Richard 188
  Simeon 67
  Vance 137
LaChance
  Emma 187
  Florence 146
  Fred G. 86
  Marlene 162
LaClair
  Anna 200
  Celinda 200
  Frank 200
  George 200
  Gerald 200
  Irene 200
  Jane 200
  Jeffrey 200
  John 200
  Kathryn 200
  Kathryn Agnes 200
  Lloyd 200
  Margery 200
  Regina 200
  Regina Kathryn 200
  Walter 200
  William 200
LaClaire 200
LaCroix, Jacob 67
LaFave
  Andrew 77
  Francis H. 77
LaFrance
  Clara 197
  Joseph 77, 86
  Kenneth 92
  Michael 134
  Mr. and Mrs. Samuel 77
LaGray
  Helen 77
  Henry 77
  Margaret 167
Lake Champlain 104
Lake Ontario 104
Lake Ozonia 98, 102, 110, 174
Lake Ozonia School 37
Lake Placid 4, 120
LaLouvesc 3
LaMay, Mary 136
LaMoy, Victor 173
Lancto, Philomena 167
Lang
  Elizabeth M. 77
  Fred 31
  Fred W. 77, 86
Lantry
  C. P. 177
  Joshua and Nellia (Lyons) 177
LaPage
  Alphonse and Philena Gardner 151
  Betty 200
  Floyd 197
  Mike 197
  Natilie (Nettie) 151
  Paul 197
LaPoint
  _____ 162
  Donald 92, 163
  Douglas 163

Douglass 163
E. Douglas 92
Earl 48, 162, 163
Earl J. 26, 86, 145
Elisabeth P. 35
Elizabeth 162
Gary 163
Guy A. 162
Halcyon 92, 163
Halcyon L. 162
James 163
Jeanne 163
Jeffery 163
Jerry 63, 162
Marion 195
Marion Douglass 145, 163
Michelle 163
Roy W. 162
La Rock, Carrie 135
LaRocque, J. 117
LaRose
  Charles W. 92
  Frank 187
  Louis H. 78
  Nelson, Mr. and Mrs. 78
  LaRouche
  Earl A. 78
  George 78
  Henry, Mr. and Mrs. 78
  Lauzon
  Rev. J. R. 33
  Rev. J. Rodrique 32
Lavac 131
LaValley 61
LaVare, Arthur 92
Lavaseur, H. 62
LaVoy
  Abraham 140, 169
  Alton 140, 169
  Alton and Eileen Jandrew 169
  Arnold 167
  Carl 184
  Carla Ann 169
  Carl and Glencie Palmer 169
  Carl H. 92, 140, 169
  Charles 118
  Clemence 172
  Effie 168
  Effard 92
  Efford 140, 169
  Elmer 168
  Frank F. 167
  Gladys E. 167
  Glenda Mary 169
  Gloria 167
  Harold 140, 169
  Herman 167
  Jerry 167
  Joyce Marie 169
  Lawrence H. 167
  Lewis 172
  Lewis and Maggie Mashtare 167
  Margaret 167
  Paula Marie 169
  Raymond 167
  Rita Ann 169
  Robert 167
  Ruth 167
  Walter J. 167
Lawrence, Mass. 128
Lawrenceville 119
LeBoeuf
  Alfred 171
  Evariste 21
Lee
  Alice 152
  Allen 152
  Arliegh 152
  Phyllis 152
  Ronald 151
  Ronald and Isabel Finlayson 152
LeMieux
  Anabel Ellen 171
  Charles 47
  Charles Paul 172
  Charlie 40, 42, 46

Fred 61
Fred W. 78, 86, 171
Ida Mae 171
Joseph 92
Josephine 33
Joseph Arthur 171
Laura 172
Laura Isabel 171
Lionel Oscar 172
Mamie F. 171
Mayme Beyette 78
Paul 33
Paul and Josephine 171
Paul and Josephine Morin 170
William 92, 170
William Wilfred 171
Charles 47
Charlie 40, 42, 46
Fred 61
Fred W. 78, 86
Joseph 92
Josephine 33
Mayme Beyette 78
Paul 33
William 92
Lennon
  Grace 26
  Grace B. 190
  Jennifer 190
Leonard, Harriet M. 192
Levansworth, Henry 196
Levesque
  Alfred 131
  Andrew and Orellia 131
  Charles 131
  Charles Eugene Bishop 131
  John 131
  Mary Ann 131
  Paul 131
Levine, Martha 110
Lincoln, Abraham 1
Lindsay
  Edson 175

Parepa 35
R. P. 19, 118
Linkinson 1
Listovitch
  Carol 135
  Charles 135
  David 135
  Denise 135
  John 135
  Mark 135
Little
  Donald 154
  John 154
  Louise 154
Littlejohn, James 189
Little Valley Union School 121
Lodge #100, I.O.O.F 63
Lohr, Elmer 194
Londerville, Frank 119
Long Pond 196
Long Pond Road 106, 196
Lontagne, Vina Susice 132
Lucas, Vita 171
Luck, Violet 136
Ludic, Clarence E. 78
Lucrick
  Edith 79
  Mary 79
  Otis H 79
  Walter A. 79
lumber camps 125
Lunderman, Pete 144
Lyons, Richard 203

M

"Ma Smith's" 21
MacDonald
  Alexander 11, 26, 35, 96, 122, 179
  Dallas 141
  Duane 141
  Edith 35
  Edith O'Neil 35

Jessica 141
MacFarland, Esther 29
Macfarland, Peter C. 111
Maher
  Martin 157
  Mary (Mamie) 157
MAI 41
Malone 26, 42, 44, 45, 50, 62, 98, 133, 136, 137
Malone Evening Telegram 41
Maloney, Agnes 160
Mannix, Dorothy 143
maple syrup 19, 113
Marcheteau 172
Marcheterre 172
Marcy 105
  William L. 105
  William L., Capt. 104
Markey, M.D. 97
Marks, _____ 186
Maroney, Robert 19
Marshall, Charles 36
Marshall Bros. 18
Martin
  Albert 92
  Don 194
  Donald 62
  Elmer 182
  Emma 133
  Gerald 134
  Gerald, Jr. 134
  Geraldine 134
  Howard 143
  Leon 134
  Marion 134
  Odina 182
Mashtar
  Anna 172
  Clarica 173
  David 172
  Francis and Phebe (Duguay-Flavia Dewyear) 172
  Jennie 172
  John 67, 172
  John, Jr. 172
  Joseph 172
  Margaret 172
  William 173
Mashtare
  Alice 173
  Anna 165
  Bessie 173
  Bessie _____ 173
  Carrie 173
  Clifford 168
  David and Nellie Story 173
  Della Mae 173
  Dorothy 187
  Dorothy Louise 173
  Earl L. 168
  Edward 173
  Edward and Ruth Winkle 173
  Floyd 173
  Francis 168
  Harold Edward 173
  Henry 173
  John 165
  John and Matilda Stone 165
  Joseph and Margaret Debiew 173
  Margaret 165
  Milon W. 173
  Ray 173
  Rose 173
  Timothy 173
  William and Phebe Deno 173
Massena 14, 18, 26
Mayflower 189
Mayflower Compact 189
Mayville
  Francis 14, 92
  Lloyd 93
McCann
  Michael 163
  Robert 163
McClung, Holly, Mrs. 148
McCollum

INDEX • 387

John 192
McDonald Oil Co. 18
McGarvey
  Edward 19
  Harold 93
  Kenneth G. 93
  Willard 93
McKenna
  Genevieve 171
  _____ 151
McKennon
  Emma 154, 173
  Isabelle 174
  James and Isabelle 173
McKennon family 174
McLane
  Harry N. 36
  Mrs. R. R. 36
  R. R. 35
  Robert R. 123
McLaughlin, Margaret 172
McLeod Hotel 125
McMahon, F. C., Rev. 33
McNeil
  D. I. 21
  Martha 18
  Oscar 18
Meacham
  Beatrice 175
  Christopher 175
  Deborah 175
  Edna 175
  Ethel 175
  Everett 93, 175
  Frederick 93, 175
  Genevieve 137, 175
  George 175
  George, Jr. 175
  Gilbert 93
  Gilbert L. 175
  James J. 175
  Kay 175
  Lena M. 175
  Linda 175
  Michael 175
  Mildred 175
  Milon 175
  Nancy 175
  Norman 176
  Philinda Sochia 137
  Robert 175
  Stephen 176, 177
  Sylvester 31
  Thomas 176
  Thomas, Jr. 176
  Vern 137, 175, 194
  Viola 175
  Wesley 175
  William 175, 194
Meacham Lake 7, 12, 154, 176
Meehan, Rev. J. L. 33
Meigs
  Ferris J. 5, 106
  Titus B. 106
Merrick
  Bert 79
  Gladys 146
Merrill, Maude L. 120
Methodist Church 22
Methodist Episcopal Church 30
Meyers, James 36
mica 13
mica factory 13, 134
Mica Hill 102
Middlebury College 122
Millares, Manuel 196
Millbrook 155
Miller, F. E. 30
millinery 119
Mitchell
  Emily E. 164
  John and Mary Sherkey 164
Moffett
  Clara Smith 135
  John 135
Mohawk Indians 1

Moira 5, 6, 50, 116, 119, 126
Monarch, Amelia 194
Moody
  Adelbert E. 123
  D. E. 97
Mooers 123
Moose
  Carol 136
  Edward 136
  Kathleen 136
  Kay 186
  Nora Cheney 136
Morbito, Charles 150
Morey
  Jackson and Della Wilson 188
  Lavina 187, 188
Morey, Beth 141
Morgan, _____ 173
Morick, Alice 141
Morin
  Jane R. 153
  Josephine 170
Mormon religion 176
Morrick, Betty 136
Morrison, Bradley 189
Morristown 50
Mosher
  Kenneth 36
  Rose Marie 197
  Stanley 197
Mosier
  Charles 132
  David 132
  Debra 132
  Donna 132
  Gloria 132
  Jeffrey 132
  Joseph 132
  Merry Ellen 132
  Stephen 132
Mott, Buell 186
Mountain View Cemetery 152
Mount Assumption Institute 41

Mourick, Edward 93
Mourick, Frederick 93
Mt. Azure Observatory 170
Mulholland
  Albert 93
  Floyd 93
  Henry 79
  Ralph R. 79
murder 108
Murphy
  Glenn B. 79
  J. J., Mrs. 119
  J. J. A. 118
  John 174
  John D., Mr. and Mrs. 79
Murray
  David 132
  Jane 144
Mushtare
  Frank and Elizabeth Bruly 175
  Henry 93
  Mary Ann 175

N

Nash
  Charles Amos 153
  Paul 153
National Basketball Association 43
Nelson
  Charles Bernard 93
  Malina 150
Newman
  Sarah 143
  Wayne 143
New York Central Railroad 6, 131, 170
New York Homeopathic Medical College and Hospital 124
New York State Police 62
Niche, Doris 199
Nichols
  Gerald 93
  Winifred 93

Nicholville 4, 18, 36, 110, 111, 120, 126, 177
Nicholville Road 62
Niles
  Alma 191
  Archie 106
  Glenford 93, 146
  Merle 18
Nisoff, David F. 167
Noll, _____ 188
Noonan, Mary A. 187
Norfolk 199
Normandeau, Fr. G. J. 31
North Bangor 128
North Country League 41, 44, 50
Northern Adirondack Railroad 5, 6
North Lawrence 126
Northwest Bay Road 4, 104
Norton, Warren 85
Norwich 135
Norwood 42, 50
Nowicki
  Ernest 132
  Joseph 132
  Laura Ann 132
  Michael Richards 132
  Yvonne 132
Noyes
  Brandon 199
  Nillie D. 199
  Nillie Walter 199
Nunn
  Lawrence 186

O

O'Connor
  John 163
O'Doherty, Rev. L. 33
O'Neil
  Arthur 14, 179
  Arthur S. 26, 80
  Barney Stephen 177
  Bernard P. 93
  Catherine 177
  Charity 177
  Cornelius 177
  Dorothy 179
  Edith C. 179
  Ella S. Grimes 179
  Florence 179
  Franklin 178
  Fred 178, 179
  Frederick E. 179
  H. E. 10, 11, 19, 35, 96, 124
  Harold G. 179
  Henry E. 14, 26
  Henry Edward 179
  Herbert 179
  James M., M.D. 178
  Jennie 178
  Jeremiah 177
  John 177
  Joshua 177
  Katherine 178
  Margaret Traver 177
  Mary 177
  Maurice 177, 178
  Michael 177
  Nellie 177
  Ophelia 80
  Rex 132
  Rexford 93
  Rexford Charles George 132
  Rexford George 132
  Rose 132
  Thomas 4, 177, 178
  Thomas J., Rev. 177
  W. T. 7, 26, 117
  W. T., Sen. 124
  William 21, 96, 179
  William T. 10, 96, 108, 178, 201
  William Thomas 178
O'Neil & Hale 179
Odd Fellows 145
Ogdensburg 27, 41, 50, 141
Ogdensburg Free Academy 50

Ogdensburg Trust Co. 27, 191
Olmstead 161
Oneida National Bank and Trust
  Co. 27
Oneita Rebekah Lodge #264 63
Order of the Eastern Stars #455 63
Orton, Riley 180
Ouellet, F. J., Rev. 125
Ouellette, Fr. 33
Ouellette, F. J., Rev. 32, 33
Overton, Carl 36

P

Page
  Eugene F. 80
  Fred A. 80
  Frederick A. 86
  Nettie 189
  Peter, Mr. and Mrs. 80
  Watson 7, 21
Palmer
  Alva Jane 182
  Ann _____ 180
  Ardie C. 185
  Arthur C. 182
  Azro 182
  Azro I. J. 180
  Azro Irvin Joseph 182
  Beniah D. 180
  Betsey 180
  Betty 180
  Carrie 180
  Charles Asa 185
  Clara Marion 185
  Darlene Nancy 184
  Dean William 186
  Doris Grace 186
  Douglas 182
  Douglas (Sonny) 184
  Douglas and Lillian Bray 184
  Elijah A. 180
  Eliza A. 180
  Elizabeth 153
  Elzira 150, 180
  Eric Potter 186
  Ernest Charles 185
  Ernest G. 81
  Ervin 180, 182
  Ervin and Sarah Jane Ramsdell
    186
  Ervin J. 180
  Erwin 93
  Eva Marion 185
  Flora U. 180
  Gerald L. 182, 187
  Glencie 169
  Glencie Helen 184
  Henry S. 68, 180
  Homer E. 180, 182
  Hoyt 180
  Ida 185
  Idella Blanche 186
  Idelle B. 185
  Iva J. 182
  James and Sarah Brown 185
  James William 186
  John L. 182
  Jones J. 180
  Joseph Hoyt and Elizabeth Simpson Dolloff 180
  Lena E. 127
  Lloyd 93, 182
  Louise 180
  Louise A. 186
  Luna 180
  Madora J. 180
  Manchester 186
  Mary Jane 180
  Milton H. 180
  Patricia 153
  Paul Edward 153
  Percy 93
  Ralph Willie 186
  Ravina 180
  Reginald 186
  Rita 199

INDEX • 391

  Rita Harriet 184
  Rowena Sophia 186
  Sally 180
  Sibley (Buck) 153
  Sibley J. 182
  Sophia 81
  Susan O. 185
  Theo E. 182
  William 185
  William James 185, 186
  William James and Sophia Palmer 185
  Willie James 186
  Ziba A. 180
Paradise
  Eva 162
  Gerald E. 93
Parishville 41, 177
Parka, John Jr. 93
Parks
  Betty 155
  Even 135
  Frank 93
  Lloyd 182
  Jack 155
  John 135
  John, Mr. and Mrs. 81
  Kenneth 94
  Leo 85
  Leo S. 86
  Morton 155
  N. M. 118
  Overt 35
  Robert 94
  Roger 155
  Roy 94
  Vernon 85
  Vernon "Dutch" 19
  Vernon D. 86
  Vernon D. (Dutch) 160
  Vernon, Mrs. 161
  Walter L. 81
Partlow, Angus A. 144

Pastine Theater 61
Patnode
  Amber 198
  Anne 198
  Barbara 198
  Beverly 198
  David 198
  Jamie 198
  Jeanne 175, 198
  Kierstin Yager 198
  Kory David 198
  Leo 198
  Leo (Corky) 198
  Nancy 198
  Thomas 198
Patraw 186
  Barbara _____ 187
  Beatrice 187
  Blanche 187
  Clyde R. 81
  Clyde Robert 186
  Edith 187
  Edna 187
  Edward 180
  Eloise 187
  Eugene 187
  Freda 187
  Gary 200
  Glenford P. 85
  Helen 182, 187
  Janet M. 187
  Lois 81, 82
  Peter 186
  Preston P. 81, 186
  Ray H. 82
  Ray Homer 186
  Roy 187
  Thelma 187
  Wendell and Blanche 187
  Wendell E. 186
  William 173, 180
  William (Bill) 187
  William A. 186

William Aaron 187
Patreau 186
Patton, Henry and David 111
Paul, John 85
Paulist Order 177
Paul LeMieux & Sons 170
Paul Smiths 6
Peck
  Harriet Blanche 186
  Franklin and Ada 109
  Otis W. 68
  Robert 94
Peer, Stephen 187
Perkins, Christena 186
Perley D. Moore & Co. 10
Perry
  _____ 134
  Arthur F. 85
  Laura 150
  Martin 68
  Violet 143
Philadelphia Dental College 122
Philips, Arlene 132
Phillips
  Royal 174, 186
  LeRoy 31
Phipps, John 68
Pierce
  Agnes 191
  Fannie M. (Tilly) 168
  Henry M. 68
  Julia 37
  Morris and Katherine Walsh 191
Pierrepont 126
Pittsburgh Desmoines Steel Co. 101
Plattsburgh 41, 126
Plessis 122
Ploof
  _____ 150
  (Percy) Keith 188
  Alice 187
  Alvina 187
  Amanda 198
  Anice 187
  Bruce 198
  Bryon Richard 188
  Carol 188
  David 153
  Dennis 153
  Donald L. 94, 187
  Earl G. 187
  Edith 187
  Edward 94, 187
  Edward (Bud) 153
  Elizabeth Farmer 151
  Enola 188
  Evelyn 188
  Florence 188
  Francis and Maranda Jesmer 187
  Frank 153, 187
  Frank A. 187
  Frank and Mary Noonan 187
  Gerald L. 94
  Howard 187
  Ian 198
  James 153
  Jean 188
  Jerald L. 187
  Joan 188
  Joe 22, 30, 102
  Joe and Lavina 188
  Joseph 187
  Joseph (Joe) 188
  Joyce 136, 188
  Keith 102, 188
  Keith and Elizabeth 189
  Leona E. 187
  Leonard 187
  Leonard, Jr. 188
  Leonard and Emma LaChance 188
  Lilah 187
  Lloyd 188
  Lois 188
  Margaret 187
  Martha 187

Mayfred 187
Michael 188
Nowelle 188
Patricia 188
Percy Keith 151
Penny 188
Peter 187
Peter and Mary Richards 187
Rita 162
Royal F. 187
Ruth 188
Seymore L. 188
Shirley 188
Ploof's Falls 11
Plouffe 187
Plumb, Maurice W. 101
Plunkett
  David 135
  Gary 135
  John 135
  Larry 135
  Robert 135
Pondysh
  Carol 163
  Dale 163
  Raymond 163
  Tom 163
Poole, Joan 132
Popp, Dorothy 195
Poquette, Joseph 175
Poquette residence 102
Port Kent 111
Port Kent Road 104, 110, 196
Port Leyden 12
postmaster 179
Pothook Hill 111
Potsdam 42
Potsdam Normal School 120
Potter
  Bernice A. 186
  Elsie C. 186
  Ezra I. 186
  Henry T. 186

Ira 186
Ira and Clara 185
Leon S. 186
Lyman A. 186
Mary R. 186
Sarah 186
Sophia F. 186
Sophia P. 185
William H. 186
William S. 186
Powell, Muriel 141
Powers, D. W., M.D. 97
Powlesland, Stewart 36
Pratt, Lillian 141
Prentice, Glencie L. 200
Prespar, Madge 94
Prespare
  George 21, 82
  George, Jr. 82
  Millard H. 85
  Robert 134
Price
  Henry 187
  Charles 94
Pringle, Ralph 36
Prior
  Phil, Jr. 141
  Philip 94
Pritchard
  Dorothy 134
  Mary 35
  Mary C. 35
Proctor, A. H. 127
Proulx, John 101
Purchase Street 14

Q

Quesnel, Louis 32

R

R. G. Giffin & Son 18
Rabitaille
  Eugene 182

Racquette River 1
Radcliffe
  Audrey 162
Radloff
  Charles 82
  Earl C. 82
  Louis 194
  Reese 18
Rafter
  David, Mr. and Mrs.
  Frank 173
  George A. 82
  George Alex 86
  James 173
railroad 5, 131
Rakish, Shirley 158
Ramsdell
  Carrie 189
  Daniel 189
  Daniel and Hannah 189
  Eunice 189
  Farrington 189
  Farrington and Lois Fitts 189
  Fred 104, 190
  Fred S. 31
  Fred Smith 189
  Gideon 189
  Gideon and Sarah 189
  Herbert Nelson 189
  John 68, 189
  John, Jr. 189
  John and Polly Rice 189
  Joseph 189
  Lois 189
  M. B. 35, 96
  Mary (Polly) 189
  Melvin Blanchard 190
  Nathaniel 189
  Nathaniel and Phebe 180
  Nelson 30, 68, 125, 189, 190, 191
  Nelson, Rev. 31
  Nelson and Eliza Smith 189
  Prudence 189
  Robert 189
  Sarah Jane 180
  Thomas 189
  Winifred 193
  Winnifred 190
Raymo
  Hugh 19
  Sarah 110
Raymond
  Frederick L. 94
  Valina (Raymo) 143
Redear, Cyrus 68
Red School House, District #5 110
Red Tavern Hotel 110
Red Tavern Road 110, 196
Redwood 122
Reed, Otto 94
Reed, Robert 94
Regenie, Felix 143
Regent Theater 61
Regis
  Joseph M. 194
  Arthur J. 82
  Mr. and Mrs. Joseph 82
  St. John Francis 3
Reid
  Mary 83
  Robert A. 83
Revolutionary War 195
Reynolds, Margaret 160
Reynolds Brothers 111
Rice (Roice), Polly 189
Rice Mountains 98
Richards
  Francis R. 68
  James 94
  Lincoln 187
  Oren 5
  Valerie 132
Riggs, Helen Augusta 145
Rising
  Julius 4, 139
  Myhitible (Hitty) 139

Phoebe Howard 139
Samuel 139
Rivard, _____ 134
River Road 107
Rivers
  Bernard W. (Sonny) 175
  Chad 198
  David 68
  Doris Ann 175
  Elaine 175
  Larry, Jr. 198
  Lawrence 175, 198
  Melanie S. 198
  Ray John 94
Riverside 21, 22
Riverside Church 109
River Street 14, 21, 61, 96
Rivito
  Frank 94
  James 94
Robarge, George 118
Robert
  Leon 136
  Marshall 136
  Marshall, Jr. 136
  Paul 136
Roberts
  Don 198
  Jeremy 198
  Joshua 198
  Nathan 198
Robeson, Mrs. 62
Robitaille, Emerilda 194
Rocchi, A. 97
Rockaway Valley 121
Rockhill, Roger 184
Rockland, Ontario 134
Rodgers, Jimmie 40
Rollins
  Alphonzo 135
  Rhoda 192
Roosevelt
  Franklin 40
  Theodore 178
Root, Edith G. 185
Roscoe
  _____ 150
  Lee 142
  Lloyd 142
  Wanda 142
Ross
  John G. 68
  Mariam 133
  W. J. 111
Ross' Park 152
Ross's Store 14
Ross' Store 61
Rovito
  J. 51
  James 44, 45, 46, 48, 49, 50
  Jim 44, 52
Rowell
  Agnes Pierce 191
  Lynn A. 83
  Lynn Avon 190
  M. A. 35
  Mark 26
  Mark A. 36, 190
  Mark and Jennifer Lennon 191
  Percival L. 83, 86, 190, 191
  Percy 27, 48, 158
Rumley, Rose M. 141
Rusaw, Julius 85
Russell
  Bernard 94
  E. M. 119
  Roy 85
Rust
  Marvin 163
  Ryan 163
  Tonya 163
Rusterholtz
  John H. 162
Ruth, Babe 40
Ryan, T. J. 62

S

"South Woods" 31
Sabrey Hill 14
Saints 45
Salisbury 120
Salisbury Village School 121
Sampson
  Jerry J. 83
  Robert and Jerry 111
Sandhill Cemetery 151
Sandwich College 125
Sanford
  Lawrence 187
  Jonah 111
Sanford Millhouse 111
Santa Clara 4, 5, 6, 8, 32, 36, 97, 98, 106, 108, 109, 110, 111, 116, 125, 193
Santa Clara House 8
Santa Clara Lumber Co. 5, 131
Santerre, Edward 150
Saranac Hollow 139
Saranac Lake 4, 19, 97, 98, 123, 137
Sather
  Helen Mary 193
  Oscar S. 193
  Oscar S. and Ann Viola 193
  Peter and Louise 194
Saucier
  Leonard E. 193
  Theodore 193
Saunders
  Amy 34
  Leslie 191
  Leslie H. 126
  Leslie M. 29
  W. J. 127
  Willard J. and Ellen E. 126
Saunders & Saunders 127
Sausville, George 85
Sawyer
  Antoine 135
  Cameron 137
  Douglas J. 84
  Max 137
  Max, Jr. 137
  Mr. and Mrs. Richard 84
Scharbach
  Bertha 158
  John and Sarah Oberriter 158
Scharf, Vern A. 94
Schenk
  Ira 94
  William 94
Schillic, Doris 182
Schuyler, Patrick P. 84
Schwartzberg, Josh, D.O. 98
Scott, Walter L. 187
Scovil, Mary E. 197
Sealy, G. A. 35
Servant, Henry 94
Sexton, Mathew 150
Seymour, Charlotte 200
Shampine, Charles 68
Shanley 7, 107, 133, 196
Shanley Road 107
Sharp, Lottie 195
Sharpstene, John 36
Shatraw, Katherine 135
Shattuck, George L. 84
Shaw, Elizabeth A. 190
Shaw Brothers 10
Shaw Tannery 96
Sherman, George C. 106
shingle mill 155
Shoemaker, M. M. 30
Shuflet, Mrs. Philip 34
Skerry 182
Slaunwhite, W. Roy, M.D. 98
Smith
  Alma J. 192
  Bessie 192
  Cammie 151, 192
  Charles P. 135, 192
  Charles P. and Grace 193

Clifford 193
Eliza C. 125
Francis A. 192
Fred N. 192
Gar 132
George 31
George D. 192
Grace 193
I. Clayton 192
Jennie E. 192
John 6
John A. 36
Joseph Perkins 192
Lucy 192
Myrtle L. 192
Otto 21, 62
Paul 106
Thomas 192
Thomas B. 193
Wendell 94
Willard 192
William 95
William J. 86
Snell, Anna 142
Snickles, Betty 163
Sochia
  Alice 194
  Almeda 194
  Angelina Young 139
  Beatrice C. 194
  Bernard 194
  Carrie 139
  Cecil R. 194
  Diana 194
  Dorothy 194
  Edison E. 194
  Eldora May 194
  Eli 95
  Elsie May 194
  Ethel M. 194
  Everett, Jr. 194
  Everett and Helen 194
  Everett Lynn 193
  Exzildia 194
  Floyd 194
  Frank 194
  Frank and Almeda 193
  Frank Joseph 193
  Harold M. 194
  Harvey 194
  Howard 95
  Janice 194
  Judy 194
  Lawrence 194
  Leo 194
  Leon and Chloe 193
  Martha 133, 194
  Mary 194
  Mildred 194
  Philinda 175, 194
  Roger 194
  Rose 194
  Stanley 95, 194
  Theodore 139
  Waldo 194
  William 194
Soetemon, Peter W. 69, 101
Somers
  Colson 68
  G. Arba 68
  Maude 180
  Ora 35
  Thomas 180
Soteman, Peter 200
Soucy, Thomas 132
Sourwine, Ray 152
Southworth
  Clayton 195
  Clayton C. 195
  Gertrude 163
  Gertrude J. 145, 195
  Harold 195
  Lena M. 195
  Ogilvy 145, 195
  Ogilvy S. 68
  Ogilvy Sylvester 195

Ogilvy S. and Martha Carpenter 145
Robert 195
Southworth Building 61
Sovay
 Oleta 95
 Elzear 187
Spancake, Lambert L. 36
Spanish-American War Veterans 69
Spapiro, Dr. 97
Spaulding
 Edward 10
 Francis 10
 Solomon R. 10
Spaulding & Bumstead 10
Spinner, Ruth 133
Split Rock Road 19
Spring Cove 32, 111, 125
Spring Street 14, 26, 106
Spruce Street 19
St. Ann's Catholic Church 31
St. Ann's Catholic School 36
St. Ann's Cemetery 135, 171, 172, 202
St. Ann's Church 31, 32, 33
St. Ann's Society 63, 171
St. Anne's Cemetery 141, 196
St. Ann Street 63
St. Germain, Anna Levesque 131
St. Hilaire, Emmett 169
St. Hyacinthe 125
St. Jean Baptiste Society 171
St. Lawrence Baptist Association 31
St. Lawrence County 119, 120
St. Lawrence River 1
St. Lawrence University 108
St. Lawrence Valley League 41
St. Peter's 32
St. Regis Church 31
St. Regis Coal Co. 18
St. Regis Creamery 14, 178
St. Regis Creamery Co. 14, 124, 178
St. Regis Falls 4, 5, 6, 7, 13, 18, 26, 29, 31, 33, 36, 39, 40, 41, 42, 45, 50, 51, 52, 62, 63, 96, 97, 101, 107, 108, 109, 110, 111, 117, 119, 120, 122, 123, 124, 125, 126, 127, 128
St. Regis Falls-Nicholville Road 102
St. Regis Falls Central School 35, 36, 146
St. Regis Falls High School 41
St. Regis Falls Legion Hall 105
St. Regis Falls Middle School 34
St. Regis Falls National Bank 26, 27, 123, 124, 158, 178, 179
St. Regis Falls Newsletter 190
St. Regis Falls School Board of Education 35
St. Regis Falls Union School 34, 122
St. Regis Falls Universalist Church 30
St. Regis House 21
St. Regis Lakes 7
St. Regis Leather Co. 10, 117
St. Regis Light & Power Co. 11, 124, 178
St. Regis Lumber Co. 117
St. Regis Palle Cemetery records 87
St. Regis Paper Co. 14, 17, 106, 131, 154
St. Regis River 1, 7
Starks
 Arthur 154
 Linda 197
 Margaret 197
 Mary 197
 Robert 197
Star Theater 61
State Assembly 178, 179
State Senate 178

stave mill 154
Stearns, H. W. 111
Stevens, Ella 135
Stewart, Howard 95
Stocum, H. H. 30
Stone
  Antoine and Marguerite Berno 172
  Joseph 68
  Matilda 172
Stony Brook 176
Story
  Nellie 172
  Wallace 95, 106
Strand
  Anna 196
Strauss
  Joe 153
  Margaret 153
  Paul 153
sugar barrels 14
Suits, Vernon 181
Sullivan
  Helen 143
  Nora 119
Sunnyside Cemetery 152
Supernault, Lila E. 167
Super Saints 48, 50
Surprise
  Anna Viola 194
  Clara 152
  Frank 69, 194
  Frank H. 84
  Frank and Mary Frances Aubery 194
  Mary 84
Susice
  Alfred 132
  Bert 131
  Daniel 132
  Ernest 132
  Ida Mary 131
  Jennie May 198
  John 131
  Joseph 132
  Julius 131
  Katherine Cayea 131
  Patricia Ann O'Neil 132
  Peter 132
  Richard A. 95
  Shirley 173
Sweet
  Michael G. 198
  Tesa 198
  Todd 198
Swift, Jane Ann, Mrs. 191
Swinburne, John 123
Swinburne Dispensary 123

T

"The Patch" 157
Taberg 122
Tanner, William 97
Tannery Street 21, 61
Taylor
  Frank L. 86
  Morris 85
Taylor University 121
Tessier, Alan 36
Tetrault, E. A., Rev. 33
The Adirondack News 26
Thomas
  Almeda L. 193
  Emma L. 192
  Matthias E. 68
  Wilber and Julian 193
Thompson
  Donald 197
  Henry H. 87, 197
  Raphael 197
Tierney, John 62
Tiesdel House 174
Titus
  Josephus 139
  Kirby 4, 139
Town Lock-up 96

Traver, Jeremiah and Zilpha Byron 177
Tremblay
  Florestine 142
  Joseph and Josephine Raynot 142
Trim
  Alvin 195, 196
  Alvin and Alvira Drew 195
  Angela Jean 169
  Benjamin 195
  Burlan 196
  Daniel James 169
  Eva Mae 195, 196
  Fay 106, 195, 196
  Fay and Rose 196
  Fay Hubert 195
  Frank 195, 196
  Frank and Carrie 195, 196
  Gerald 196
  Gerald, Jr. 169
  Gerald and Paula 169
  Joyce 196
  Rebecca Lynn 169
  Will 196
  William 195, 196
  William R. 151
  William Rubin 195
Trim's Crossing 111
Trim Hill 110, 111
Trim Road 37, 106, 196
Tripeny
  Angelica 197
  Anna 197
  Bernard 197
  Charlotte M. 197, 199
  Ernest C. 197
  Evelyn 197
  John 197
  Margaret 197
  Marie 197
  Maude 197
  Raphael, Jr. (Budd) 197
  Raphael and Anna 197
  Raphael and Anna Strand 199
  Raphael W., 3rd 197
  Raphael W., Sr. 196
  Rita 197
  William 196, 197
  William and Angie 197
Tripenyville 199
trolley 102
Troop "B" 62
Trout Lake 110
Tryon
  E. P. 26
  Eva 35
  F. L. 120
Tryon's 61
Tuell, Anne 172
Tupper Lake 5, 6, 8, 41, 45, 46, 63
turntable 131
Tweed, Malcolm 101
Tyler
  Eddie 135
  Fred 135
  Frederick 135
  Jimmy 135
  John 135
  Kathleen 135
  Richard 135
  Robert 135

U

Union School 127
University of Vermont 126
Unwin, Joan Ploof 27
Uplands 8
Upper Jay 127

V

"Ville du Harve" 159
Valley Forge 195
Velay 3
Vermont Evaporator Shop 19
Vilas, Samuel F. 5
Villnave

Daniel A. 187
Thomas 187
Vining, Peter S. 31
Visneau, Matilda 136
Votra
  Harold 95
  John L. 87
  Lee 146

W

"wolf ring" 114
"Wonder Five" 172, 199
Waddington 41
Wadhams, Bishop 33
Wager, Harry W. 36
Wait
  Albert 197
  Almon and Jennie 199
  Almon and Mary 197
  Almon Elsworth 197
  Almon Gary 198
  Almon L. 198
  Archie 197
  Brenda Lee 198
  Crystal Lynn 198
  Edna Bouchard 198
  Margaret 197
  Myron A. 197
  Myron and Clara 197
  Odena Mary 197, 198
  Veronica Ann 198
Waite 197
  Ernie 197
Waite Road 197
Wait Road 37, 112
Waldman, Joseph 95
Walker
  _____ 180
  A. D. 30
  Jimmy Jo 198
  John 31
  Kathy 198
  Russell 198

Ward
  Beverly 134
  Clarence 143
  Emerson 134
  George 134
  Geraldine 197
  Jane 143
  Paula 143
  Richard 134
  Sharon 134
  Thomas 143
Wardner
  Joseph E. 101
  Joseph Jr. 95
  L. M. 97, 118
  L. M., Dr. 11
  L. M., M.D. 68, 97
  Lena 63
  Leroy, Dr. and Mrs. 127
  Leroy M. 96
  W. 35
  W. A., Dr. 35
  W. A., M.D. 97
  W. Allen 127
Wards, William E. 68
War of 1812 104, 105
Washington, George 195
Waste, Harvey 68
Waterloo 123
Watertown 19
Watson Page Lumber Co. 11
Waverly 2, 4, 6, 97, 101, 111, 116, 123, 128, 176, 177
Waverly House 7, 21, 62, 118
Webb & Stevers 19
Webb
  Benoni G. 19
  J. W. 19, 118
Webb's block 118
Weeds, Smith & Conway 126
Weller, Earl N. 35
Wells
  Arthur 148

Basil 146
Della 148
Francis 148
Gerald 148
Geraldine 148
Harold 148
John 148
Lucille 148
Oral 148
Orie Peter 148
Philip 148
Westmoreland 122
West Parishville 126
Westport 4
White
  Aaron Lee 198
  Carl Michael 199
  Carlton 184, 199
  Carlton Strand 199
  Carol 199
  Dona Rae 199
  Douglas James 199
  Frank and Angeline 199
  G. 51
  Gary Carlton 199
  Gerald 45, 199
  Harriet 199
  Helen Marie 199
  John 199
  John Patrick 199
  Mabel 199
  Pamela Lynn 199
  Susan 199
  Tamara Lee 199
  Theron A. 198
  Tisha Lee 198
  Verne 84
  Vernon J. 87, 199
  W. 51
  Walter 84, 197, 199
  Walter and Charlotte 199
  Walter F. 199
  Willard 44, 46, 47, 50, 199

White Hill 109
Wilcox, Grant J. 135
Wilkins
  Bernard 194
  Roy L. 87, 194
Wilson
  Margaret 178
  Orin L. 128
  Ruth 134
Winkle
  Elmer and Margaret Shockey 173
  Ruth H. 173
Winter
  Lan 200
Winters
  Carl 18
  Flossie 142
  Forest and Glencie 200
  Forest E. 200
  Gerald 200
  Helen S. 200
  Henry 180
  Kathryn LaClair 200
  Lan 200
  Linda 200
  Mattie _____ 200
  Regina 19
  Sharon 200
  Stanley 95
  Wallace 200
  Wallace Henry 200
  Walter 95, 200
  Walter Lan 200
  Wilta W. 200
Winters family 19
Witcher, Lydia 135
Wolcott, Elmer 167
Wolfe, Cecilia 172
wolves 114
Wonder Five, The 39, 41, 42, 43, 45, 47, 48, 50, 51, 52
Wood
  Charles 145

John E. 95
Lye Joseph 95
Philemon 68
Thomas P. 85
Woods
  E. 51
  Milfred 84
  Mr. and Mrs. Antoine 84
  Nelson D. 85
  Phyllis 186
Woodward, Mildred 155
Working Girls' Vacation Society 8
World War II 42
World War II Veterans 88
World War I Veterans 70, 87
Wright
  Ella J. 179
  Richard H. 158

Y

Yerrick
  George 174
Young
  Alexander 200
  Angelina 193
  Antione 68
  Arthur 201
  Charles 201
  Charles H. 96, 201
  Chloe M. 193
  Ernest E. 85
  Eudora 180
  Frank 26
  Frank A. 85
  Frank and Jane 26
  Frank Stanley 201
  George 200
  George M. 85
  Grace M. 192
  Henry 200
  J. Stanley 95
  Jacob 200
  James 200, 201
  James and Caroline 201
  James H. 10, 179
  James Henry 200, 201
  Jamie 201
  Jane Donaghy 201
  Janet 201
  John 200
  Margaret 200
  Nelda 201
  Opelia 201
  Ophelia 179, 201
  Orpha Berry 201
  Robert 200
  Robert and Phebe 200
  Stanley 201
  Theodore 200
  William 200, 201
  Willis 200

TEACH Services, Inc.
P U B L I S H I N G

We invite you to view the complete
selection of titles we publish at:
www.TEACHServices.com

We encourage you to write us
with your thoughts about this,
or any other book we publish at:
info@TEACHServices.com

TEACH Services' titles may be purchased in
bulk quantities for educational, fund-raising,
business, or promotional use.
bulksales@TEACHServices.com

Finally, if you are interested in seeing
your own book in print, please contact us at:
publishing@TEACHServices.com
We are happy to review your manuscript at no charge.

www.ingramcontent.com/pod-product-compliance
Lightning Source LLC
Chambersburg PA
CBHW070932230426
43666CB00011B/2406